MW00620512

CONTESTING
COMMEMORATION

CONFLICTING WORLDS

New Dimensions of the American Civil War

T. Michael Parrish, Series Editor

CONTESTING COMMEMORATION

THE 1876 CENTENNIAL, INDEPENDENCE DAY, AND THE RECONSTRUCTION-ERA SOUTH

JACK NOE

Louisiana State University Press Baton Rouge

Published by Louisiana State University Press
lsupress.org

Copyright © 2021 by Louisiana State University Press
All rights reserved. Except in the case of brief quotations used in articles or reviews, no part of this publication may be reproduced or transmitted in any format or by any means without written permission of Louisiana State University Press.

Chapter 4, "The Centennial and the Politics of Representation," is derived, in part, from an aritcle published in *Southwestern Historical Quarterly* in October 2016 (CXX, 2), avialable online at www.muse.jhu.edu.

Chapter 5, "White Southerners and African Americans at the 1876 Centennial," is derived, in part, from an article published in *American Nineteenth Century History* in September 2016 (17:3), avialable online at wwww.tandfonline.com.

Designer: Barbara Neely Bourgoyne
Typeface: Whitman

Jacket photograph: The Statue of Liberty's torch on display at the 1876 Centennial Exhibition in Philadelphia. Courtesy Library of Congress.

Library of Congress Cataloging-in-Publication Data
Names: Noe, Jack, author.
Title: Contesting commemoration : the 1876 centennial, Independence Day, and the Reconstruction-era South / Jack Noe.
Other titles: Conflicting worlds.
Description: Baton Rouge : Louisiana State University Press, [2021] | Series: Conflicting worlds : new dimensions of the American Civil War | Includes bibliographical references and index.
Identifiers: LCCN 2021002212 (print) | LCCN 2021002213 (ebook) | ISBN 978-0-8071-7558-3 (cloth) | ISBN 978-0-8071-7616-0 (pdf) | ISBN 978-0-8071-7617-7 (epub)
Subjects: LCSH: Fourth of July celebrations—Southern States—History—19th century. | Nationalism—Southern States—History—19th century. | Southern States—History—1865–1877. | Southern States—Politics and government—1865–1950. | Southern States—Social conditions—1865–1945. | United States—Centennial celebrations, etc.
Classification: LCC F216 .N64 2021 (print) | LCC F216 (ebook) | DDC 975/.04—dc23
LC record available at https://lccn.loc.gov/2021002212
LC ebook record available at https://lccn.loc.gov/2021002213

Contents

Acknowledgments vii

Introduction 1

1. Antebellum and Wartime Fourths of July 14

2. Contesting the Southern Fourth of July 31

3. Humbug or Opportunity: Debating the Centennial 57

4. The Centennial and the Politics of Representation 97

5. White Southerners and African Americans at the
   1876 Centennial 120

6. July Fourth 1876 in the South 155

Conclusion 173

Notes 181

Bibliography 211

Index 225

Acknowledgments

This book started life as a research project at the University of Leeds and owes much to my steadfast supervisor there, Simon Hall.

Other friends and colleagues at Leeds offered support and encouragement along the way: many thanks to Gina Denton, Kate Dossett, Andrew Lunt, Lauren Mottle, Sabina Peck, Simone Pelizza, Giovanni Pozzetti, Claudia Rogers, Mark Walmsley, and Jonathan Wright. Thanks are also due to historians Alwyn Barr, Susanna Gold, Carl Moneyhon, and Patrick Williams for providing useful advice during the project's early phases. Chris Hayashida-Knight helped make a short residence at Penn State fruitful and shared a useful conference paper with me.

At Queen Mary, University of London, Noam Maggor, Daniel Peart, Joanna Cohen, Matthew Griffin, Connie Thomas, and David Tiedemann provided some really useful feedback on chapter drafts and made later revisions easier.

I'm grateful to Louisiana State University Press for publishing the book, in particular editor in chief Rand Dotson, Conflicting Worlds series editor Michael Parrish, and senior editor Neal Novak. Copyeditor Elizabeth Gratch has done a thorough and thoroughly marvelous job: thank you. I'd also like to thank my anonymous peer reviewer for their cogent, insightful, and encouraging comments.

Ron Peterson, Kat Marran, and Janet Wilson read chapter drafts and provided valuable feedback: thanks again! Beatrice Ballarini offered some timely technical advice—grazie.

My thanks and appreciation to all of these people and to Jack T. and Gail Noe, Jeremy Noe, Jacopo Pili, Howard Lewis Russell, Pablo Tempesta, and Martin White.

Chapter 4 is derived, in part, from an article published in the *Southwest Historical Quarterly*, October 2016. Chapter 5 is derived, in part, from an article published in *American Nineteenth Century History*, September 2016.

CONTESTING
COMMEMORATION

Introduction

Between May and November 1876, a grand world's fair, America's first, was held in Philadelphia's Fairmount Park. The International Exhibition of Arts Manufactures and Products of the Soil and Mine—more commonly known as the Centennial Exhibition, or simply the Centennial—attracted more than ten million visitors in the six months it was open, one-fifth of the nation's population. It introduced Americans to both popcorn and the ice cream sundae, and Alexander Graham Bell was on hand to provide curious crowds with demonstrations of his new invention, the telephone.[1] One contemporary newspaper declared that the fair was "impossible to describe. Nothing but seeing it with your own eyes can give you any conception of its magnitude. Suffice it to say that everything that was grand, beautiful, useful and ludicrous was there, not only from our own beloved land but from every nation I have ever heard of and some I have not heard of!"[2] The Centennial was more than mere spectacle, though. Held just eleven years after the end of the Civil War and commemorating one hundred years of national existence, the exhibition, along with local events held all over the country in that anniversary year, presented an opportunity like no other for whites, Blacks, northerners, and southerners to reflect on and engage with ideas about their identity as Americans. Running in tandem with a bitterly contested presidential election that would decide the future of Reconstruction and the nation, it served as a performative expression of post–Civil War American nationalism as well as a rhetorical proxy utilized by the white South to reject any immediate or unconditional re-embrace of that nationalism. This study analyses post–Civil War reunion and reconciliation, using white southern reaction to and involvement with these celebrations as a lens through which to explore the economic, social, and political aspects of reunification and the tensions that lay behind the development of a post–Civil War American identity. The discussion of white southerners will, throughout, be countered with a parallel narrative focused on African Americans, another demographic whose world was upended by the Civil War. The book examines, in a comparative light, African Americans' engagement with national identity and their use of commemoration to stake a claim to full citizenship and American identity in the post–Civil War era.

There has been valuable work in recent years on the post–Civil War South and the nettlesome question of sectional reunion and reconciliation. Historians such as Gregory Downs, Anne Sarah Rubin, and Richard Zuczek have demonstrated that white guerrilla-style terrorism, a defiant and resistant white public mood and the fact of federal military control of the South, make it plausible to argue that a state of quasi-war persisted throughout the period of Reconstruction. Though it was a delicate and politically volatile process, the end of Reconstruction saw reunion accomplished with the states of the former Confederacy once again operationally part of the Union. David Blight's influential work has argued that sectional reunion was achieved at the expense of African Americans, with the war's emancipatory aspects largely overlooked in favor of a reconciliationist view that accommodated both northern and southern whites. This work's study of freed people's use of Revolutionary memory and commemoration to claim their status as full citizens builds on Blight's treatment of African American focus on preserving memory of the Civil War as an emancipationist struggle. Meanwhile, Caroline Janney has stressed the gaps between political reunion and genuine reconciliation, skillfully highlighting sectional antagonism and alienation that persisted long into the twentieth century. Recognizing that reconciliation is a different, trickier question altogether, this book zeroes in on the lacunae between reunion and reconciliation in that brief, albeit key, time frame in which reunion was achieved.

There has been considerable attention paid to the importance of Civil War memory and commemoration in the process of reconciliation. In addition to the scholars mentioned already, W. Fitzhugh Brundage, William Blair, and Karen Cox have all contributed useful work on the tensions inherent in commemorating the achievements and the dead of both sides in an ostensibly reconciled nation, while M. Keith Harris has demonstrated, through his study of the commemorative activities of both Union and Confederate veterans, a distinct lack of true reconciliation.[3] Along the same thematic lines, Timothy J. Williams's work has highlighted the diaries and narratives of captives in Union prisons and their role in molding a prevalent Lost Cause, pro-Confederate memory.[4] The little that has been published on the Centennial Exhibition, however, has been largely concerned with the fair itself and its design, rather than with how Americans actually experienced the event and inscribed it with meaning.[5] Mitch Kachun and Philip Foner are admirable exceptions to this trend in their explorations of African American engagement with the exhibition. Kachun's work is centered around Black attempts to create a usable past by using the Centennial as a space in which to articulate an American identity, while Foner's contribution is essentially a dispiriting account of Black exclusion and white (northern) indifference.[6] John Hepp has described the Centennial as a "liminal space" reflecting an America poised between an agricultural past and an industrial future.[7]

This book pursues that theme of liminality but does so in terms of identity and national belonging. In her recent monograph on the Centennial, Susanna Gold uses the myriad works of art displayed at the Centennial to interrogate the fractured state of America identity in the 1870s. Gold touches on white southern reaction to the exhibition, a theme that will be explored fully here, stating that "the fragile veneer of optimism that attempted to conceal any lingering Civil War tensions would prove to be unsustainable, headed for collapse on the

Centennial grounds."[8] Lyn Spillman's work, meanwhile, has framed the Centennial as a locus of national memory and shared identity. Spillman addresses the issue of southern Centennial resistance, pointing out attempts by Centennial promoters to counter it by appealing to shared Revolutionary heritage.[9] Kathleen Ann Clark's definitive study of Black southern commemorative culture contains a brief discussion of the Centennial that reinforces Spillman's emphasis on the reconciliatory aims of its organizers. Clark acknowledges southern ambivalence toward the Centennial, but her argument that white southerners were "fully-fledged participants in Philadelphia" does not stand up to close scrutiny.[10] However, her emphasis on the role of women in commemoration is an important contribution that is followed up here. Caroline Janney, in demonstrating the very slow road to reconciliation in the twentieth century, has ably highlighted the role of women's groups such as the United Daughters of the Confederacy in "provid[ing] an antidote to the Blue-Gray gush" of reconciliatory sentiment.[11] In this book's concentrated focus on an earlier time frame, however, a picture emerges of *some* white women seeing a shared sense of wartime loss as mothers and wives as a path to reconciliation.

Finally, the late W. Burlie Brown, writing in the midst of 1970s Bicentennial hoopla, showcased some interesting and colorful source material in a localized study of white Louisiana's engagement with the Centennial but seriously underestimated the reach and importance of the exhibition when he characterized it as "miniscule" in comparison with that of the Bicentennial.[12] This book will demonstrate the ubiquity of this national anniversary in mid-1870s southern culture as well as the ways in which the commemoration amplified ideas of regional distinctiveness and served as a rhetorical proxy for the political and social divisions of the era.

Brundage, in pointing out the fictions involved in commemoration, warns that collective memory—that version of history ratified by commemoration—should not be mistaken for an objective record of the past. When certain factions/groups/interests are involved in depicting their version of events as objectively true, he argues, in order for these depictions to be viable, they merely need to be believable to their intended audience.[13] Sometimes presenting a particular version of events in order to shape collective memory involves suppressing memories as much as celebrating them; for example, Brundage cites Austrian depictions of that country as a victim of rather than participant in the Nazi regime.[14]

Brundage's admonition, as exemplified in the contested history of the Civil War, echoes the ideas of French historian Pierre Nora. Nora postulates a chasm between history and memory, seeing the latter as irretrievable and the former as a problematic and incomplete reconstruction.[15] Scholar Bruce Baker, though, has warned that extrapolating Nora's ideas about French history into a study of the American South can lead to "false comparisons and conclusions."[16] He is correct: here history and memory do mingle. In the words of Matthew Dennis, "Popular memory, particularly in the pluralistic United States, is constructed, incomplete, and itself at least partially dependent on formal history, which filters into the popular consciousness."[17] One significant way in which this filtering takes place is through commemorative, usable rituals such as the Fourth of July and the Centennial of 1876. The commemorations in question here were informed and shaped by ideas around sectional identity, a construct that was at the same time both part of and distinct from Americanness.

THE DEVELOPMENT OF AMERICAN SECTIONALISM

While southern identity and interests were discernible from the beginning, American nationalism remained a fluid and elusive concept in the first decades of the nineteenth century. Historian Cecilia O'Leary has described a nation where "one's notion of country more often than not was affixed to an individual state," with even Fourth of July celebrations more reflective of localism and local cultures than anything national.[18] The South wielded significant influence in the formation and early history of the United States: a southern, and particularly Virginian, ascendancy during these decades allowed the region to define what it meant to be American. Virginian George Washington was the leader of the Revolutionary army that won independence, Virginian Thomas Jefferson authored the Declaration of Independence, Virginian James Madison was the central figure in putting together the Constitution, and Virginians occupied the White House for thirty-two of the republic's first thirty-six years. Southerners exercised influence in protecting what was by the last part of the eighteenth century already *their* peculiar institution of slavery: the three-fifths clause of the Constitution was a concession to the southern bloc in allowing the slave states to count each slave as three-fifths of a person for purposes of allocating congressional representation.

When civil war did eventually break out in the 1860s, a repeated southern claim was that the Confederacy was the true embodiment of the ideals of the founders, that it was the North who had betrayed these ideals and caused the rupture of the Union. Historian James McPherson endorses this view, arguing that it was the North that "deviated from the mainstream of historical development . . . the breaches that opened between the regions came mainly because of developments in the North . . . the South's concept of republicanism hadn't changed; the North's had."[19] Robert Bonner has delineated a "proslavery constitutionalism"—an effort by antebellum southerners to frame a vision of American nationhood that while not explicitly about slavery featured a "decentralized version of state sovereignty" that allowed the institution to flourish.[20] Aiming to define America, not dissolve it, this represented the southern side of what was essentially a tug of war over what sort of nation the United States would be.

Cecilia O'Leary, juxtaposing the birth of "true" American nationalism with the North's efforts in the Civil War, has observed: "Northern men and women who previously had recognized only local, regional, ethnic, and religious allegiances hammered out the meaning of patriotism as they fought to preserve the Union."[21] In other words, the northern vision of America became America, and southerners were relegated to simply being southerners, their sectional interests seen as merely that, sectional. This solidification of an American national identity at the time of the Civil War can be linked with the sacralization of the concept of the "union" in American—or at least, northern—thought. Scholar Paul Nagel has described the Unionism of the Federalist period as no more than a "stratagem for the occasion."[22] Washington's description of it as being "the main prop of your liberty" reinforces the idea of Union being a tool, or means, as does Jefferson's 1804 statement that the Union was of "little importance" to the happiness of the American people and that he was sanguine about the possible development of "Atlantic and Mississippi Confederacies."[23]

This evolution of the idea of "Union" into being an end in itself, as voiced by northern politicians such as Daniel Webster, William Seward, and most critically, Lincoln, was viewed apprehensively in the South. There was certainly some strong Unionist sentiment in the South, but as historian Paul Quigley observes, it tended to be "only [for] the Union as they defined it."[24] On the eve of war in 1861, the *New Orleans Bee* summed up the danger perceived in absolute union: "The dogma of the perpetuity and imperishability of the Union carries with it the right to coercion for its enforcement . . . the very term 'union' implies voluntary association . . . if any of the parties should be forced to maintain a compulsory compact, it would cease to be a Union, and would become despotism."[25] Similarly, the *Richmond Enquirer* warned of "the immense mischief that may be introduced under the Trojan Horse of the word 'Union.'"[26] It was this inferred threat in the idea of indivisible union that most disturbed white southerners.

WHAT WAS THE SOUTH?

But what, then, was the antebellum South? Did it constitute a discrete and concrete entity, and if so, what defined it? Avery Craven, writing in the 1950s, questioned the existence of "a" South prior to the 1850s, arguing that it had been "too much a bundle of contradictory and conflicting interests to see itself as an entity."[27] More recently, William

Freehling has convincingly described a land of gradations and regions dissolving into each other, a region containing so much variation that he, like Craven, concludes that it cannot be considered a South.[28]

But does Freehling's portrait of a land of gradations and regions dissolving into each other negate the traditional idea of a solid, definable South? Certainly, the Mississippi planter who in 1857 contrasted southern "high-toned gentlemen descended from cavaliers" with Yankee antecedents in the "narrow-minded, sanctimonious bigots who landed at Plymouth Rock" saw a clear cultural distinction between himself and his northern counterparts.[29] And writing twenty years earlier, J. H. Ingraham, a native of Maine who settled in Mississippi, declared that "the inhabitants of the South [are] dissimilar to those of the North. The difference is clearly distinguishable, through all its grades and ramifications and so strongly marked as to stamp the Southern character with traits sufficiently distinctive to be dignified with the term 'national.'"[30] Later historians, as has been noted, have questioned this Manichaean view, but the writings of Craven and Freehling would no doubt surprise John Calhoun. The South Carolina political titan died in 1850, having spent the previous two decades fighting to preserve the political power and way of life of a region that according to some historians of a century hence, did not really exist. Calhoun, showing where his ultimate loyalty lay, had written in 1838 that he was "utterly opposed [to government by an absolute numerical majority] . . . [it] would destroy our system and destroy the South."[31]

Avery Craven's denial of John Calhoun's South as an objective entity was cited in a collection of essays whose title, *The Southerner as American*, telegraphs its intentions. Published in 1960, the essays were clearly aimed at promoting national unity and rehabilitating the white South in a time of racial and sectional discord. In one essay, Charles Sellers writes that the "American Experience knows no greater tragedy than the Old South's twistings and turnings on the rack of slavery," obscuring the somewhat greater tragedy befalling the enslaved.[32] This observation is in itself evidence of a southern mindset that reached into the twentieth century; Sellers goes on to depict an antebellum white

South struggling with its own conscience over the slavery issue and recognizing the paradox of upholding, at the same time, both slavery and liberty. (William Cooper has offered a more compelling analysis of the slave owner's view of liberty: "Without control of their slaves, white Southerners agreed, they could not possess their own liberty. Slavery and liberty were inextricably intertwined in the Southern mind.")[33] Sellers backs up his portrait of the antebellum southerner as ardent American by citing, but not quoting, editorials from *DeBow's Review* (a leading antebellum southern periodical) that inculcated American patriotism.[34] *DeBow's* also, however, contained passages like this, in an 1850 argument for increased southern self-sufficiency: "Who conducts our commerce, builds our ships . . . who supplies the materials and the engineers for our railroads—where we have any? The North. Who educates for us our children? The North. Various propositions have been brought forward in the view of preserving the South from the . . . dangers of the times."[35] The article is not completely lacking in nationalist sentiment ("great indeed is the value of this federal union"), but the overall tone is distinctly sectional and propagates the idea of a discrete South; an entity that, despite its lip service to American nationalism, *DeBow's* prioritized over the nation as a whole: "There must be an end, somewhere, of concessions . . . it becomes the South to determine how far its safety will admit of concession. The stand should be made there."[36] Implicit in this passage is the idea that the South's "safety," indeed its very existence, was threatened by the North.

The United States, from its inception, was composed of sections. They were not always precisely or easily demarcated, as William Freehling has shown; one section dissolved into another almost imperceptibly, and east-west and cultural and societal differences muddied the waters still further. But a strong and definite southern regional identity was forged over the 1820s and 30s, largely out of southern fear and resentment over challenges to the "peculiar institution." As David Potter wrote, "The slavery issue gave a false clarity and simplicity to sectional diversities which were diffuse and complex."[37]

Just as the North was successfully setting itself as the template for what America would be, the antebellum crisis sparked by the slavery issue allowed the heavily slavery-dependent Deep South to do the same on a regional scale, leading the more moderate and less slavery-dependent Middle and Upper Souths into the ultimate declaration of southern identity, the Confederate States of America. What effect, then, did the war that broke out in 1861 have on southern identity and regional cohesion?

CONFEDERATE NATIONALISM?

The view that the Confederacy failed to develop a sense of true nationalism is perhaps best expressed by Paul Escott. Stating that a sense of Confederate nationalism "had to grow and inspire Southerners if they were to emerge from their ordeal as an independent nation," Escott examines class divisions within the Confederacy, highlighting working-class resentment at what might be considered a struggle to preserve the way of life enjoyed by wealthy slave owners: "During the war tensions and bitterness of the Southern class system surfaced strongly, as southerners of slight or modest means looked up from their daily struggle to stay alive and saw that many wealthy individuals seemed to enjoy the position of a privileged class."[38] Evidence of class-based divisions and low morale in the Confederate South is easy to come by, and it is unquestionable that the war caused, or exposed, deep divisions in white southern society. But as historian Benjamin Carp writes: "Whether or not slavery and secession served the interests of all white Southerners in 1860–1861, a significant portion of Southerners believed that they did. They were nationalists because their community of interests was embodied in the Confederate nation."[39] There were also comparable divisions in the North, as demonstrated by the political strength of the antiwar "Copperhead" Democrats and the 1863 anti-draft riots in New York City.

Historians such as Carl Degler, Charles Sellers, Kenneth Stampp, and Bell Irvin Wiley all contributed to a historical portrait of an antebellum and wartime South that was more or less "American," but Drew Gilpin Faust has raised an obvious and pertinent question: if southern nationalism is to be dismissed, how to explain the Confederacy and the war, which did not end when things began to go badly for the Confederacy but dragged on for four long and draining years?[40] There was more, then, than the appearance of southern nationalism; the Confederate experience did inculcate a discrete and distinct white southern identity. Indeed, as Quigley has pointed out, "By the end of 1861, nationalism was an inescapable and an increasingly consequential feature of life in the South."[41]

There are myriad examples of a southern nationalism that endured in the face of plummeting Confederate fortunes, but the nationalist sentiment is most clearly indicated by the lengths to which Confederates were willing to go in order to preserve their independence.[42] In November 1864, Jefferson Davis proposed that the Confederate government purchase, train, and arm forty thousand slaves, the survivors of whom would be rewarded with emancipation.[43] Escott stresses planter resistance to the idea, arguing that planters' actions throughout the war "showed that their basic commitment was to slavery rather than independence and Confederate nationalism."[44] The evidence suggests, however, that over the course of the war, much as Union war aims widened to include emancipation, Confederate priorities shifted somewhat from protection of the "Peculiar Institution" to preservation of national independence.[45] Robert Bonner points to Confederate secretary of state Judah Benjamin's recognition of the diplomatic value to an independent Confederacy of "even a gradual move away from slavery."[46] A letter to an Augusta newspaper in March 1865 provides further evidence for this shift. The writer argued that Confederate emancipation would deprive the Union of its moral imperative for continuing the war, enabling a peaceful resolution that preserved Confederate independence and, critically, the racial hierarchy: "It may be abolished without violating the great principle of subordination, which we have all regarded as the essential feature of Southern civilization."[47]

If in 1861, southern emphasis was on redeeming an America ruined by the Yankees, four years of war had replaced that priority with a focus on surviving as a separate nation. Jefferson Davis, by 1864, was talking no longer about George Washington but about self-determination: "We are fighting for independence, and that—or extermination—we WILL have."[48] In the aftermath of the failed Hampton Roads peace conference in 1865, mass public meetings were held in Mobile, Richmond, Lynchburg, and other towns. Jefferson Davis appeared and spoke before ten thousand spectators at the Richmond meeting. The *Richmond Enquirer* reported: "President Davis was greeted with thunders of applause . . . he said . . . he felt a proud and ecstatic joy to see his countrymen looking . . . disasters . . . in the face and plucking from adversity new courage and resolution . . . All must be laid on the altar of country . . . let us unite our hands and hearts, lock our shields together . . . before the next summer solstice falls, it will be the enemy who will be asking us for conferences and occasion in which to make known our demands."[49] This in February 1865, when Confederate military defeat was a foregone conclusion.

The Confederacy had gone to war in 1861 in order to defend slavery; four years later, there was a willingness to sacrifice the same institution in order to preserve their independence and nationhood, with the government not only entertaining the notion of arming and freeing Black men but taking steps to do so. Even with the necessary caveat that this flexibility was being applied to the legal practice of slavery and not to the region's racial hierarchy or white hegemony, this is a remarkable testament to the effect that the Civil War had on the South and its perception of itself. What follows, then, recognizes a Confederate nationalism forged between 1861 and 1865 and, through the lens of commemorative activity, examines what happened to that nationalism when there was no more nation.

Historian Don Doyle has stated that former Confederates met defeat "with stoic resignation" and that there were "remarkably few guerilla bands offering resistance, no pockets of irreconcilable opposition to reunion with the United States."[50] This is arguable; certainly, the number of Black people slaughtered during Reconstruction (and afterward) demonstrates a sustained resistance to any kind of reunion that recognized African American citizenship.[51] This white guerrilla-style terrorism, a defiant and resistant white public mood, and continued federal military control of the South make it plausible to argue that a state of quasi-war persisted well after Appomattox. An 1873 South Carolina newspaper editorial certainly suggests an undimmed loyalty to the Confederacy: "Whatever the politicians seeking place may say, the heart of the people is as true now to that cause for which they gave and suffered so much as it was when the colors of the South were floating most bravely."[52] At this same time, the re-formed United States was planning an ambitious world's fair to mark its one hundredth year, and this book zeroes in on this particular moment in the long process of reunion and reconciliation. As white southerners alternately shunned or engaged selectively and conditionally with this celebrations of American nationhood, African Americans embraced the opportunity to stake their claim to full agency and citizenship. The commemorative activity of the Reconstruction era was inseparably intertwined with its politics, and ostensibly unifying and celebratory commemorations of the nation's founding served as arenas for reflecting the deep sectional, partisan, and racial divisions of an unreconciled nation.

1

Antebellum and Wartime
Fourths of July

"The Yankees have robbed us of too much already. We have no idea of giving up the national anniversary—not a bit of it. The Fourth of July is ours . . . Long live the Confederacy and huzza for the old Fourth of July."[1] This was the response of a Louisiana newspaper to the news that units of the Confederate army, in the first summer of the Civil War, intended to celebrate the "glorious old Fourth of July."[2] Independence Day marked the creation of the nation that these southerners were breaking away from yet would remain a highly politicized and contested commemoration. Indeed, the Fourth of July had provided a mirror for sectional, racial, and partisan divisions almost from the beginning.[3] Independence Day was generally perceived as celebrating American nationalism, but that concept was understood differently from place to place, and in the words of historian Len Travers, "Nationalism may have seemed little more than localism writ large."[4] Any post-Revolutionary sense of unity in the new United States was short-lived: between the inaugurations of Washington and Jefferson, Americans developed two parallel imagined communities—two national identities—existing side by side, each denying the legitimacy of the other.[5] The Jefferson-led Democratic-Republicans were, broadly, more democratic, pro-French, and anti-British, while the Federalists were pro-British, anti-French, and more hierarchical and traditional. By 1800, these two parties were holding separate Fourth of July commemorations in most towns and villages across the country, and these opposing rituals served as vehicles for creating partisan "bubbles." Participants in alternative celebrations were decried as foreigners, "outside the circle of true Americanism," delegitimizing them as opposition and as Americans.[6] As Federalists conflated Republicans with the French and Republicans tied the Federalists with the British, the Fourth of July was turned into a day of "rancour, hatred and unfriendly contention."[7]

There was a commonly adhered to routine for Independence Day rituals, and interestingly, there does not seem to be much evidence of regional or party-based variation in the form of the celebration. Most observances began with a parade or procession, which would lead to a church, courthouse, town square, or other locale, where the ceremonies would take place. This would involve prayers, orations, patriotic songs, and reading of the Declaration of Independence, followed by food and drink and, with the drinks, toasts. These could be numerous—one celebration in Georgia included the raising of eighty-seven toasts. The variation came in the content of the speeches and toasts, which served as summations of the political stance of the faction holding the celebration. An 1801 Republican gathering in Massachusetts saw toasts to the memory of George Washington politicized by criticism of Federalist proposals to erect an ostentatious tomb for the late president: "The memory of Washington—More durably embalmed in the affections of Republicans than in the most *costly Mausoleum*. Three cheers!"[8] A Washington militia group responded with twelve cheers to this toast in 1814: "The Principles of Federalism: the political creed of the best and wisest men in our country—the safety and existence of the nation depend on their prevalence."[9]

The political specificity of these events is further evidenced by notices such as this one from 1812: "The Republicans of the town of Windsor . . . will celebrate the anniversary of American Independence on the 4th of July ensuing at the meeting house in the West Parish . . . Refreshments will be provided by Rufus Root, Esq."[10] Meanwhile, toasts offered at this Federalist Fourth, characterizing the Jefferson and Madison administrations as "bad nurses," highlight the partisan rhetoric employed at these celebrations: "To the United States: While rocked in the cradle of constitutional liberty, their infancy was healthy and vigorous and their early decrepitude is owing to bad nurses and physicians, not to original defect in the natural constitution."[11]

Women did not offer toasts or make speeches but were nonetheless an integral part of these celebrations. One celebrant in South Carolina remarked in 1793 that "the fair were not excluded from our pleasure, but their firmness, their resolution, their patriotism were again an embellishment to their charm."[12] Len Travers makes the interesting point that to some extent the performative aspects of these commemorations were *for* women—that female presence at Fourth celebrations provided an affirmation both of the commemoration itself and the men's performances.[13] The announcement of a Mississippi Fourth celebration in 1838 corroborates that argument. Trumpeting "liberal and efficient measures to celebrate our National Birthday in a becoming manner," a local newspaper made the point that festivities would "occur in the cool of the morning, and at an hour when the ladies would choose to appear."[14]

The second decade of the nineteenth century found the Federalist Party in eclipse and the Democratic Republican Party in ascendance, resulting in a relatively tranquil "Era of Good Feelings" capped off by James Monroe's unopposed election as president in 1820. This tranquility was reflected in Independence Day commemorations. In 1817, New Englander Isaiah Thomas noted in his diary that Federalists and Republicans celebrated the Fourth together in Worcester, Massachusetts, and that "every thing was done to the satisfaction of both parties: neither the oration or the Toasts gave the least offense."[15] Travers sees, at the same time, a diminishing of the Fourth's relevance, with the day "losing its immediacy and power to persuade Americans of their homogeneity in the face of rapid geographic expansion, new national concerns, and budding sectional issues . . . the nationalist message of July 4 became increasingly diffused."[16] This decline in significance was slowed by one event: the nearly simultaneous deaths of Thomas Jefferson and John Adams on 4 July 1826, the fiftieth anniversary of independence. The impact of this double departure was considerable. But as a regional bias in memorial orations—favoring either Adams or Jefferson depending on the location of the eulogizer—hinted, commemorative unanimity did not outlive the Era of Good Feelings.[17] Americans were gradually being driven apart over the issue of human slavery, and uses of the Fourth over the following three decades reflected that.

As white southerners used the Fourth to celebrate the slaveholding republic that they felt was intended by the founders, abolitionists and Black Americans saw the same day as an opportunity to promulgate a philosophy that undermined the bedrock of southern life and to demand liberation. Indeed, Frederick Douglass's refusal to commemorate the Fourth was as powerful a statement as the affirmative parades, speeches, and picnics that were going on around him. In repudiating the Fourth, Douglass still marked it and used it: "What, to the American slave, is your 4th of July? I answer; a day that reveals to him, more than all other days in the year, the gross injustice and cruelty to which he is the constant victim. To him, your celebration is a sham; your boasted liberty, an unholy license; your national greatness, swelling vanity . . . There is not a nation on the earth guilty of practices more shocking and bloody than are the people of the United States, at this very hour."[18] Free Black Americans, as indicated by these remarks, tended to shun celebrations of Independence Day in the antebellum decades.[19] Black groups often held alternative meetings on 5 July—as did an 1832 Ohio gathering, whose members were told: "We have met on this 5th of July, not under the mock pretense of celebrating the 4th of July, for that would betray us in a want of sound understanding . . . this day causes millions of our race to groan under the galling yoke of bondage."[20] In 1827, free Blacks in Fredericksburg, Virginia, *did* gather on the Fourth to commemorate the abolition of slavery in New York, which went into effect that day. On this occasion, the Declaration of Independence was read, toasts to liberty and equality were offered, and the account furnished to *Freedom's Journal* encouraged Black engagement with the day: "The Fourth of July 1827 is a memorable epoch and ought ever to be dear to the minds of the present and succeeding descendants of the African race. Its return should be annually celebrated."[21] In 1848, Frederick Douglass's Rochester, New York, paper reported on the "anniversary of American hypocrisy." Commenting on the enthusiastic celebrations in that city, the paper noted that "theirs is a white liberty."[22] A few years later, the same paper used the Fourth to point out the shortfalls in American liberty by reporting that "they celebrated the Fourth of July at Columbus, Ga. by the sale of one hundred slaves! What a land of liberty this is!"[23] Still, in their avoidance of the day, these dissenters testified to the power that commemorative rites exercised over people's sense of identity and belonging, something that would be seen again in white southern reaction to the Centennial celebrations of 1876.

Rather than the Fourth, then, the antebellum period saw widespread Black celebration of Freedom Days that commemorated British emancipation of West Indian slaves on 1 August 1834. These African American celebrants, in Mitch Kachun's words, "hoped to establish a commemorative tradition, to articulate their historical consciousness to the American public, and to leave a legacy for coming generations."[24] Black abolitionist Absalom Jones prescribed solemnity as a hallmark of Emancipation Day observation, in deliberate contrast to the increasingly boisterous white Fourth of July celebrations, from which Blacks were largely excluded: "Let us be sober-minded, humble, peaceable, temperate . . . frugal in our apparel."[25] While 1 August observances initially lacked firecrackers and other frivolities associated with the Fourth, they were political statements in public spaces, involving parades and processions.[26] While white abolitionists sometimes organized their own 1 August rites and attended Black-run celebrations, the celebrations tended to be under Black control. Black abolitionists often chafed under white dominance of the movement, and Emancipation Day observances gave them an opportunity to demonstrate their own initiative and make their own statement through commemorative ritual.[27]

As the years passed, Emancipation Day began to take on some of the more boisterous characteristics of the Fourth. Frederick Douglass described an 1859 gathering at Geneva, New York: "The ringing of bells, firing of guns, and the sound of music with the gay, fluttering throngs which arrived by every train gave proof of the general joy. The great good nature and boisterous merriment of the colored people, though at times not over regardful of good taste, seemed to awaken in the white people a good deal of mirth, but it was mirth without malice . . . to many of us the first of August is like the white man's 4th of July, a day of freedom from ordinary restraints . . . without any marked concern for . . . decorum. There were a few at Geneva who carried this 4th of July-ism a little too far, but they were the exceptions."[28] Here Douglass exhibited the concern with white opinion that marked Black social movements all the way into the twentieth century as well as the prewar popularity of Emancipation Day. After war and emancipation, however, African American citizens would embrace Independence Day celebrations as a vehicle for confirming that citizenship, a shift that will be examined in chapter 2.

Celebrations of the Fourth evolved in subtle ways that reflected changes in American politics and society. Reflecting the growing popularity of civic groups and fraternal organizations, Fourth of July parades included increasingly higher representation from such groups. As implicit statements of identity, they offered different, and competing ideas of America and Americanism. In the early nineteenth century, there was an increasing utilization of the Fourth by local and civic associations. These associations, which people used to identify themselves with groups and causes, point up the linkage of commemoration with identity. As these associations tended to be a feature of middle-class or bourgeoisie life, they also served to reinforce the idea that commemoration was under elite control. Some associative groups linked with movements, such as abolitionism or temperance, used commemorative ritual to advance their causes. When Charlotte, North Carolina, saw an Independence Day in 1842 organized by local temperance advocates, it was typical of other observances, with a reading of the Declaration and more than fifty toasts, although the glasses raised contained nothing but "pure, cold water."[29] Five years later, at another temperance-centered celebration, a newspaper account noted that in spite of the lack of alcohol in the toasts, "the racy pun, the sparkling jest, and witty repartee circulated most merrily."[30]

The involvement of local civic organizations, membership of which helped to define an individual's identity, thus helps to establish linkage between commemorative activity and identity, both personal and national. It also points to the role of local elites in managing commemoration. Mary Lou Nemanic has described ways in which post-Revolutionary elites attempted to build and reinforce national unity by substituting formal and solemn nationalistic rites for the rowdiness often displayed by the lower orders on early Fourths.[31] While they were unsuccessful in curtailing all bumptious elements of the celebration (English diarist Frederick Marryat wondered in 1837, "The Americans may have great reason to be proud of this day, but why do they get so confoundedly drunk?"), they did manage to largely replace the practice of setting bonfires and blowing up homemade firecrackers with civic firework displays under the control of local leadership.[32] Kurt Ritter and James Andrews, working on the assumption that editors knew their audiences, have argued that the orations and toasts published in early-nineteenth-century partisan newspapers provide reliable windows into the thoughts and feelings of ordinary Americans of the time.[33] Len Travers disagrees, seeing the printed record as the record of an elite with its own agenda. Travers's working class was more into celebrating the Fourth with drinking, parades, fireworks, and sporting activities.[34] But the majority of people at any given time have priorities beyond the political, and their participation in and acceptance of particular commemorative activities can fairly be interpreted, irrespective of alcohol consumption or rowdy behavior, as a statement of belonging to a faction, community, or nationality.

Mitch Kachun, meanwhile, has pointed up the didactic uses of commemoration by pointing out that July Fourth parades were "designed explicitly to teach the public the lessons of patriotism as well as their own place in the social order."[35] A participant in an 1847 Fourth in North Carolina acknowledged the part played by the local "worthies" in orchestrating the celebration: "Our little town was alive yesterday, in honor of the '4th' . . . the worthies took an abundance of trouble . . . and expended themselves in fireworks. There was besides the illuminated Courthouse with its flags and banners, gunpowder and fire enough in general to have satisfied the heart and aspirations of Old Zachary [Taylor?] himself."[36] As this account indicates, the Fourth was generally celebrated enthusiastically in the white South throughout the antebellum period. One account, from 1839, proclaimed that "in the midst of an era of unparalleled party excitement, the Fourth of July has never been commemorated with more universal, fervent and sincere outpourings of patriotism. While this feeling prevails, no fears need be entertained for the duration of the Union."[37]

What this sort of optimism overlooked was that white southerners were celebrating a different sort of Union—one that was defined by the rights of the member states to hold human property. Independence Day was, of course, a commemoration of the Declaration of Independence, and that document was put to use in differing ways that reflected the concerns and the divisions of the nineteenth century. Abolitionists took the Declaration's assertion of equality literally and used the Fourth to point out the gap between the ideals in the document being celebrated and the reality of a slaveholding society. William Lloyd Garrison used the day to challenge American self-congratulation, calling the Fourth "the time-honored, wine-honored, toast-drinking, powder-wasting, tyrant-killing Fourth of July—consecrated for the last sixty years to bombast, to falsehood, to impudence, to hypocrisy."[38] In his study of historical memory in the United States, Michael Kammen reproduces an 1845 painting in the primitive style depicting people gathered in a park setting, with food-laden picnic tables under a fluttering American flag. Contextualizing the image as depicting merely a "festal" occasion, Kammen obscures the juxtaposition of political and commemorative by not noting that the celebration shown was specifically an antislavery Fourth picnic, held at Weymouth Landing, Massachusetts.[39]

Meanwhile, as many southern whites who were reluctant or ambivalent defenders of slavery gradually morphed into active proponents of the institution, they opted for nonliteral interpretations of the Declaration they were celebrating. Future president John Tyler, during the Missouri Compromise debates of 1820, clarified that the idea of human equality as expressed in the Declaration, "although lovely and beautiful, cannot obliterate those distinctions in society which society itself engenders and gives birth to."[40] John Calhoun went further by describing the Declaration's ideals as "a false and dangerous notion" and spoke of the "great . . . error" committed by its drafters.[41]

And so though there was, in William Blair's words, a "cautious reevaluation of the Union" in southern distancing from July Fourth activities, there was not yet any wholesale abandonment of the holiday.[42] In 1849, the *Raleigh Register* stated that "there are but few places in the Union where . . . the day is celebrated with more lively enthusiasm."[43] Similarly, six years later, a Knoxville paper boasted that the Fourth in that city would "surpass in grandeur and interest anything of the kind ever witnessed in this end of the state!"[44] The account went on to describe the planned procession and fireworks, before concluding: "All of the world and the rest of mankind will be here. Come one, come all, and see how we do it up in the Queen City of East Tennessee!"[45] This parochial focus and local boosterism recurs frequently in these accounts and would be even more prominent when the white South engaged with the American Centennial a couple of decades later. So, as Fourth observances were so locally driven and controlled, with orations and toasts having distinctly regional or cause-centered flavor, their popularity in the late antebellum South should not be misinterpreted: the Fourth was seen and used there as a vehicle for promotion of a particular version of the United States. Writing five years before secession, a Wilmington editor highlighted its polemical uses: "Thousands of preachers and orators at the North will avail themselves of the opportunity to instil hatred of the South and her institutions . . . We cannot, therefore, look forward to the influence of the day with the same hopeful feelings that used to animate us on such occasions."[46]

In 1854, a Charleston newspaper remarked upon the resilience of Independence Day celebrations, asserting that the day was "one of the 'peculiar institutions' of our country, about whose extension there is not likely to be any doubt."[47] As use of the phrase *peculiar institution* and reference to a noted abolitionist indicated, however, the sectional conflicts of the decade were inextricably bound up with this editor's thoughts on the Fourth: "Even the Garrisons of the land are compelled to honor the day and recognize its special prominence in the Calendar by the impotent assertions of fanaticism, spleen and blasphemy which they utter on it."[48] This sort of "blasphemy" was on display two years later in Framingham, Massachusetts, where an Independence Day gathering was held with the stated intention of rescuing the Fourth "from the ordinary popular descecration and consecrate[ing] it to the cause of impartial and universal liberty, by striking a mortal blow at the existence of slavery in our land."[49] In 1857, the *Texas State Gazette* linked the Fourth to the sectional crisis, calling it a day "for serious reflection" upon the obligation of citizens whose democracy was threatened by "false and dangerous doctrines . . . [and the] attacks of demagogues."[50]

As the sections drew further apart, there was some attempt to use the Fourth to bridge the division. Adam Criblez, in his study of midwestern Fourths, has described efforts by community leaders in that region to focus on their "shared revolutionary legacy" and revive interest in "old-fashioned," patriotic Fourth of July celebrations.[51] Similarly, in New Orleans, the *Daily Picayune* condemned the lack of will among local officialdom to organize or fund Independence Day celebrations in 1857: "Next Saturday will be the glorious fourth . . . what is to be done, if anything must be done quickly."[52] In Richmond, Virginia, one newspaper editor pined nostalgically for the "joy and merriment" of the "country" celebrations of his youth.[53] In 1860, Mississippi governor John Pettus, when asked what the South would "do" with the Fourth of July in the case of disunion, responded promptly, "We will make a new one."[54] But sectional divisions, rooted in African American slavery, were leading inexorably to the breakup of the nation celebrated on 4 July. In 1859, the *Indiana State Sentinel* used the occasion of the Fourth to ponder worriedly, "What shall be our future?"[55] The short-term answer to the *Sentinel*'s query came in 1860–61, when the Union did break apart. As first the Deep South and then states such as Virginia, Tennessee, and

North Carolina seceded and banded together to form a slaveholding republic, questions of sectionalism were transformed into questions of a new nationalism and new identities.

WARTIME FOURTHS

In early 1861, just as the Union was breaking apart, the words of a Georgia planter's wife pointed up the complicated relationship between Americanism and southern identity in a region on the cusp of war. In a letter to her adult son, Mary Jones reflected that

> an indescribable sadness weighs down my soul when I think of our once glorious but now dissolving Union! Our children's children—what will constitute their national pride and glory? We have no alternative, and necessity demands that we now protect ourselves from entire destruction at the hands of those who have . . . obliterated every national bond of union, of confidence and affection. When your brother and yourself were very little fellows, we took you into old Independence Hall, and at the foot of Washington's statue I pledged you both to support and defend the Union. *That Union* has passed away, and you are free from your mother's vow.[56]

A couple of years later, Virginian Isaac Handy, captive in a Union prison, versified in his journal that "it [the American flag] steals from his master the contented old slave / and it gives the old Negro a comfortless grave."[57] Neither Handy nor Mrs. Jones was directly addressing the question of Independence Day celebrations when she disavowed her pledge in Independence Hall, but the same impulse led many Confederates to distance themselves from that most American of holidays. Still, there remained some voices of support for continued celebration of the Fourth of July in the wartime South.

The impulse to continue celebrating the Fourth of July was largely the result of a widespread southern belief that the newly formed Confederate States of America (CSA) were the true embodiment of American ideals. As the *Southern Monthly* put it: "The government of the Confederate States is in conformity to that established by the fathers of the American Revolution, and a continuance of the government they established."[58] The *Raleigh Register* endorsed this view and laid claim to the Fourth at the same time: "[There is] no reason why the birthday of Liberty should be permitted to pass unheeded . . . the principles asserted on the Fourth of July 1776 were those of man's competence for self-government and the South . . . has but reasserted those principles."[59]

Indeed, at his Richmond inauguration ceremony on 22 February 1862, scheduled to coincide with George Washington's birthday, Jefferson Davis stood beside a statue of the first president and declared, "On this birthday of the man most identified with the establishment of American independence, beneath the monument erected to commemorate his heroic virtues and those of his compatriots, we have assembled to usher into existence the Permanent Government of the Confederate States . . . the day, the purpose and the memory seem fitly associated."[60] Positioning himself and his compatriots as the true heirs of Washington, Davis denied any revolutionary intent in secession, insisting that the South was only resisting the perceived threats posed by Lincoln's Republican Party and seeking to protect the ideals of the Founding Fathers. The *New Orleans Daily Picayune,* for one, reinforced this claim with its description of the Confederacy as merely "acting over again the history of the American Revolution of 1776."[61] The *Charleston Mercury* insisted, in that first July of the war, that the Fourth "is truly our Independence Day. It is the North that should properly refuse to recognize it. That region has distinctly repudiated all the ideals of July 4, 1776."[62]

But the North largely managed to conflate its version of Americanism with America itself, a feat summed up by Paul Quigley when he commented that since it had been the South that left the Union, "the institutional embodiments of American nationalism remained in Northern hands."[63] This resulted, almost inevitably, in southern detachment from the Fourth once war was underway. The process had, though, begun earlier, as evidenced by a bill placed before the South Carolina legislature in December 1860. The bill, presented in the same month that the state withdrew from the Union, fixed several dates, such as Christmas and Good Friday, as official state holidays but omitted the Fourth of July. The *Mobile Advertiser* took exception to this omission: "Must we give up everything to the North, Fourth of July included? Does the Fourth of July belong particularly to the North? Are its glorious memories the property of the North more than the South? They are vandal hands that would violate the patriotic sanctity of the Fourth of July."[64] In the North, meanwhile, the *Worcester (MA) Spy* remarked simply that the Carolinians' course was the correct one since they no longer had a "right to celebrate the Fourth of July as a holiday."[65]

Just after the first Independence Day of the Civil War, the *Charleston Courier* described the commemorations in the outlying Georgetown district of South Carolina. The account, attributed to "Rifleman," contained no references to the Declaration of Independence but did point out that the occasion had kicked off with a reading, "in a clear and audible voice," of South Carolina's Ordinance of Secession.[66] Numerous orations were summarized, and the common theme running throughout was patriotism—but a very specific Confederate brand of patriotism. "Dr. Sparkman" spoke of the "merits of our cause, also showing the many benefits which the South will derive from separation."[67] A Colonel J. H. Read urged, "in warm and patriotic language, the intuition of patriotic principles into our children." Their appetites having been "sharpened" by listening to the "patriotic and well-timed addresses," the celebrants sat down to a table "well-filled with all the delicacies of the season." The account concluded that the dinner was "highly creditable to the getters-up of it and . . . it was not at all diminished by the presence of old Abe's sharks on our coast, which is cheering evidence that we can live without the aid of the Yankees and can get up a true Southern dinner, ample enough for a Prince."[68] Here we see the Fourth of July being appropriated by white southerners to ratify secession and their own independence.

The same year, in a similar vein, a Mississippi newspaper commented that "the 'Glorious Fourth of July' was celebrated with enthusiasm in the chief towns and cities of the South. Our people very correctly concluded that they were better entitled to do so than the Yankees . . . It seems astonishing that anyone should ever for a moment have entertained a dream of our being bullied out of our right to the Fourth of July by the Yankee government."[69] Meanwhile, in Louisiana, the *Daily True Delta* insisted that "the Yankees have robbed us of too much already. We have no idea of giving up the national anniversary— not a bit of it. The Fourth of July is ours . . . Long live the Confederacy and huzza for the old Fourth of July."[70]

But in Augusta, Georgia, the *Constitutionalist* disagreed. Expressing "strong and abiding confidence in the justice of our cause and the strength of our arms," the newspaper nonetheless argued that it would be prudent to avoid public commemoration of the Fourth during wartime, but "when our new Republic shall have been firmly established and the glorious principles of the Declaration of Independence fully vindicated we may, in the exuberance of our gratitude to kind Heaven . . . celebrate the old Independence Day and with it the new Independence Day, with all the noisy demonstrations of the past."[71]

On the occasion of the war's second Fourth, a Richmond newspaper argued for the South's continued observance, arguing that the Confederacy was fighting for the values represented by the Declaration, while in the North, "sanctimonious Yankee orators will read this declaration to gaping crowds and desecrate the memory of the illustrious statesmen of '76 by attempting to justify this iniquitous war against the people of the South."[72]

In Union-occupied Nashville, local authorities requested churches to ring their bells to mark the Fourth of July 1862; all but one refused, with two clergymen stating that they would "rather have their churches burned down than grant the request."[73] Referring to the "so-called anniversary of our national independence," the *Edgefield Advertiser* in South Carolina opined that the day's glory "is now departed, and that forever."[74] In response to urgings to continue observing the day, the

Advertiser asserted that the Fourth, despite having been "respectfully" celebrated throughout the South for decades, had

> for a long time been *par excellence*, the great day of Yankeedoodle-dum proper . . . when the South, under the exactions of an oppressive government, began year by year to find less joy in an anniversary which seemed a mockery amidst her wrongs, the men of the North... increased the fervour of their patriotic demonstrations. It was evident that the day, while in name a commemoration of past events, was in reality a rendering up of hallelujahs to a government which was doing whatever its increasing powers enabled it to do, for the aggrandisement of one section at the expense of another. Now that the Union is defunct forever, it is natural that the day should be buried with it.[75]

At the same time, this writer refused to relinquish southern claims on the legacy of 1776 but advocated consecrating a new commemorative date for a new nation: "It is true that we at the South have in one sense the only just claim to proper celebration of the day. In selecting another anniversary for the South, we can carry to it all our reverence for the past and encircle it with all our hopes for the future."[76]

The fall of Vicksburg on 4 July 1863 could only have furthered Confederate aversion for the Fourth. John Pemberton, Confederate commander of the besieged fortress town on the Mississippi, if not exactly celebrating it, still made use of the holiday. Asked about the timing of his surrender to Union forces, Pemberton explained that "the answer is obvious. I believed that upon that day I should receive better terms. Well aware of the vanity of our foes, I knew they would attach vast importance to entrance on the Fourth of July to the stronghold of the great river, and that to gratify their national vanity, they would yield then what could not be extorted from them at any other time."[77]

Independence Day observations the same year in Washington, DC, would provide a neat illustration of Quigley's argument about northern appropriation of the "embodiments" of American nationhood and the resultant alienation of white southerners from Independence Day rituals. The federal capital's commemoration of the Fourth involved the installation of the statue representing "freedom," which still sits atop the dome of the U.S. Capitol. Reflecting upon the plans for this celebration, one southern journal compared Abraham Lincoln's administration to the tyranny of Roman emperors: "Mr. Lincoln is learning his lessons in the art of enslavement very well . . . it is well known that tyrants seek to amuse or captivate by shows and spectacles the people whom they would enslave. The gladiatorial combats of old Rome kept the populace entertained while the Caesars plundered the treasury and ran riot in their palaces . . . Old Abe . . . is beginning to profit from the lessons of history and this Freedom celebration in Washington is intended to delight the Yankees, from whom Freedom has taken her everlasting flight."[78]

Concomitant with this Confederate detachment from the symbols of American nationhood, there developed a discrete Confederate nationalism; part and parcel of this was a disengagement with the Fourth of July that was nearly total by the latter part of the war. Even in the face of newly constructed Confederate identity, however, the Fourth still had its rhetorical uses. When the *Augusta (GA) Constitutionalist* remarked on the Fourth of July 1864, it made no mention of local observations or oratories but utilized the occasion to claim, "Southern statesmanship and Southern heroism combined achieved the independence of the States." It also, crucially, stressed the nationalist goal of the war: "Already the history of our young Republic is written in blood . . . the patriotism of our people will soon be rewarded with peace and independence. The 4th of July 1865 will, we firmly believe, dawn upon the Confederate States as one of the acknowledged powers of the earth, for we see through the smoke of battle the eagle perched on our victorious standards."[79]

This vision of victorious standards was, of course, faulty. When the war ended in 1865, former Confederates were left with a nation lost and a world they perceived as turned upside down. These feelings were summed up piquantly in one southern woman's diary entry: "Oh God we are a subjugated people . . . this is too bitter. I would bear bravely as long as there was hope but now . . . the town is garrisoned . . . a Yankee wretch at every corner and we are under Yankee rule. Negroes free!"[80]

2

Contesting the Southern Fourth of July

In 1860 an Alabamian penned a description of the Independence Day holiday, the last before secession and war: "We had a splendid picknick and barbecue at the Steam Mill on the Glorious Fourth; at least we had some rareties there in the shape of iced water and lemonade, it looks rather strange to see ice in such warm weather . . . there was musick of the drums and calaranets [sic]. Then the Declaration of Independence was read by Mr. McAlily. The people were then told that dinner was ready and to march after the drum, the gentlemen escorting the ladies. But every lady rushed helter skelter for the tables as if they had nothing for breakfast."[1] Just a few years later, however, the Fourth of July no longer meant lemonade and "calaranets" to white southerners; four years of civil war had rendered Independence Day anathema to them. The source of this antipathy was, broadly, twofold: bitter postwar feelings toward the victorious federal government and a deep resentment at what was seen as Reconstruction's reversal of a natural racial and social order.[2]

David Blight has summed up the problem of Reconstruction with a question: "how to make the logic of sectional reconciliation compatible with the logic of emancipation?"[3] The answer to that, in the short term, at least: it was impossible. White southerners, in the words of historian David Goldfield, "saw in [their] black neighbor both the reason and the fact of [their] defeat" and were simply not willing to accept their former bondsmen as coequal and free citizens.[4] As Gregory Downs has vividly described it, "Slavery had to be pried away from the body politic like a tick from the skin."[5] In this earliest period following cessation of battle, reunion was still metaphorically, and to an extent literally, accomplished at gunpoint, and reconciliation was scarcely on the horizon. If the meaning of the Declaration of Independence had proven malleable for antebellum debates on slavery, that was no longer the case in 1865. Pauline Maier comments that the Declaration, "in Lincoln's hands, became first and foremost a living document for an established society, a set of goals to be realized over time."[6] The society, and the version of the United States, that Lincoln had established was not the one envisioned and fought for by white southerners. This would be clearly reflected in attitudes toward Fourth of July commemoration.

AFRICAN AMERICAN CELEBRATION OF INDEPENDENCE DAY

White South Carolinian Emma Le Conte encapsulated white southern sentiments concerning Independence Day when she vented to her diary on that 1865 Fourth that "the white people shut themselves within doors and the darkies had the day to themselves—they, and the Yankees."[7] Le Conte continued, disconsolately, "I could have listened to the roar of cannon at our very doors all day and thought it music were it celebrating our independence but well, well, what is the use of talking about it?"[8]

In Austin, Texas, a local (white) newspaper, in describing the first postwar Fourth in 1865, reported that "the negroes made a regular holiday affair of it, gadding about, and seemed to be hugely satisfied with the proceedings."[9] In the same year, the New Orleans Tribune, an African American paper, provided a description of the Fourth in Mobile, Alabama: "The ever memorable fourth was celebrated here by the colored population in fine style."[10] The Tribune, however, made it clear that the Fourth was about more than "gadding about" to Mobile's Blacks. After a recitation of various groups marching in the Mobile parade, the paper's correspondent noted that "a large number of enfranchised citizens turned out to witness the demonstration. Many [whites] looked 'daggers' but could not prevent it [the parade]."[11] After recording that the procession "passed off quietly and with satisfaction," the *Tribune's* correspondent devoted the rest of the report to an assessment of the political situation in Mobile. Complaining that the federal troops stationed in the city were "negro-hating . . . Western troops from Illinois and Indiana . . . the meanest and lowest men I ever met with in my life," the report concluded, "A [political] meeting was to come off in the evening but the Rebs and Copperhead Union soldiers threatened to kill all they met, which frightened our timid leaders, who concluded not to meet."[12]

In Washington, DC, which, bordered by slaveholding states both to its north and south, had remained culturally southern, the first postwar Fourth "passed off without any celebration save by the colored people, who gathered in the number of several thousand. The tone of the speeches all favored negro suffrage."[13] Also in 1865, a Freedman's Bureau report from South Carolina evidenced the assertion of both Black rights and civil presence as well as the sort of reaction it triggered in white southerners:

On the Fourth of July the colored firemen represented that Mr. Casey, the Chief of the Fire Department (heretofore an active secessionist) had forbidden them to parade their engines, although white firemen had permission. I saw Mr. Casey, warned him against making any such distinction, had the guards removed from engine houses, and in the afternoon the Freedmen prevailed. But after proceeding a short distance they were attacked by a brutal crowd, their engine was wrested from them, and they themselves were compelled to take flight. Such was the opposition which secessionists manifested to the only class of Southerners whose loyalty has been unswerving, and who, as a class, were the only citizens who desired to celebrate the Day.[14]

In 1867, the *New Orleans Tribune's* account of the Fourth in its own city reinforced the intersection of commemoration and politics in Black

Independence Day observations. The *Tribune,* reporting that "a large number of loyal citizens yesterday assembled at the Mechanics' Institute to celebrate the great national anniversary of the independence of the United States," described a racially mixed platform, which included Black legislator Robert H. Shannon, white Republican attorney Henry Dibble, a "carpetbagger" from Indiana who read the Declaration of Independence, and Louisiana native and white Republican "Scalawag" John R. G. Pitkin.[15] Pitkin, who congratulated his audience on being "no longer freedmen, but FREEMEN" went on to remind them that the "Republican party stands the representative of the cause of equality" and, paradoxically, warned against the use of the ballot for "partisan favour."[16]

The Fourth's importance as a vehicle for affirming Black citizenship in the immediate postwar years can also be seen in an account of an 1868 observation in Columbia, South Carolina, a commemoration with military overtones that would have been impossible for an enslaved people: "The negroes celebrated the day by parading their various political societies, with banners and commanding officers wearing swords; and these assembling in a grove upon the edge of town resolved themselves into a Republican mass meeting. The Declaration was read . . . after which . . . the discussion was of course political and severely Republican."[17] This account, from the *New York Times,* went on to comment on the festivities that came after the speechmaking and politicking: "There were a good many drunken negroes to be seen and heard, but the breaches of the peace were few and unimportant."[18] The *Times's* correspondent described a procession involving "a motley array of grotesque, fancy and comic characters . . . some dress as women, some as priests, military officers, monkeys, birds and monsters of nameless kinds" that paraded through the streets for a number of hours, offering the "rabble a great deal of boisterous amusement."[19] Though the *Times's* description of Columbia's Fourth is reminiscent more of an anthropologist detailing the bizarre rituals of some remote tribe than of a description of fellow citizens celebrating a shared holiday, the account does credit the Black celebrants with some serious po-

34

litical intent. Two years later, in contrast, Georgia's *Columbus Enquirer,* after commenting that for white Georgians, the Fourth of July's "spell was broken," dismissed African American commemoration of the day as "barbecues and fandangos [with]. . . a tolerably free indulgence in whisky and sundry abortive attempts to get up a dance."[20]

WHITE SOUTHERNERS AND INDEPENDENCE DAY

Southern white dismissal of the Fourth remained widespread throughout the first years of Reconstruction, leading the *New York Times,* in 1869, to wonder why the day was celebrated "almost exclusively by negroes" in the region.[21] The query provoked a sharp response from the *Louisville Courier Journal,* highlighting a widespread southern attitude: "Can't the thought peck its way through the radical skull, that a people disfranchised, subjected to military tyranny, governed . . . by negroes, denied the right of trial by jury, liable to be seized at any hour of the day or night without process of law . . . may naturally feel little disposed to celebrate the Fourth of July? . . . the memory of which can force upon their minds a horrid consciousness of the contrast between what they were and what they are."[22] The Kentucky newspaper here registered its dismay at the upending of a white supremacist social order, the disfranchisement of a segment of the southern white population, and resentment toward those it deemed responsible, but interestingly, it did not repudiate the Fourth itself, or what it stood for, in resisting commemoration of the day.

In 1866, the *Houston Telegraph,* in what a competing Republican paper called a "bilious effusion," did not disown the Declaration but claimed that the Fourth had been "turned against" white southerners: "The fourth of July remains a holiday for the United States as a nation, and will, we suppose, continue to be celebrated north of Mason and Dixon's line, but it will be passed over with indifference in the South. We have no pleasant recollections connected with it; the platitudes of the Declaration of Independence have been turned against us. In garrison towns, cannon may be fired; their sound will fall heavy on the dull air, military bands may march through the streets escorted by crowds of negroes, the people will remain at home pursuing the dull routine of their daily enjoyments."[23] The newspaper made clear that the postwar Fourth was a day for "negroes" and occupying federal troops; two groups that, as far as the *Telegraph* was concerned, did not comprise "the people."

Another Texas journal, the *Honey-Grove Enterprise*, made explicit the link between southern distaste for the Fourth and a political landscape in which white southerners felt themselves deprived of "liberty." In describing the Fourth of July in 1870, the Democratic organ noted: "No music, no banners, no feast, no sounding of drums, no jubilee in a land whose liberties are dead and among a people to whom such things would be but a mock and an empty, foolish parade."[24] The sentiment was echoed by, interestingly, a northern Democratic journal, the *Cincinnati Enquirer*, when it commented that "one of the results that have followed the accession of the Republican Party to power is the practical destruction of the 4th of July . . . the universal text of all our Independence celebrations was once the personal liberty that was birthright of every American citizen . . . that Declaration of Independence that we used to read with so much gusto and eloquence . . . will sound queerly to those of our fellow citizens who are in the South."[25] In 1870, the *Richmond Whig* commented on the dearth of Fourth observances in the white South ("our people pretty much got out of the habit of celebrating it during the war") and observed that there was no "heart" for celebrations at that time. The *Whig* then made what would come to be an oft-repeated truism for white southerners over the coming years: "(Our people) . . . can never forget that the wisdom, courage and devotion of many Southern sages and heroes bore a conspicuous part in the winning of American independence. The day belongs as much to the people of the South as to the people of the North."[26]

The idea that the South had played a key role in the Revolution and could claim a distinct role as heirs of the founders, an idea that had never been entirely abandoned during secession and war, was frequently cited by white southerners seeking to bring about a change in attitudes toward the Fourth as the Centennial of independence neared. Emphasis on the southern involvement in the Revolution cleared a path to an embrace of Independence Day, and eventually Americanism, that enabled white southerners to claim their Revolutionary legacy and status as Americans while making no concessions concerning the rightness of the Confederate cause or the supposed cruel unfairness of their present status. Closely tied to this evocation of eighteenth-century history was the reassertion of Democratic political control that was taking place in stages across the South throughout the early and middle 1870s. And it is this, more than any geographical considerations or intra-southern dissimilitude, that accounts for variations across the region in southerners' willingness to reengage with the Fourth (and with American identity).

After Democrats took control of the Texas State House in 1872 and then recaptured the governorship the following year, the *Dallas Weekly Herald*'s description of Independence Day 1874 showed how closely linked resumption of the Fourth was with Democratic political success: "Various parties and social gatherings took place in the city and suburbs, of which we have no special report, but general good feelings prevailed through our community and one feeling was manifest very generally: that since Texas is restored to her rights, Arkansas is on the high road to the same felicity, and faint ray of light has appeared even over poor Louisiana, southern men assert their inherited right to a full share of the glories which encircle the Fourth of July."[27] The cumulative effect of these incremental Democratic gains led to a turning point of sorts for white southern engagement with the Fourth in 1875, one that can arguably be linked to a particular wing of the Democratic Party.

After the election of Ulysses Grant as a Republican president in 1868, some Democrats, referred to as "New Departure Democrats," had begun to take a pragmatic view of the political landscape and decided that the path to regained power was through acceptance of the new political realities. According to Eric Foner, New Departurism only "underscored the chasm between the parties on fundamental issues and the limits of Democratic willingness to embrace change."[28] New Departure Democrats did make some appeal to the Black vote but were more interested in convincing the wider body politic that they were ready to put the war behind them. Foner calls their embrace of Black civil and political rights "grudging" and contrasts their public utterances about a new era with private mutterings about undoing "the evil of black suffrage as early as possible."[29] This faction of the Democratic Party was arguably more open to a southern embrace of American identity and values represented by commemorations such as those for Independence Day and the American Centennial of 1876 than other factions within the party.

One of the figureheads of this movement was Atlanta's Henry Woodfin Grady. Grady would gain nationwide fame as the editor and part owner of the *Atlanta Constitution* in the 1880s but first promulgated the idea of a "New South" in the pages of the *Atlanta Herald* in 1874. The New South ideal of the mid-1870s and 1880s had strong links to the New Departure movement within the Democratic Party of the late 1860s and early 1870s; in the words of historian Michael Perman, "Advocates of the New Departure and proponents of the New South, were, if not interchangeable, certainly operating in parallel."[30] This faction of the party favored a pragmatic approach accepting the reality of Black suffrage and the advisability of economic reform, and not coincidentally, it was the New Departure–leaning *Herald*, under Grady, that finally achieved some success in promoting celebration of the Fourth by white southerners. While stressing that it was "a Democratic paper always," in the summer of 1875, the *Herald* laid out the southern right to commemorate the Fourth: "As far as the South is concerned, the war is ended . . . why should not our Fourth be a soulful and sincere occasion of joy? Is it not the birthday of our country, the country that our forefathers died to establish . . . Did not we of the South bear honourable part in that revolution . . . Did we not furnish to that cause the Patrick Henry who gave it birth and volume? the Jefferson that gave it shape, and the Washington that gave it victory?"[31]

With the southern claim on Independence Day established, the

Herald went on to outline the kind of commemoration it wished to promote: "We want to see the old Fourth revived. Not revived as mere form, but as an enthusiasm . . . and when it comes we want to see our people meet it—not timidly and with lack-lustre countenances, but bravely, joyfully, with heads erect and cheeks aflame, as men rejoicing in their own right, honouring their own memories, and proclaiming the glory that is their own birthright and inheritance."[32] The newspaper sent out invitations to a select group of prominent Georgians, and their responses provide a useful sampling of attitudes to the Fourth and sectional reunion in the year before the Centennial. M. Keith Harris has remarked on the "very specific terms" under which some white southerners were willing to engage in reconciliatory efforts, and this is clearly reflected here.[33] For example, congressman William Felton insisted in his reply that the observation of the Fourth should never have been abandoned in the first place, since "all that was implied by the '4th of July' was the design of Southern brains and the achievement of Southern arms."[34] Felton acknowledged the reconciliatory potential of the day: "Let this day be . . . a witness between the North and South that we will not 'pass over to each other for harm'—a memorial of perfect amnesty."[35] The congressman, however, made clear just who was granting amnesty to whom by pointing out that "the South has never been untrue to the principles of self-government enunciated in that Declaration. As a section it has never sought to interfere with the constitutional rights and privileges of other sections."[36] This response was typical. Judge James Jackson, who could find "no sensible reason for Southern men to decline to participate" in Atlanta's Fourth, reiterated the importance of the South's contribution to the Revolution and interpreted the Civil War as a southern attempt to maintain Revolutionary ideals. Jackson reminded the *Herald*, "We again proclaimed [the principles of 1776] . . . in 1861 and fought for their maintenance for four bloody years."[37]

The *Herald* collated these responses along with some of its own editorials into a pamphlet, which it intended as an answer to "the slanders which Radical politicians are heaping upon the South," highlighting yet again how closely tied these debates were to the struggle over the region's political future.[38] The newspaper believed that this pamphlet, which was both conciliatory and unapologetic, highlighted the white South's readiness to accept a place in the Union once more, while holding fast to its own distinct Revolutionary heritage and accepting no blame for the war. As Democratic senator Thomas M. Norwood wrote in accepting the *Herald*'s invitation to Atlanta, "If our liberties have been lost, we, as Georgians, have the proud consciousness that the sin lies not at our door, or the door of the South."[39] The implication here, as in Felton's letter, is that in accepting reunion, the South was demonstrating magnanimity. Similarly, Thomas Hardeman, chairman of Georgia's State Democratic Executive Committee, expressed the hope that the North had, perhaps, learned from its supposed wrongdoing: "The struggle through which we have just passed, though disastrous to us, may yet be an instructive lesson to our conquerors, teaching them that the encroachments of liberty and power inevitably result in revolt and revolution."[40] The pro-Fourth argument was succinctly summed up by Georgia superior court judge G. J. Wright: "Although our country is not in the condition we would prefer to have it, yet it is our country, and the only one we have. Then each citizen should strive to correct its evils and add to its blessings."[41]

The *Herald* did receive some negative replies from die-hard Confederates who wanted nothing to do with the Fourth. Robert Toombs, formerly secretary of state for both the United States and the Confederacy, insisted that only when "the principles proclaimed by our ancestors in 1776" were reestablished would he join in any commemoration of the nation's birth.[42] Toombs, placing the blame for secession and war exactly where he believed it to lie, went on that he refused to shake hands "over the bloody chasm" with "those who dug it." Toombs followed the standard template in laying claim to the principles of 1776 and in apportioning blame to a chasm-digging North, but he was unable to bring himself to put the benefits of reconciliation ahead of bitterness.[43] Another recalcitrant Confederate, former congressman Absalom Harris Chappell, illustrated in his response to the *Herald* how intertwined the debate was with the political and racial upheavals surrounding Reconstruction. Citing "the harrowing spectacle of Negro and carpet-bag lawlessness, misrule and ruin," Chappell compared Republican control of the South unfavorably with eighteenth-century British rule: "I take it for granted that you do not propose . . . to glorify our deliverance during the last century from the mild, maternal British yoke, just as if we were unconscious . . . that we had come under another yoke infinitely worse than the one we threw off ninety-nine years ago—a yoke the most galling and ignominious the world ever knew."[44] As Chappell elaborated on this theme, he made clear how central the idea of racial role reversal was to white southern repugnance for the Reconstruction-era regimes: "So long as that vile yoke is upon our necks, so long as we have enjoined upon us . . . a government . . . the aim of which is to make us slaves of our former negro slaves and the Northern miscreants who use them . . . as the easy means . . . of debasing us. Let the Fourth of July, if commemorated at all in the South, be kept as a season of patriotic mourning and indignation."[45]

Chappell's observation that the Fourth was suggestive of sadness and humiliation did not necessarily imply repudiation of the Fourth itself, nor that of the nation that was born out of the Revolution. He was simply unable to divorce commemoration of the Fourth from the "infinitely worse" yoke that he saw the South as then being under, a stance that reinforces historian John Bodnar's argument that commemoration is as much concerned with the present as with the past.[46] Chappell's comments also highlighted a white southern reluctance to credit African Americans with any sort of agency, preferring to depict their former bondsmen as pawns of unscrupulous "Northern miscreants." This, of course, was a central tenet of white southern resistance to Republican control. Anne Sarah Rubin has quoted a postwar white southerner as having complained that "George Washington if he now lived would be less than a Negro."[47] Rubin has expounded on the southern view that northerners had no real interest in Black rights or equality and that the racial policies being implemented during congressional Reconstruction were only tools to humiliate (dishonor) the white South. South

Carolina general and future governor Wade Hampton, for instance, complained to President Andrew Johnson in 1866 that the deployment of Black federal troops in his state was a "direct and premeditated insult to the whole Southern people."[48] The idea that Black enfranchisement and political engagement was only desired as a means to humiliate and dishonor former Confederates served to delegitimize Reconstruction governments, and debates around the resumption of Independence Day celebrations proved a handy way of making that point.

The *Herald*'s hopes for commemoration that year were realized, and in his oration on Atlanta's big day, Georgia governor James M. Smith reiterated much that the state's notables had emphasized in their letters to the *Herald*. Noting that white observations of the Fourth had not been common in the South for many years, the (Democratic) governor insisted that this was "not for want of appreciation of the principles of '76 on the part of the people of the South. We have an especial property in them and an especial right to be proud and to celebrate them. The Declaration was drafted by a Southern man. The proposition was first made by Southern men. The army of the Revolution was led to victory by a Southern man. I shall not allow anyone to deprive me of the privilege of rejoicing on this anniversary."[49] Smith then went a step farther than most of the *Herald*'s correspondents in not only establishing southern claim to the ideals of 1776 but allowing a place in his ideal of America for both South and North: "The principles of the Declaration are the principles upon which I stand and upon which the Southern people stand and I am willing for everybody to get on it . . . I am glad to have the Northern and the Southern people commingle together on this platform. The people, the real people, of the North are not opposed to it and they lack only the opportunity to manifest their devotion to it unmistakably. I tell you, when the . . . honest masses of both sections, meet and strike hands, the tricksters and soulless demagogues had better get out of the way, for their doom will be sealed."[50] Crucially, however, Smith distinguished between "real people" in the North and the reviled Radicals held responsible for current conditions in the South, or what Absalom Chappell had referred to as the "vile yoke." Of course, although their support was slipping by 1875, the Radical Republicans still had the support of many real people in the North, but this kind of distinction allowed white southerners a path to reconciliation without having to concede anything.

Atlanta's celebration was one of the largest of 1875 but far from the only one in the South that year. Descriptions of 1875 observations of the Fourth in Norfolk and Lynchburg, Virginia, and Savannah, Georgia, all noted that the day was more generally observed than it had been since the outbreak of war.[51] A correspondent for the *Charleston News & Courier*, reporting on the commemoration in Augusta, Georgia, declared that the "harmony of these festivities . . . [is] significant of the spirit of the times. The silver-winged spirit of Peace . . . hovers over our late distracted country."[52] A delegation from a white South Carolina militia group, the Charleston Riflemen, attended the same celebration, however, and a spokesman for this group, a Mr. George R. Walker, delivered remarks that reiterated the fact that while observations of the Fourth were resurgent in the white South, intraregional bonds remained stronger than national feeling: "Carolina and Massachusetts have clasped hands. But in the rejoicing I have to assure you that Carolina has not forgotten and never will forget that though she has joined hands with her old enemy, she is yet bound closer than by hands by the Great Ruler of the Universe, as a Siamese twin, to her sister Georgia—in heart, in soul, in geography."[53]

Reporting on the festivities for the *Charleston News & Courier*, a correspondent identified only as "Vidette" noted that "everyone seemed to think a new era of good feeling had dawned . . . it is a fact worthy of notice . . . that a United States flag was borne in a white procession in this city for the first time since the war . . . along the line of the parade the Stars and Stripes fluttered to the breeze from the housetops and from the windows of private residences and I am happy to state that there were no outrages." Vidette surmised that the absence of outrages may have been attributable to the presence of federal troops and concluded the report, "Let us have peace."[54] This report led to a small skirmish in the pages of the *Augusta Chronicle* when one reader took issue with the description of American flags fluttering in the Charleston breeze, stating that "they may have been [there]—we hope they were, but we didn't see them. Our people had too much household duties incumbent upon them for this, and withal, they had no 'Stars and Stripes' except in their hearts."[55] This seemed to imply a reluctance to either admit renewed appreciation of the Fourth or disclaim allegiance to the Stars and Stripes. Vidette's remarks about the lack of any "outrages" drew a particularly sharp retort. Apparently resenting the implication that an outrage might have been expected, this correspondent insisted that the day's festivities were "as far from outrage as the North Pole is from the South." And the correspondent, identifying him or herself, significantly, as "Georgian," then issued the challenge: "Whence cometh thou, 'Vidette'? Massachusetts, New York, Indiana, or Brooklyn [?]"[56] This was all a storm in a teacup; after several exchanges in the pages of the *Chronicle,* Vidette made it clear that the remarks about outrages were meant facetiously, with the remarks intended in a "Pickwickian sense."[57] What the exchange illustrates, however, is how sensitive to slight, real or perceived, white southerners were and how fragile the reunion that Vidette celebrated was: South Carolina may have "clasped hands" with Massachusetts, but Georgia remained her "Siamese twin," and Georgian sought to dismiss Vidette's account as that of a Yankee interloper from "Massachusetts, New York, Indiana, or Brooklyn."[58]

Several hundred miles to the west, an Arkansas newspaper published a letter, carrying the evocative byline of "Rebel," demonstrating that sentiment for a renewal of the Fourth could be found in other parts of the South: "Let us have a demonstrative Fourth of July celebration. There has not been one in the south for many years with any heart in it. We were not sure that anything was left us to be thankful for."[59] Rebel leavened this plea with some rhetoric that, typically, was as much about southern self-aggrandizement as it was reconciliation: "The people of the south are too noble to be churlish and we always mean what we say. We said fight, say now peace and let it be peace in every sense. We can take equal glory in the time when Cavalier, Puritan and Huguenot all stood together."[60] Little Rock proved receptive to Rebel's suggestion: the city observed the Fourth not only by the closing of businesses and offices but by the "popping of the friendly cracker and the banging of the lively revolver."[61]

There were, however, still serious reservations about the Fourth. In New Orleans, the *Daily Picayune* commented on "the day we do not celebrate" by observing that "people no longer congregate in clammy throngs to superintend the firing of brass-barrelled pistols and watch the appointed idiot work off . . . accumulated eloquence."[62] The Louisiana journal made clear, though, that it was not repudiating the day itself or the nation that had been created in 1776. Like much southern rhetoric around Independence Day celebrations in 1875, the *Daily Picayune* paid homage to the spirit of '76 with a sense of martyred self-righteousness:

> No doubt we honor the heroism and revere the devotion which ninety-nine years ago laid in blood and martyrdom the cornerstone of the splendid nation it is now our pride to claim . . . We cherish in grateful hearts the memories of that immortal episode. Perhaps we do these things the more intensely and fervently because of our sense of being denied a full and equal participation in the liberties and privileges for which our common forefathers offered up their lives . . . the Fourth of July can hardly be called the day we celebrate, however sacredly we may keep its noble memories—however faithfully we may wait the fulfilment of its gracious promise.[63]

Here the newspaper struck a familiar note, with its assumption that the white South had been victimized and unjustly deprived of the rights implied in the Declaration. Moreover, linkage of the Fourth with the political landscape is again made explicit with the claim that Reconstruction entailed white southerners' exclusion from the "gracious promise" of the Fourth.

Also in New Orleans, the *Bulletin*, described by its editors as being opposed to "carpet-baggers, scalawags and usurpers," featured a description of that city's Fourth.[64] The report began with a look back at antebellum Fourths in New Orleans, when "there used to be countless numbers of militia companies filling our streets with gay uniforms . . . the roar of artillerys and the peal of musketry . . . thrilled our pulses."[65] The *Bulletin's* correspondent compared that scene to 1875, when "twenty-five or thirty people . . . [watched] a sable pageant . . . carrying gorgeous ensign of the Republic, hanging limp and rag-like on a yellow pole," ascribing the contrast to the "iron hand of war, the edict of the conqueror."[66] The *Alexandria Gazette,* in reporting on the Fourth in Manassas, Virginia, made clear that where white southerners did celebrate Independence Day, their commemorations were kept clearly distinct from those of African Americans: "The Fourth was observed here by the colored people only, who had a tournament and picnic . . . The whites, generally, attended the celebration at Woodbridge [seventeen miles distant] and came back immensely pleased with their trip, while the superabundance of ticks kept them active and merry and sufficed to relive the monotony of their wearisome ride."[67]

In Montgomery, the original capital of the Confederacy, the *Advertiser* noted a rekindling in the "Southern bosom . . . of that old fire which in other days warmed the heart on each recurring anniversary of American independence."[68] The paper invoked the familiar trope of southern allegiance to the ideals of 1776 and reminded readers that while the Fourth remained a day that marked the South's "transference from one sort of bondage to another—from allegiance to one despot to enforced obedience to a senseless, soulless mob," the region could not be expected to celebrate it. With white Democrats gaining political control in an increasing number of states in the old Confederacy, however, the *Advertiser* conceded that although "we have not celebrated a fourth of July since 1861—an exception shall be made in favour of this. No paper shall be issued from this office until next Monday evening—the typo's [sic] must have a chance to celebrate with the rest, the 99th anniversary of American Independence."[69] The paper then concluded with a reference to the following year, which would see white southerners grappling further with questions about the United States, its history, and their place in it: "After this comes the Centennial—the American year of Jubilee."[70]

INDEPENDENCE DAY AS CONTESTED SPACE

White Republicans and former Unionists in the South, meanwhile, had never abandoned the Fourth: William Brownlow was a wartime Unionist, newspaper publisher, and Reconstruction governor of Tennessee. His newspaper, the *Knoxville Whig*, took a distinctly unreconciliatory stance in promoting the celebration of the Fourth in 1866. Noting the lack of Independence Day activity among southern whites, the *Whig* remarked that "it is natural that a people should remain silent who despise the American Union, hate and spit upon the flag, and still look to and hope for the overthrow of the government—the very remembrance to such traitors that about 90 years ago a body of 'Radicals' got together in a little Quaker town called Philadelphia . . . and declared that they were free and independent . . . we say the very remembrance of these facts arouses the ire of these traitors seeking the overthrow of the Government. No wonder such people decline to celebrate!"[71]

Here we see Revolutionary memory being contested—even as southern Democrats stressed their own entitlement to the founders' legacy, Republicans linked their current identity as Radicals with the radical activity of eighteenth-century patriots. Brownlow biographer Merton Coulter noted further Radical use of the Fourth, remarking that when the Fourteenth Amendment was submitted to Tennessee for ratification, Brownlow called a legislative session for 4 July 1866, "for what could be more patriotic than to prepare for ratification on the 'Glorious Fourth!'" Dunningite historian Coulter continued that "the Tennessee radicals also made merry in their celebrations over the state, both for the Fourteenth Amendment and the Fourth of July."[72] The following year, several prominent white Republicans publicized a July Fourth commemoration in the *Whig*. Their letter expressed the unlikely hope that their celebration would help "convert all the Conservatism and Rebelism in the country to the true household of faith."[73]

Republican Fourths followed the same outward pattern as Democratic gatherings. One account of a Tennessee Fourth in 1866 described a gathering that could outwardly have been for either party—with prayers, a procession, a picnic, and a reading of the Declaration of Independence. As had been true for Fourth celebrations from the beginning, the difference was in the content of the speeches, toasts, and resolutions offered. This particular celebration included endorsements of the Reconstruction amendments to the Constitution: "Resolved: That it is wise and proper that the late proposed amendments to the Federal Constitution should be ratified by ¾ of the states."[74] The participants also resolved that they were "firmly attached to the great principles of our Republican form of government" and, in a show of support to congressional Republicans then in the process of wresting control of Reconstruction from President Johnson, "that no other branch of government is so safe a repository of the power to reflect such principles as that of the Senate and the House of Representatives."[75] Another similarity in the account of this Fourth with countless others was recognition of the role of "the ladies" in the day's events. Tribute was paid to their "culinary skill and good taste . . . energy and efficiency" in the planning and preparation of the picnic. Acknowledgment of women's culinary contributions to commemorative gatherings was a recurring motif in accounts of nineteenth-century Fourths, but unfortunately, the record is generally silent about their thoughts or engagement with the meaning of the events. They were most certainly present for the celebrations, and we can surmise that presence and participation itself goes some way toward situating women within the political landscape.

Sometimes celebrating in tandem with white Republicans, African Americans in the South continued to use the Fourth not only to commemorate the Revolution but to make political statements about the present and to articulate their claim to the rights of citizenship. In 1875, T. B. Stamps, an African American businessman and legislator, demonstrated this practice in a Fourth of July oration at Hahnville, a predominately Black town in Louisiana.[76] Stamps drew on familiar themes, beginning his talk by paying homage to the patriots of 1776: "The American people, oppressed with grievous burdens, onerous taxation, an odious stamp act, and denied the right of representation in the law-making power of the British government, declared their freedom and independence."[77] The orator went on, however, to remind his audience of Black exclusion from the promises of the Declaration: "But, fellow citizens, memorable as were those great events in our national life, and grandly noble as were the deeds of the Fathers of the Republic, their acts and works were but for naught until within a few years since. For ninety years the American people in their Declaration of Independence . . . declaring the liberty and equality of all men they yet held four millions of human beings, their fellows, in cruel and abject bondage."[78]

Stamps then got to the heart of the matter as he saw it, the importance of the franchise in protecting Black citizenship in the face of a politically resurgent white South: "The colored people of the south today constitute a large part of the law-making power, the sovereignty of these states . . . all of us being voters . . . and all of us both can and must see to it that the great boon of freedom . . . shall be held as a priceless gem, never, never to be lost, guarded as the Christian does his soul . . . see to it first of all, that your suffrage is loyal. That this flag . . . is never tarnished by our vote. That no ballot of ours belie the gratitude we owe the republic in freedom!"[79] Implicit within Stamps's message, in his stress on "loyal" suffrage and gratitude owed the republic, is an endorsement of the importance of the Republican Party to the achievement of Black citizenship. African Americans thus celebrated the Fourth, and their citizenship, *because* of Reconstruction, while white southerners' re-embrace of it was predicated on Reconstruction's revocation.

The same day as Stamps's speech, Louisiana's Black lieutenant governor, Caesar Antoine, delivered the oration of the day at Shreveport, where, making clear the partisan nature of the event, the *New Orleans Republican* described it as an assemblage of "Republicans from all near sections of the country."[80] Antoine also reviewed Revolutionary history but did not dwell on the Union's antebellum failure to live up to the promises of the Declaration. Instead, Antoine itemized and discussed the postwar constitutional amendments and concluded that "these guarantees should cause every man . . . to rejoice that he is an American citizen . . . We, the newly enfranchised citizens should bow . . . to Almighty God that the intentions of the Framers of the Declaration of Independence have been carried out and we have been made citizens of this great Republic."[81] Antoine here stressed the citizenship of every Black American man. Black women were also part of these commemorations, and as in the case of their white counterparts, we can generally only surmise what their motivations, thoughts, and feelings were. One indication of their political engagement is found in a patronizing description by a white reporter of a Fourth celebration and Republican rally in Atlanta, where there were many women who "seemed to enjoy the thing amazingly" and indicated political engagement through a "vigorous waiving [sic] of handkerchiefs."[82]

As that description suggests, white accounts of Black Fourths did not stress enfranchisement or citizenship. Kathleen Clark has cited white descriptions of "antiquated maumas" at a Charleston Fourth in 1867 who "had their wares exposed to the rapacious gaze of dusky promenaders." The following year there were similar accounts of "dusky daughters cavorting with sable gallants."[83] This trope of Black sexualization, which would become a fixture of the Jim Crow era, served to discount the political intent and agency behind Black celebrations. Another "useful" trope was one of Black propensity to violence and disorder. In 1875, a Charleston newspaper commented condescendingly that the Fourth had been celebrated "with becoming eclat by the colored folk" but went on to describe a general row in which "pistols, knives, sticks and rocks were indiscriminately used."[84] An account of trouble at a Fourth celebration in Vicksburg, Mississippi, in 1875 was relayed in this rather offhand account in a white New Orleans paper: "The negroes had a Fourth of July celebration at the courthouse today. Some difficulty occurred among the audience during the speaking when firing commenced. Several negroes were wounded and three . . . were fatally shot . . . all quiet now."[85]

A similarly blasé tone was adopted by other white papers reporting the story. The *Macon Telegraph*, for instance, reported news of the melee without any investigation into the causes of the difficulty but assured its readers that "no further trouble is anticipated."[86] Other accounts presented a fuller picture. The *New Orleans Republican* made clear that it was a Republican, racially mixed gathering: Black chancery court clerk G. W. Davenport organized the meeting, and white (Republican) deputy sheriff J. W. Gilmer served as "president" of the event, which drew about two thousand attendees.[87]

The commemoration opened with a reading of the Declaration of Independence followed by patriotic band music. After (white, Republican) Judge George Brown, of the state circuit court, delivered a well-received address on the Revolution, Mississippi's Black secretary of state, James Hill, addressed the gathering. A correspondent for the African American *Christian Recorder* opined that Hill's remarks, "though not ultra or acrimonious, were nevertheless not so guarded and discreet, as we thought they ought to have been."[88] The *New Orleans Republican* reported more specifically that Hill's remarks referenced Black participation in the Revolution, citing Crispus Attucks, the African American killed in the Boston Massacre, and claimed that "the band of white men who threw the tea overboard in Boston harbour a hundred years ago were led by a negro."[89] A white attendee (presumably Republican) objected to these remarks. Another white man, Republican John Hill, encouraged Secretary Hill to continue speaking, whereupon yet another white man, Harvey Andrews, struck Hill.[90]

The *Christian Recorder*'s account continued: "When he [James Hill] had been speaking about twenty minutes, a file of white men were noticed coming into the room, and immediately arranged themselves in regular file along one side of the house. Within five minutes a scuffle began at the head of their line—on the left of the crowd, and then a pistol shot followed, whereupon the whole line presented revolvers and ordered the meeting to disperse. The colored people as usual took panic and made one grand rush for the door."[91] The correspondent went on to describe the arrival of more armed white men and concluded:

"Those fearful Winchester rifles were turned upon the defenseless mass of colored humanity. I suppose as many as one hundred shots were fired in the space of two minutes. Two men were killed and a number wounded; some of whom have since died . . . Thus ended the ninety-ninth year of American freedom (?)."[92]

These accounts of the incident at Vicksburg provide a useful counternarrative to those of the white, Democratic newspapers. The commemorative and political context for the gathering was made clear by the *Recorder* and the *Republican,* as was the violent white response to Black rhetoric that was not sufficiently "guarded and discreet." Both factors are absent from the white accounts, which read as if violence were a natural by-product of any Black gathering. It is clear, too, that white Democrats found it expedient to equate whiteness with the Democratic Party and Blackness with the Republican. So, despite the fact that white Republicans were present and involved with the Vicksburg observances, the affair was widely dismissed as a "negro" celebration. The white, Democratic *Monitor* of Vicksburg, again conflating race and political affiliation, remarked in reference to the violence in the Mississippi town: "The whites have borne all they will bear. Their passions have been so wrought upon by the outrages and insults they have had to endure that the least thing is sufficient to rend away the frail barriers and precipitate a conflict."[93] The *New Orleans Republican* riposted, making clear the significance of the Fourth in the Reconstruction era political landscape: "A Fourth of July oration is one of those things calculated to rend the barriers around law and order. This riot and negro massacre['s] purpose and effect was to break up a celebration of the anniversary of the declaration of American independence."[94]

The political situation in Vicksburg was one ripe for violence of this sort: the city itself was governed by conservative Democrats, while the county remained under the control of Republicans. Sheriff Peter Crosby, a county official, was a Black Republican. In December 1874, a posse of about five hundred white citizens, aggrieved by the notion that they were overburdened by taxes that benefited propertyless African Americans, essentially ran Crosby out of town. The state's Republican governor, Adelbert Ames (who would similarly be forced from office a year later), offered little assistance to Crosby beyond suggesting that the sheriff organize a Black posse to restore his authority in Vicksburg. Crosby did so, and his band was met by a considerably larger white militia as it approached Vicksburg. The Black force agreed to retreat and, even as it did so, was fired upon by the white militia, which then proceeded to sweep the county, attacking African Americans. After this paroxysm of violence, which left two white men and approximately three hundred African Americans dead, Governor Ames requested military support from President Grant to enforce Crosby's reinstatement. The sheriff was soon gone for good, however: he left the state after being shot in a brawl with his deputy, J. W. Gilmer, who would be one of the officiants at the town's ill-fated Fourth commemoration. In the words of historian William Harris, the racial and political turmoil exemplified by the Independence Day trouble "inspired the cause of white-line militancy and . . . set an ominous stage for the campaign and election of 1875."[95]

The 1875 celebrations in Memphis, Tennessee, demonstrated a white, Democratic effort to neutralize African Americans' use of the Fourth. The *Memphis Daily Appeal,* noting that "no demonstration was made among the white citizens," devoted many column inches to a description of a local celebration organized by an African American group, the Independent Order of Pole-Bearers.[96] The Pole-Bearers extended invitations to various white notables to address their Independence Day gathering, among them Confederate generals Nathan Bedford Forrest and Gideon Pillow. The group was motivated, according to an address on the day by their spokesman to utilize the "sacred day" in order to banish discord: "We earnestly pray that our future generations may proudly recall this auspicious period as the moment in which fraternal discord has taken its leave forever from . . . the hearts of united American brotherhood."[97] Forrest, a founder of the Ku Klux Klan in the late 1860s, spoke in generalities and patronizing platitudes, assuring the African American celebrants that "my interests are your interests and your interests are my interests . . . I want to elevate you to take positions . . . wherever you are capable of going . . . I don't propose to say anything about politics."[98]

Gideon Pillow's remarks were more substantial. The general echoed Forrest's sentiments that "the interests of the white and colored races in the South are inseparably intermingled" as well as offered an avowal to "purposely avoid all discussion of political questions—this is a day dedicated to the commemoration of a nation born to freedom."[99] Washington's *National Republican,* in reporting on the speech, noted that Pillow "naturally found it extremely difficult to do so."[100] Pillow proceeded to deliver a thoroughly political diatribe, reiterating that freed people and white southerners were "natural friends" but that African Americans had been

> misled by bad men of the Republican Party who were seeking to use your votes to get into power and into lucrative office. These places they wanted for their own selfish purposes. They pandered to your prejudices, they told you that you should have forty acres and a mule and that the rebels would put you back into slavery. By your votes many of them reached positions they were not worthy to fill and they practiced frauds . . . and robbed the country of vast amounts of money. If you had not thus put yourself in the hands of the enemies of Southern white people but [instead] had placed your confidence in them, and co-operated . . . [it] would have greatly advanced your interests.[101]

Here Pillow not only dismissed Black political agency by portraying African Americans as dupes of white Republicans; he effectively blamed them for white bitterness and, by extension, the violence that characterized the Reconstruction-era South. Pillow concluded, with what would prove a harbinger of things to come, by advising his audience that politics was a white man's game: "My colored friends, give up politics as a pursuit . . . it does not feed and clothe your wife and children. That man is your best friend who tells you how to return to your friendly relations with your old friends and neighbors."[102]

The racial prejudice of men like Pillow, and indeed of nineteenth-century society generally, is hard to overstate, as are the challenges that the freed people of the South faced following Appomattox. Gregory Downs, arguing that the military occupation of the former Confederacy constituted a continuation of war, has clearly demonstrated that it was only the presence of federal troops that enforced emancipation. He further posits that the federal government's continued use of war powers after the ostensible end of hostilities in spring 1865 "confirmed that the war was fundamentally a political, not just a military conflict."[103] This ongoing conflict made reunion, let alone reconciliation, problematic, to say the least. Downs pinpoints 1871, and the end of direct military rule in the South, as the return to "peacetime," but if we see the war as a political struggle, it makes sense to view the ongoing tribulations of Reconstruction as something less than "peace." This impression is reflected in continuing white avoidance of Fourth observances through the early 1870s. As the southern political landscape of the 1870s was contested terrain, so, too, were Fourth of July celebrations. They were an arena in which identity, citizenship, and belonging could be claimed or denied and in which race and political affiliation were inextricably intertwined.[104]

These commemorations were symbolic of nationalism and an identity that white southerners had rejected, and even as they tentatively and conditionally reclaimed that identity, they were emphatically unwilling to share it with their erstwhile bondsmen. Emphasis on Black "violence" served as a means of delegitimizing Black claims to the Fourth and, by extension, American identity. Other commemorative activity also overlapped with the politics of the era: in New Orleans, for example, conservative Democrats used the occasion of Robert E. Lee's death in 1870 to thwart Louisiana Republican rule. While local Republicans adopted a deferential and respectful tone in offering obsequies for Lee, conservative Democrats organized a massive memorial service, attended by thousands, where speakers, in the words of historian Michael Ross, "defended secession, the Confederacy, and white supremacy."[105] This use of commemoration for political ends represented an early evocation of the cult of Lee that would be so prominent in the

"Lost Cause" mythos that informed and informs so much of American Civil War memory.[106]

John Bodnar has described the contests involved in creating a "past worthy of commemoration" as a struggle for supremacy between advocates of various political ideas and sentiments, arguing that commemoration of the past has more to do with the present than with anything else—that commemorative activity is intended by leaders to "calm anxiety about change or political events" and to promote feelings of solidarity.[107] In the immediate aftermath of defeat, former Confederates left the day to "the Yankees and the darkies," but as it became necessary to negotiate a future within the United States, New South voices such as those in the *Atlanta Herald* began to drown out the diehards in a conversation inspired in large part by the looming anniversary of independence.

The rhetoric highlighted by the *Herald*'s 1875 project points up a split within the white South: if absolute rejection of the celebration can be linked to the "Bourbon" planter class, it seems plausible that New Departure white Democrats, the relatively liberal wing of the party that favored a more cooperative relationship with the federal government, would be the element most likely to push for Independence Day celebration. Historian Susanna Lee has highlighted the need of white Southerners to "at least pretend" a certain level of reconciliation in order to regain a measure of normality in their lives, a pragmatism that can be seen in Paul Gaston's delineation of the more flexible New Departure approach.[108] In his words, it betrayed "a less unreserved dedication to it [nationalism] than they were willing to admit. Underlying the professions of nationalism . . . were calculations of concrete gains for the region . . . the nationalism that the New South prophets preached had as its basic goal the recouping of the losses the South had incurred because of her long commitment to militant secessionism."[109] Similar considerations would come into play during discussions around the Centennial Exhibition.

3

Humbug or Opportunity
DEBATING THE CENTENNIAL

In the summer of 1869, before any firm plans for a commemoration of the centenary of American independence had been made and as Radical Reconstruction reached its apogee, the *Weekly Telegraph* of Macon, Georgia, made clear how closely linked white southern ideas about the politics of Reconstruction would become to discussions of the Centennial. After facetiously suggesting that Philadelphians could celebrate the occasion by taking half a million people up in a gigantic hot-air balloon or constructing waterworks that would spout the entire contents of the Delaware River five miles high, the newspaper concluded: "Let them close up the performances by paying off the national debt, and making a general bonfire and illumination of the bonds, the greenbacks . . . then Reconstruction Acts, the Fourteenth and Fifteenth Amendments, the Civil Rights bill and negro suffrage and start out in 1876, at sun down, upon a respectable and sensible basis for the future administration of national affairs."[1]

Five years later, with a magnificent world's fair in Philadelphia being planned, white southern sentiment was still less than enthusiastic. In January 1874, an Alabama newspaper proprietor remarked acerbically that "the spirit of liberty that dwelt in Independence Hall a hundred years ago finds no lodgement in the hearts of these mock patriots who are engineering this great Centennial Humbug."[2] His comment high-

lighted the extent to which the International Exhibition of Arts Manufactures and Products of the Soil and Mine, the Centennial, with its
twin themes of American progress and reunion, proved problematic
for the white South.

CENTENNIAL ORIGINS

Great Britain's Great Exhibition of 1851 and the 1855 Exposition Univer-
selle in Paris set the template for a series of world's fairs that both defined and reflected the world of the nineteenth and early twentieth centuries. These "curious secular rituals" were designed to be entertaining,
didactic, nationalistic, and commercially beneficial, not necessarily in
that order.[3] In the words of one historian, "Millions of visitors strolled
through the sites [of the fairs] were taught, indoctrinated and mes-
merised by them."[4] America's first world's fair, the Centennial, had its
origins in a plan conceived by a group of men, including John Bigelow,
former American ambassador to France; General Charles Norton, U.S.
commissioner to the Paris exposition of 1867; Professor John Campbell
of Wabash College in Indiana; and Colonel M. R. Muckles of Philadelphia. The Franklin Institute of Philadelphia became involved, petition-
ing Philadelphia's city government to authorize the use of Fairmount
Park for a centennial celebration. The municipal authorities created a
seven-man commission to investigate the possibility. The movement
gained momentum when the Keystone State's legislature appointed
a ten-man commission to join Philadelphia's seven and presented a
request to Congress to grant federal imprimatur to the idea. Then in
March 1870, Republican Pennsylvania congressman Daniel Morell introduced a bill calling for an official centennial celebration in Philadelphia.

A year later, on 3 March 1871, Congress adopted the proposal, making specific reference to the national, inclusive character of the proposed commemoration:

Whereas it is deemed fitting that the completion of the first century of our national existence shall be commemorated by an exhibition of the natural resources of the country and their development, and of its progress in those arts which benefit mankind, in comparison with older nations; and whereas, as the exhibition should be a national celebration, in which the people of the whole country should participate, it should have the sanction of the Congress of the United States; therefore, Be it enacted . . . that an exhibition of American and foreign arts, products and manufactures shall be held under the auspices of the Government of the United States, in the city of Philadelphia, in the year eighteen hundred and seventy-six.[5]

The bill authorized the creation of a National Centennial Commission, answerable to Congress and responsible for planning, organizing, and operating the exhibition. The bill also established fiscal protocols: commissioners were not to be paid for their services, and most significantly, "the United States shall not be liable for any expenses attending such exhibition, or by reason of the same."[6] The National Centennial Commission was to be composed of one commissioner and one alternate from each state or territory, who were appointed by the president upon the nomination of the various governors. Each state then formed their own state commissions, or boards (the nomenclature varied), charged with the often thankless task of raising both enthusiasm and funding for their respective states' presence at Philadelphia. It was envisioned that each state, as well as many foreign countries, would have their own dedicated exhibition spaces at Fairmount Park.

At the commission's inaugural meeting in the spring of 1872, the members elected officers to oversee its operations. Most prominent among them were former Union general, Connecticut governor, and congressman Joseph Hawley as president and fellow Union veteran and Cincinnati businessman Alfred T. Goshorn as director general, whose position was described as the "chief executive officer of the Exhibition."[7] Both men were Republicans; Hawley, in fact, was president of the Republican National Convention in 1868, and in 1872 and 1876, he served on the convention's Committee on Resolutions. These political affiliations would reinforce white southern suspicions that the Philadelphia fair was a sectional and political endeavor.

In the absence of a federal subsidy, the first priority for the commission was to finance the Centennial, with much of the funding expected to come from private investors. In June 1872, Congress created a Centennial Board of Finance, authorized to issue stock in shares of ten dollars each, with the stockholders sharing proportionately in any profit realized by the exhibition. Each state was assigned a quota in sold shares, based on population. The commission issued an open letter to the American people, widely reprinted in newspapers across the country in the autumn of 1872, stressing the national character of the exhibition: "To this grand gathering every zone will contribute its fruits and cereals. No mineral shall be wanting; for what the East lacks the West will provide. Under one roof the South will display in rich luxuriance her growing cotton and the North, in miniature, the ceaseless machinery of her mills converting that cotton into cloth."[8] The commissioners went on to encourage the purchase of shares as a patriotic duty: "The Commission looks to the unfailing patriotism of the people of every section, to see that each contributes its share of the expenses and receives its share of the benefits of an enterprise in which all are so deeply interested."[9]

The response to these pleas was decidedly uneven. By the end of 1875, Pennsylvanians had purchased nearly three times their quota, acquiring almost $3 million in Centennial stock. Things were different, though, in the states of the former Confederacy. Alabama had been assigned a quota of $258,000 in sales of Centennial stock; after a year, only twenty-two shares (amounting to $220) had been sold. William Byrd, the Cotton State's representative on the National Commission, wrote to Lewis Waln Smith, the commission's secretary, that he was "chagrined . . . I was prepared for a failure but not for such a one."[10] He elaborated: "I have had an uphill road to travel—I could not get the Governor, who is a Republican, to present the matter to the Legislature. But like Congress, they provided for Vienna [an 1873 exhibition in Austria], but not a cent for the Centennial. What a commentary on American patriotism! But I shall not give up the good cause—it can be made a success in spite of the politicians. We can get the people in it and the demagogues will be in it at the swell-tide, head and ears."[11] But Byrd, himself a Democrat and former Confederate, faced a real struggle. The Centennial itself came a mere eleven years after Appomattox, and when the preparations, planning, and public relations efforts began, the Civil War had only been over for about seven years, inauspicious timing for a celebration of American unity.

CENTENNIAL THEMES

A central theme of the celebration was patriotism and reunion. In 1872, Centennial commission president Joseph Hawley released an "address" that depicted the upcoming exhibition as an inclusive and uniting experience that would restore the "kindly and fraternal" relations that had existed before "this terrible war."[12] Hawley expressed the hope that Americans "from every corner of this broad land [would] . . . gather by land and by sea to the City of Brotherly Love and with kindly and loving hearts, exchange the warm grasp of common brotherhood under one and the same nationality. And exult that now, at last, the stripes as well as the stars unite in proclaiming liberty to every son of man, and once more float over a reunited, harmonious and happy people."[13]

In the Centennial commission's first round of meetings, in 1872, similar sentiments were expressed. A Wisconsin delegate noted that although his state had done "her full part to quell the rebellion and restore the Union," he was convinced that the Centennial would "do more to reunite all the elements of this nation into one grand whole than any event which has occurred in the century."[14] Florida commissioner J. S. Adams, a Republican transplant from Vermont, voiced the hope that the exhibition would lead Americans North and South to "shake hands in a common destiny, a common love, and for the glory of our flag and our common country."[15] Alabama's William Byrd, a genuine southerner and Democrat, voiced agreement with his colleague: "I have been a Southern man all my life, either by misfortune or good fortune . . . if this is to be a National Exposition, I want it to be one. I do not want it to be sectional."[16] All of these statements were published and therefore intended for public consumption. But at least in the case of William Byrd, private correspondence already quoted showed the same commitment to a "patriotic" Centennial. Similarly, the *United States Centennial Almanac* (1874) expressed the aim of making the Centennial "a work of pride, of patriotism, and reconciliation."[17]

In 1873, Texas's Centennial commissioner, William Henry Parsons, addressed a letter to his state's legislature that underscored the desire of the exhibition's organizers that the celebration be a national one, designed to help heal sectional wounds: "We assume that the celebration of the 100th Anniversary of American Independence is neither a sectional nor a party question, but one that should enlist the sympathy, excite the patriotism and ensure the cooperation of all sections and all parties of our common country."[18] Parsons's hope would be largely unfulfilled, however, and southern ambivalence toward the Centennial was reflected in the lack of financial investment in the fair by the states of the former Confederacy. The state of Pennsylvania and city of Philadelphia appropriated $1 million and $1.5 million, respectively, to help fund the exhibition. Foreign investment was substantial: the United Kingdom spent $250,000 on its exhibit at the Centennial, France $120,000, Germany $171,000, Sweden $125,000, and Ecuador $10,000. Pennsylvania invested a further $50,000 on its official state building at the fair, with Massachusetts expending the same amount, and the young state of West Virginia raised $20,000 for its building. In the end, of the southern states, only Arkansas and Mississippi would fund exhibition space at Fairmount Park.

The Floridian Vermonter J. S. Adams, in addition to the hopes he expressed regarding the Centennial's healing and reunifying role, also highlighted another key theme of the exhibition, envisioning it as a "national, profound tribute to the majesty of labor."[19] Adams was framing the

Centennial as a celebration, and a statement to the world, of American ingenuity and technological prowess. The *Philadelphia Ledger* remarked that the fair should express "the progress of the United States in all that benefits mankind . . . How vast that progress has been and how multitudinous the material illustrations of it are—no one needs to be told."[20] Despite the proto-industrialization espoused by adherents of a New South, the former Confederacy remained an overwhelmingly agrarian region, and themes of reunion and manufacturing would not have been likely to encourage white southern engagement with the exhibition.

CENTENNIAL DEBATES

Some southerners, motivated apparently by no more than a visceral hatred of the "Yankees," responded to the idea of the Centennial with disdain. A letter from Confederate admiral Raphael Semmes to the *Mobile Register* typified this response: he attacked the Fourteenth Amendment's provision against erstwhile Confederates (including himself) holding elected office, referring to "this Constitutional proscription" as a "brand of infamy and shame which has been burned, as it were, into the very forehead of the state."[21] Arguing against Alabama's participation in the Philadelphia festivities, Semmes made it clear that he saw the Centennial in a political context, characterizing it as "this radical love-feast." The admiral went on to link, in florid and emotional prose, Confederate loyalty to Centennial resistance by asking, "Will you dare . . . admit, by the presence of your representatives at Philadelphia on the 4th of July 1876 that those who sleep in their bloody winding sheets were rightly branded by the . . . United States as insurrectionists and rebels?"[22] A San Francisco paper made reference to Semmes's political leanings when, after remarking that Semmes would never be reconstructed "until he has been unjointed by some skilful demonstrator of anatomy," mused about "what an invaluable stump-speaker Semmes would make for that wing known as 'Bourbon Democracy.'"[23] The *Augusta Chronicle*, meanwhile, adopted a more measured but no less dismissive tone than Semmes: "If the citizens of the North, East and West feel like celebrating the hundredth anniversary of a nation's freedom, let them go ahead. We have not had enough liberty in the South during the past eight years to feel like spending much money or exhibiting much enthusiasm on the occasion."[24]

When the Alabama legislature debated appropriating funds to mount an exhibit at Philadelphia, opponents of the measure fulminated against the thought of their state being represented at "this Yankee humbug."[25] Even legislators in favor of the funding agreed that the South had been "oppressed and outraged by fanatics" but argued that participation at the Centennial could "sow the seeds that will eventually rout out the tyranny that now oppresses the entire land."[26] Their reasoning echoed the New Departure line that the most prudent course for the South was one of engagement rather than intransigence. One proponent of this approach, Senator John Terrell, made explicit the link between Centennial engagement and politics by arguing that he believed "the days of Radical Reconstruction were over" and that Alabama would be "welcomed to the National Exposition as heartily as Massachusetts or New York."[27] This link is also evident in a suggestion by the *Augusta Chronicle and Sentinel* that southern participation in the exhibition should be "a *quid pro quo* . . . Now is the time to say to our Republican friends: no amnesty, no centennial. This will bring them to terms and remove the ban which still rests upon two or three hundred of the old Southern leaders."[28] The newspaper was referring here to the continuing disfranchisement of Confederate leaders and made clear that it saw the exhibition as a northern affair—and one that could be used for political leverage.

The belief that the South was being wronged and mistreated extended beyond the restrictions placed on former Confederate officials and demonstrated a consensus in white southern thinking that transcended the question of Centennial participation. When the Virginia-based *Religious Herald* counseled, in endorsing the Centennial, that "it is time the animosities of the war were forgotten. Upon the graves of the slain let us plant the olive," it could not help adding that no one could doubt that "the South has been needlessly injured by the acts of Reconstruction."[29]

In the spring of 1875, a kerfuffle over the oath meant to be sworn by National Centennial commissioners posed a serious threat to white southern engagement with the exhibition. A year earlier, Governor James Smith of Georgia had written to U.S. secretary of state Hamilton Fish remonstrating over the fact that the oath sent to Georgia commissioner George Hillyer required him to swear that he had never taken up arms against the United States. Smith pointed out that this condition would necessarily preclude most white southerners from serving on the commission and warned that "candor constrains me to say that if this gratuitous and wanton requirement is insisted upon, the people of Georgia will not, with my consent, take any part whatever in the proposed partisan celebration at Philadelphia."[30] For reasons that remain unclear, Smith's letter was widely reprinted a year later, raising considerable ire throughout the white South. The *Daily Picayune* of New Orleans, for example, commended Governor Smith's "manly" letter to Fish and remarked that Smith's sentiments "would find an echo in every heart this side of Mason and Dixon's line."[31] Within a few days, however, most newspapers that published Smith's letter followed it up with a "never mind." Hamilton Fish had responded promptly to Smith the previous year, explaining that a clerical error had resulted in the oath intended for northern commissioners being sent inadvertently to Georgia's Hillyer.[32] This explanation, in turn, resulted in more southern resentment. The *Daily Picayune* complained that having separate oaths for southern and northern commissioners was "ungenerous toward the South and untrue to the ostensible spirit of the Centennial celebration."[33]

ECONOMICS AND CENTENNIAL SUPPORT

Much anti-Centennial sentiment stressed northern corruption and unfairness, paying lip service to the idea of reunion but insisting on the dishonorable intentions of the northerners. Clearly positioning the question of Centennial engagement as a political matter, Alabama newspaper proprietor A. H. Keller editorialized, with reference to the Reconstruction policies of the Grant administration, "How quietly they [Philadelphians] endorse Grant's late scheme to subvert the fundamental principles of the very government whose one hundredth anniversary they are preparing to celebrate."[34] Keller cited Centennial commission president Joseph Hawley's vote, when in Congress, against continuing pensions to southern veterans of the 1812 and Mexican wars: "Many of these noble old veterans had shed their blood and lost their limbs defending the government he now makes a pretense of glorifying . . . This fellow is a fit apostle to preach Philadelphia's gospel of hate towards the South."[35]

The conflation of the Radical wing of the Republican Party with Centennial organizers was not entirely accurate, with the latter making some effort to accommodate white southern sensibilities (as will be seen in chapters 4 and 5). But such distinctions were apparently of little interest to Keller, who closed his diatribe with jabs at "Yankee" duplicity and corruption: "Policy may silence his [Hawley's] venomous tongue now, just as self-interest restrains the City of Brotherly Love from her wonted exhibition of malice towards us. She will never forgive the South because its trade is forever lost to her. Our people should do nothing to encourage this latest swindle . . . Grant urges an appropriation of a million dollars to it, but says nothing of what percentage of it he and Hawley expect to get."[36]

"Hypocrisy" was frequently cited as a northern characteristic. Equating Republican political control with lack of liberty, the *LaGrange Reporter,* in Georgia, insisted that the pretense of freedom that underlay Centennial plans was "hollow and hypocritical" and that as long as the white South was not "free," any invitation by the North to celebrate the Centennial was a "mocking lie."[37] The *Southern Planter and Farmer* also depicted northerners, specifically Philadelphians in this case, as hypocrites: "We have made no mention of the progress of this Philadelphia job, because we cannot conceive that any Virginian, or any Southerner, can have any interest in it one way or the other. It was gotten up . . .

to enrich the citizens of a community which has ever hated us."[38] The journal underlined its charge of hypocrisy by comparing Philadelphians to an ancient Hebrew sect noted for pretensions to moral superiority: "[Philadelphia's] broad-brimmed Pharisees brought in and sold Negroes to the South as long as they could and then . . . rolled up their holy eyes at the exceeding sinfulness of slavery."[39]

An Atlanta newspaper also suggested Centennial-linked corruption when it declared: "Let the Southern people keep a watchful eye on their Congressmen should this thing come to a vote. There will be at least strong presumptive evidence that every Southern man who votes to donate money to Philadelphia has been bought . . . The whole thing is a fraud and stinks with corruption . . . No Southern representative can properly vote to give away the people's money to the mean, miserly and fanatical Philadelphians."[40]

Southern accusations that the Centennial was a moneymaking scam ("The press of the South has not done its duty in exposing that huge fraud and Yankee Swindle") highlight a central aim of the Centennial, albeit one less freely acknowledged by its organizers than that of commemoration, reunion, or showcasing technology: profit.[41] The Gilded Age of unbridled capitalism was underway, and Philadelphia's leaders anticipated a lucrative windfall from the millions of visitors. The United States had been hit by a devastating financial panic in 1873, known, until the 1930s, as the "Great Depression."[42] James McCabe's contemporary history of the Centennial described the economic climate: "The panic of 1873 had almost paralyzed the finances of the country and the people had become timid and hesitating in supporting schemes which required an outlay of money . . . It [became] evident that the various states of the Union could not be depended upon to furnish their respective proportions of the funds, and that the Exhibition must depend for its success mainly upon private subscriptions."[43]

Scribner's Monthly magazine summarized the extent to which the Centennial was seen as a catalyst for economic recovery: "All good Americans are looking forward to the passage of the year 1876 with great interest . . . there is a belief we have seen the worst. Of a certain kind of business there will be more done than ever before. The passenger traffic on the railroads will be immense. All the West is coming East . . . the Southern states will be similarly moved . . . all lines of travel converging upon New York and Philadelphia will be crowded . . . There will be a tremendous shaking up of the people, a great going to and fro in the land, a lively circulation of money and a stimulation of trade."[44] The clear financial benefits the exhibition offered its host city and its merchants and entrepreneurs provided an easy target for southern critics. As early as May 1872, the *Richmond Whig* took aim at the money involved in setting up the exhibition: "The Centennial Commission today considered the report of the Committee on Plans authorizing the selection of ten architects, to be paid $1,000 each for preliminary plans for the buildings, that ten other prizes of $1,000 each be paid to other architects for sketches or drawings, and that six of the most meritorious be selected from the twenty plans to be awarded. The following are the prizes: $15,000 for the first, $10,000 for the second, $6,000 for the third, $4,000 for the fourth, and $3,000 and $2,000 for the fifth and sixth."[45] The *Whig* then made clear that it considered the enterprise a wasteful lark: "The Resolution was debated without a result. The Commission then embarked on a tug for an excursion along the river front."[46]

It seems evident that local interests held the lion's share of stock and that Philadelphians stood to gain the most from the fair's success. In the words of historian Robert Rydell, "A small number of wealthy individuals, railroads and large mercantile establishments held controlling interest" in the fair.[47] The twin themes of patriotism and profit were underscored by a letter from Connecticut commissioner William Phipps Blake to director general Alfred Goshorn, which explained, "We must fall back upon patriotism and other such incentives."[48] Linda Gross and Theresa Snyder, in their 2005 photographic history of the exhibition, described Centennial patriotism as a "mechanism" to convey American innovation and technology to the world.[49] Philadelphians certainly hoped to reap financial rewards from the exhibition, but there is no reason to believe that pecuniary and patriotic motivations were mutually exclusive. However, although Lyn Spillman has pointed out that the "most enthusiastic organizers" of the Centennial were "Pennsylvania manufacturers and merchants," it was certainly more than a commercial enterprise, or "Yankee swindle."[50]

One indication of the money at stake in the Centennial comes from the fees charged to concession holders at the fair. A newspaper report contained the following particulars: one individual paid the organizing commission $12,000 for the exclusive privilege of hiring out rolling chairs to visitors at the rate of fifty cents an hour. The right to sell soda water to thirsty fairgoers realized $30,000. The license to construct an eighteen hundred–room hotel, entirely at the licensee's expense, was sold for $10,500.[51] One restaurateur who paid the commission $24,000 to license his business reported average daily profits of $1,100 at close of the fair's six-month life.[52] I. L. Baker paid the commission $7,000 for the rights to sell his "Celebrated Sugar Pop Corn" at the exhibition.[53]

Northern industrialists, merchants, and soda water sellers were not the only ones to see potential for economic gain in the Centennial. Although some white southerners arguing for Centennial participation framed their arguments in terms of the original Union, claiming that the "anniversary of American independence is a heritage which belongs peculiarly to the Southern people and one she should never ignore," this was but a minor theme within southern pro-Centennial arguments.[54] With their economies devastated by the war and the financial panic of 1873, economic opportunity was the single most common inducement invoked by those white southerners arguing in favor of Centennial participation. The debate in Congress in late 1875 through early 1876 that eventually resulted in that body authorizing a loan—not a grant—of $1.5 million for the Philadelphia fair led the *Alexandria Gazette* to comment that wholehearted, patriotic embrace of the Centennial on the part of the white South, as long as it was being denied "equal rights" (that is, Democratic control), would be "more than any mortal of ordinary intelligence [could] . . . understand."[55] The Democratic *Gazette*, noteworthy for its embrace of New South politics, counseled what it called a "politic and . . . Machiavelian course," focused on the political expediency of cooperation with the "Yankees," with the aim of both political and economic gain.[56] A Macon, Georgia, paper weighed in on the debate, championing the same practical approach: "We are confident the refusal of the Southern members to vote the appropriation would involve greater loss than the appropriation itself; because such refusal will be used in the interests of sectional discord and repression which have already cost the South and the country hundreds and thousands of millions."[57]

When a delegation from the National Centennial Commission visited Georgia in late 1873 on a public relations and share-selling junket, a Macon newspaper quoted a toast given at a banquet for the group: "To the Centennial Committee, the only bridge which can span the chasm of the dreary past, the sole abyss in which may be buried . . . the bitter acerbities of former conflicts, the rainbow of hope which guides the future of American progress."[58] This pretty prose about postwar reunion stood in contrast to a speech delivered at the same event by Robert Patton, a former governor of Alabama. The same account reported that "Governor Patton expressed his great interest in the Centennial enterprise, his confidence in its success and his belief that it presented a most capital opportunity for Georgia to represent all of her great resources at one glance to the millions of visitors . . . It was a most stirring appeal that every citizen of Georgia should be personally interested in its success."[59] Georgia press reaction to the Centennial sales pitch reflected southern polarization about the project. The *Macon Telegraph* concluded that "the visit and its results indicate that the heart of the South beats in sincere response to the celebration of the Centennial of American liberty, and that a splendid representation of that section may be expected [at the Centennial.]"[60] The *Augusta Chronicle* was less enthused, noting that "it was true a small meeting was held and a few gushing speeches delivered, but further than this not much progress was made."[61]

Evidence of the economic opportunities southerners sensed in the Centennial was not limited to newspaper pieces. When Virginia's Democrat-controlled legislature issued a proclamation endorsing the Centennial (a few years before it voted against any financial support for the state's participation), its phraseology was telling: "Be it resolved

. . . that the time and place of holding the said Centennial are hereby endorsed. That the said Centennial Exhibition is warmly commended to the people as a means of restoring prosperity to Virginia and sincere good feeling between all the people of the United States."[62]

A Virginia delegate to the National Commission, Frederick Holliday, bemoaned his state assembly's refusal to fund a presence at the Centennial in a letter to the commission: "I fear the spirit of economy has prevailed to too great an extent in our legislature and that its members have allowed the finest opportunity that may occur in our generation to advance the material prosperity of my state."[63] And when Alabama's governor, Democrat George Houston, addressed the topic of funding an exhibit in an annual message to his state's legislature, he framed the case for participation in utilitarian terms. Houston identified the chief motivation for his state's putative involvement as being "to satisfy the peoples of other states and countries that they can do better by their industries in Alabama than elsewhere . . . to profit the State by developing and adding to its industries, wealth, and power."[64]

The *Richmond Enquirer* was bluntly dismissive of the Centennial's ostensible theme of patriotism and commemoration: "As to the sentimental part of the question—the patriotic portion—we suppose Virginia has very little of that left now." The Democratic journal, like most advocating Centennial engagement, was more concerned with what Virginia might lose out on by sitting out the exhibition, arguing that the state's course should be controlled "purely [by] self-interest. Her people take very little stock in the glory of the nation she [helped] build up . . . if she goes to Philadelphia at all, it will be merely to advertise herself from a business standpoint."[65] The *Enquirer* here made no pretense of indulging in reunion rhetoric or patriotic patter, with the bitterness and resentment of the white South baldly stated. The editorial reiterated the theme of being left behind by other southern states that would participate, arguing that not being represented would see the state "completely shut out from the advantages it would give us as a medium for advertising our material and industrial resources while others with far less claims to consideration bear away the prize."[66] The

Enquirer concluded that "the whole world will be at Philadelphia . . . and [we] should . . . make as respectable an appearance as possible." The newspaper argued that this would increase that state's "importance at home and abroad . . . but if she prefers to remain at home with her finger in her mouth, nursing her wrath, she cannot blame anybody but herself that she is passed by unnoticed."[67]

A Nashville newspaper, reporting on the inaugural meeting of Tennessee's state Centennial commission, quoted a speaker who addressed the need to "stir the people up" in order to arouse Centennial enthusiasm, and the convention resolved to educate Tennesseans about the "importance" of having the "state, its interests and products etc. represented at Philadelphia."[68] Thomas Coldwell, one of the state's national commissioners, addressed the group and explained that the scope of the Centennial embraced "every subject, pursuit and interest . . . in fact, everything on earth and under the earth." Myriad committees were formed, including ones on "Poultry," "Horticulture," "Fruit," and "Flowers, Embroidery and Needlework," all with the "vitally important" aim of ensuring that Tennessee was "properly represented" at the Centennial.[69] The opportunity for economic advancement offered by the exhibition was neatly summed up by the *Mobile Register*'s utilitarian approach to the situation. The paper huffed that any idea of patriotic motives behind the fair was "a bold humbug and open fraud" but maintained that the Centennial was "certainly a most practical and admirable scheme for collective advertising of American products, natural and industrial. As such, we would have the Southern states use it, in exactly the same spirit and manner as they would advertise State bonds in a radical newspaper or send Southern iron to a Northern foundry."[70]

POLITICAL IDENTITY AND THE CENTENNIAL

Politics, or more particularly political identity, was a key theme in Centennial-centered rhetoric. In Texas, the *San Antonio Express,* a Republican newspaper, criticized the *Herald,* a Democratic competitor, for its anti-Centennial stance. It quoted the *Herald*, in a passage that made clear the linkage between party politics and Centennial support: "We should not mingle with them [northerners] in the Centennial but stand aloof until we can demonstrate our strength in the next Presidential election."[71] The *Express* ridiculed this rigid regional and party orthodoxy: "There will be representatives from every nation and clime— there will be a display of the world's industry in competition with our own,—there will be one of the grandest congregations of men ever held on this continent, and yet the editor of the Herald will not be there, he will fold his arms and stand aloof, he will shake his haughty head when free tickets are poked under his nose."[72]

In Arkansas, Centennial commissioner George Dodge equated Democratic political control to "rightful" ownership of his state when he reported to Philadelphia in August 1875 that "our state will make a collective display of her products and resources but how large a collection and how much space I cannot positively say . . . the task seems hopeless—you can hardly conceive of the utter prostration and devastation which prevailed here up to last spring when the state was handed over to her rightful owners by . . . a kind providence . . . we will probably be compelled to abandon the idea of a state building."[73]

In Louisiana, the state assembly passed a resolution stating: "The Governor shall appoint three citizens of the state . . . who shall constitute The State Centennial Board of Managers. They are enjoined to 'take such action as will secure a full and thorough representation of the resources and products [of Louisiana] at the exhibition.'"[74] The Pelican State's legislature then undermined its own initiative by stipulating that "nothing in this act shall be so construed as to render the state liable for any pay or expenses for said commissioners or any person employed by them."[75] The polarized political atmosphere in the state is suggested by Hubert Bonzano, one of Louisiana's three Centennial managers, who wrote, presciently, to the national commission that it was

> quite safe to say that Louisiana will not make a "collective exhibition." And I may as well mention that the individual exhibits will be very

meagre as the Board is entirely without means . . . And now, as this letter may become historical, I will add that the political animosity towards the ruling state government and administration is so great . . . that the failure of the Executive, in anything, no matter how patriotic or beneficial to the state is regarded with favor rather than sorrow or shame. Such being the state of the public mind . . . I am forced to confess that little or no prospect awaits us that Louisiana's wealth and industry will be creditably represented at the Centennial.[76]

Both Dodge's and Bonzano's letters highlighted a crucial issue for the post–Civil War South, the question of home rule, or to be more precise, Democratic rule. Dodge referenced, gratefully, Arkansas's return to Democratic control in 1874, while Bonzano's letter demonstrated the animosity that Louisiana's Republican government, widely seen as an illegitimate rule by usurpers, faced. It also illustrated the overlap of the political with the commemorative in Louisianans' refusal to support anything also supported by the despised Republicans.

In contrast, Democrats in Mississippi won firm control of the Jackson statehouse in the 1875 elections. The Magnolia State's Centennial Board provided an interesting mix, headed by Alexander Warner, a former Union officer and Republican floor manager in the state senate, along with James Hoskins, a Confederate veteran; M. J. Manning, a carpetbagger Republican; and John Logan Power, who served as the board's assistant secretary and dealt with most of its correspondence. Power wrote to Director General Goshorn in the autumn of 1875: "We desire to have an exhibition and in operation the whole process of ginning, pressing and baling cotton and will have stalks in bloom forwarded early next summer. The enclosed circular will indicate that we are not altogether indifferent. Indeed, I think Mississippi will make a creditable display and I am sure that our people will attend in great numbers."[77] Two months later, Power added: "We will have a pretty good display of field crops and mill fabrics and specimens of our timbers."[78] Power's enthusiasm shines through this correspondence, the only note of negativity being a remark on the Mississippi legislature's "stinginess," though Power assured the national commission that they would be able to work around that. Power's efforts, along with those of William Byrd in Alabama, indicate that enthusiasm for the Centennial could not be predicted by party lines alone. He was a Democrat and in 1861 had served as official recorder for his state's Secession Convention, and after enlisting as a private, by war's end he was serving as superintendent of Mississippi's army records.[79] This is again indicative of a split Democratic approach to the exhibition between conservative, Bourbon Democrats and the more flexible New Departure wing of the party, which was willing to accept a measure of Black suffrage and admit the legitimacy of Republican opposition. Illustrating the depth of the divisions, one New Departure Democrat described the conservative wing of his own party as "Bourbons who would hold out against destiny itself."[80]

The pragmatic New Departure approach was more likely to see the economic and political benefits to be had from engagement with the Centennial. In Power's home state, for example, the *Hinds County Gazette* was a Bourbon organ that ignored virulent Klan activity in its vicinity, filling its pages instead with railroad matters and only mentioning the white supremacist group when it attacked Republicans for raising the issue of vigilante terror in Congress.[81] The newspaper consistently excoriated the Centennial and everything connected with it. The *Jackson Clarion*, meanwhile, a more moderate journal was demonstrably more open to the Centennial than its more conservative rival. Perhaps not coincidentally, one of its publishers was John Logan Power.

LOCAL BOOSTERISM AND CENTENNIAL SUPPORT

State and immediate locality was at the core of most white Americans' sense of identity up until roughly the last quarter of the nineteenth century. In the words of Cecilia O'Leary: "One's notion of country more often than not was affixed to an individual state."[82] The Civil War was the major factor in realigning these allegiances, and historian Melinda Lawson has delineated the way that the wartime federal government cultivated a national loyalty that for the first time overrode state and local allegiances.[83] But a bitter and defeated South was largely excluded from this new nationalism. A Milwaukee newspaper, in considering the South's reaction to the Centennial, diagnosed the region's "essential deficiency" as a lack of national feeling: "The Southron's pride attaches first to his state, then to the South, and lastly, if at all, to the Union. This is . . . a very mischievous fact. The genuine Virginian finds no satisfaction in seeing the United States lead the world in the attributes of an advanced civilization but if the Old Dominion would surpass Massachusetts he would fairly burst with pride."[84]

A sense of local allegiance and pride was another aspect of the pragmatic pro-Centennial argument and can be seen over and over again in the pro-Centennial pieces in the southern press, which invariably tell of the economic wonders to ensue if only the resources of that particular locality were to be fully represented at the Centennial. The Centennial Commission of West Tennessee, for example, set out to drum up interest in the festivities by appealing to local pride and self-interest: "We invoke the cooperation of all intelligent citizens . . . and especially the press of West Tennessee, in spreading . . . all the information and facts concerning the great exhibition and their interests in it and urging them to prepare objects to be sent to it . . . should West Tennessee lag or flag in all this she will . . . be left behind, in the background and in the dark."[85]

Here was a common theme: that of being left behind, of missing out on an opportunity that other southern states would be taking advantage of, highlighting a competitiveness that bespoke a state and even local identity that transcended regional identification, never mind national feeling. These West Tennesseans argued that the Centennial offered their region "manifold benefits" and that if they were well represented at Fairmount Park, "men of capital and genius and activity and force will come and dwell among us from all parts of the earth to share our industrial advantages to develop our material wealth and to make us rich, and powerful and great."[86] These are interesting sentiments in a region where the battle for local political autonomy was so fierce, and resentment of outside carpetbaggers and northern control so intense. A Shreveport, Louisiana, newspaper likewise trumpeted the qualities of its own region and framed the Centennial as a prime opportunity to tout them for outside investment: "There is, perhaps on this continent, no locality which presents to the capitalist and manufacturer a wider and more profitable field for investment than North Louisiana, and more especially in the immediate vicinity of Shreveport." The newspaper went on to describe the exhibition as a "great opportunity" that would "enable us to compete successfully with any portion of the Union."[87]

There was a veritable chorus of such appeals throughout the South. An editor in Columbus, Georgia, showed how specific, and how local, these arguments for the Centennial-related benefit could be: "What manufactory in the United States is superior to the Eagle & Phenix Mills of Columbus, Ga.? What city has better manufacturing advantages? If the South abstains from the Centennial Exhibition will not the unjust prejudice in favour of the North be more firmly planted in the minds of all visitors, of whom there will be hundreds of thousands? There will not be such an opportunity to advertise the resources and advantages of Georgia in a century, perhaps."[88] An Arkansas editor provided another example of interstate rivalry when he predicted that a Centennial exhibit would "place us a way ahead of some of our older brethren."[89] And J. T. Bernard, one of Florida's commissioners, assured Floridians that Centennial participation, "though it may require a small outlay, yet . . . will prove in the end a profitable investment."[90] Finally, an editorial writer in Galveston, Texas, demonstrated the strength of local and state allegiance while at the same time making it abundantly clear that the Centennial was being seen more as an opportunity than a commemoration: "There is no state in the American Union which has more to gain from the Centennial than Texas. There is no city which has so much to hope for as Galveston. As a young city, with boundless possibilities, it is our interest to advertise these possibilities before the whole world."[91]

Numerous issues of importance to Reconstruction-era Americans were interlinked with discussion of the Centennial. Among them was the topic of the railroad, perhaps the chief catalyst for the change and development of American society over the nineteenth century. Railroads, politics, and the Centennial all intersected in the state of Texas, where railroads (and politics) were often discussed in terms of one Tom Scott. Colonel Thomas Scott, formerly head of the Pennsylvania Railroad, was chosen to head up the newly formed Texas Pacific Railroad in 1871, a venture that aimed to construct a transcontinental railway from Marshall, in eastern Texas, all the way to San Diego.[92] Scott had overseen the growth of the Pennsylvania Railroad from a regional concern with about four hundred miles of track to the largest railroad system in the world, covering fifteen American states.[93] Scott's firm, which was lobbying for state support for expansion into Texas, drew considerable opprobrium. Scott was damned for being both a northerner ("[Scott's] interests and those of Texas are as wide as the Poles asunder") and for supporting the "wrong" side in the constitutional debate.[94] The latter criticism referred to a new state constitution drafted, debated, and voted on during 1875 and 1876. The *Austin Weekly Statesman* noted that a clause in the proposed constitution forbidding state aid for railroad construction made an exception for existing railroads and concluded that Scott supported the Constitution in order to suppress competition from new lines; ratification of the document would, it was claimed, secure that railway magnate "an empire that costs [him] . . . nothing."[95] The Centennial found its way into this discussion, too, with Scott being lambasted for not providing bargain fares to Philadelphia for Texans: "If the railways would entice people away from Austin to the Centennial show at Philadelphia, to which such adroit efforts are made to draw the Southern Pacific Railroad, they will make a greater reduction than 25% from present passenger rates. But isn't it nice that Austin folks must pay full fare to Galveston or Houston when they set out to the world's center—as Tom Scott sees it?"[96] The *Statesman* followed its sarcastic reference to the idea of Philadelphia being the world's center with a recommendation to seek alternate routes to the Centennial in order to avoid patronizing "trains owned by men reckless enough to demand almost full fare from poverty-stricken patriots on a weary pilgrimage to the shrine of American patriotism."[97]

When Virginia's legislature voted down a Centennial appropriation, the *Austin Weekly Statesman* linked that decision to a discussion of Tom Scott and the railroads by commenting: "It isn't Philadelphia we're against, not a bit of it. But we don't like to have Texas robbed and duped by Tom Scott. But it was Blaine's bloody shirt that staggered and shocked the legislators of the Old Dominion."[98] Here the paper seemed to be conflating two unrelated issues: Tom Scott's railroad ambitions in Texas and an incendiary speech in the Senate by Republican James Blaine against amnesty for high-ranking Confederates, tying them both in with Centennial participation. On the same page of the same issue, after declaring "it isn't Philadelphia we're against," the *Weekly Statesman* leveled the familiar charge of Yankee corruption and moneygrubbing: "If the appropriation of a million and a half of the people's money is made thereof, it will eventually go into the pockets of private individuals . . . the people of Philadelphia are preparing to skin all who may attend their Centennial show."[99] The use of the word *their* is telling here, betraying a lack of connection to the ostensibly national celebration in Philadelphia. The paper then related entirely false information about the exhibition, claiming that there would be separate admission fees charged for each building on the grounds. It went on to describe the fair as a "money-catching device of the City of Brotherly Love" and described the Centennial as "worse than sectional, it is Philadelphia."

In Dallas, the *Herald* was similarly caustic, if not anti-Semitic: "The whole concern is a big speculation . . . under the management of a joint stock company, the manipulators of which expect to gather many shekels for themselves from the credulity and gushing sentimentality of their fellow citizens."[100]

Tom Scott was often accused of corruption, but the aversion to him in Texas seems misplaced for a man who placed railroad lines through Charlotte, Atlanta, and other southern cities. The way in which Texan discourse about the railroad centered on Scott demonstrated an inclination on the part of Texans to conflate the political and the personal. It was a tendency that also manifested itself in white southerners' responses to certain members of the National Centennial Commission, as will be seen in chapter 4.

WHITE SOUTHERN WOMEN AND THE CENTENNIAL

There was one group of southerners whose arguments for Centennial engagement appear to have deviated somewhat from the pragmatic and economics-driven focus of most pro-Centennial rhetoric: white women. Centennial organizers specifically targeted women in their fundraising efforts; as historian Mary Frances Cordato has explained, "Woman's role as domestic conciliator was enlisted in the task of American reconciliation."[101] The Women's Executive Committee, headed up by Philadelphia society matrons, was formed in 1873 to raise money for a Women's Pavilion at the exhibition as well as more generally to encourage Centennial engagement. Describing the Centennial as a "golden opportunity for us to blot out the bitter past" and "come together . . . cementing the . . . foundations of our common country," the committee issued a plea to American women that "we use all our influence in the interest of peace."[102]

The ladies of Philadelphia delegated much of this work to a network of numerous state and local groups. In Florida, the mantle of Centennial champion was taken up by Ellen Call Long. The daughter of a prewar Florida governor, Long had strongly opposed secession but supported the Confederate cause once war broke out. Postbellum, however, she was a strong advocate of reconciliation. Long was intensely interested in and involved with other projects involving historical memory, among them the Mount Vernon Ladies' Association of the Union (MVLA). The association was formed in the 1850s by South Carolinian Pamela Cunningham to raise money to purchase and maintain George Washington's by then dilapidated slave plantation. The group, with branches across the United States, remained (and remains) active, dedicated to the upkeep and preservation of Mount Vernon as a historical shrine. The MVLA and its activities provide an interesting admixture of sectionalism, politics, gender, and memory as well as a foreshadowing of women's role in the Centennial.[103] Robert Bonner cites the MVLA's "validation of female patriotic organizing, prov[ing] that women could work as an independent force and offer a distinctive version of national unity amidst a crisis."[104] The project served as a focus for slavery-friendly unionism in the late antebellum years and, with Cunningham's determination to maintain southern control of the project (insisting that "Sisters of the North" would be permitted only to "offer aid"), provides an interesting counterpart to the Philadelphia-controlled Women's Executive Committee.[105]

There was overlap here between memory, commemoration, and politics, and in the MVLA's third decade, Ellen Call Long was just one of many "patriotic organizing" women involved in both the MVLA and the Centennial. Long was also a founder of the Ladies' Memorial Association of Tallahassee, one of myriad loosely connected organizations across the South dedicated to properly memorializing Confederate war dead. In the 1890s, these memorial associations would amalgamate as the influential and memory-shaping United Daughters of the Confederacy (UDC). Caroline Janney has contributed a useful study of the Ladies' Memorial Associations (LMAs) in Virginia in which she demonstrates that these groups played a "pivotal role in the evolution of women's relations to the state," representing a political response to Reconstruction.[106] Janney argues that southern white women in groups such as the LMAs and later the UDC "actively sought to hinder" reconciliation.[107] Yet Long and some of the other southern women involved in Centennial planning and promotion present a somewhat more nuanced picture.

Elizabeth Gillespie, head of the Women's Executive Committee, acknowledged to Long in late 1874 that she saw little likelihood of much money being raised in the South. She stressed, however, that "we do want you all with us, & this collaboration will *not* be National if one state refuses to shine."[108] In response, Long threw herself into Centennial work with gusto. Appealing to the women of her state, she acknowledged postwar bitterness with biblical invocations: "I know 'the heart is smitten and withered like grass' and that we have 'eaten ashes like bread.'" But she went on to outline reasons for participation that fall in line with most other pro-Centennial arguments.[109] Long appealed to state pride: "I think Florida too fair a daughter to be absent on this proud day of maternal majority, and that she herself would feel justly mortified if unrepresented on this gala occasion."[110] She refined that familiar message, though, making it gender specific, and stated that the Centennial would benefit women by "bringing their industry and intelligence into notice."[111] She then, interestingly, attempted to make lemonade out of Reconstruction lemons by arguing that the trials of the postwar years had afforded women new opportunities: "Look around and you will find the once jewelled fingers of indolence now nimbly at work, the head that once thought only to please . . . bowed with the solicitude of responsibility."[112] Long argued that war and Reconstruction had caused southern women to "develop new talents, kindle genius, and by chastening the spirit, exalted the aims of life."[113] She concluded by citing the many rebuffs she received to her arguments and made a clearly gender-specific argument for reconciliation, noting that the women of the North had suffered along with those of the South, that they had "laid their hearts' treasures on the altar of their country." She argued that women of both regions had "displayed that fortitude and self-sacrifice of which woman alone is capable. They have wept apart and yet together over the grave of buried love . . . let us gather once more with our sisters of the North, East and West under the parental wing."[114]

Her appeals had mixed results. One Florida matron wrote to Long: "I'm sorry that this attempt of yours on behalf of our oppressed state has proved abortive . . . Fifteen years bitter struggle has crushed nearly every spark of patriotism from the Southern breast, and who can wonder."[115] E. A. Perry of Pensacola reported to Long that there was "no enthusiasm" for the Centennial among "our ladies."[116] Elizabeth White, of Quincy, Florida, politely declined to join Long on the state's Women's Committee, stating that it was "scarcely necessary for me to enumerate the many 'whys' for my seemingly 'unpatriotic' inaction—I can only assure you they are insuperable."[117] Similarly, Harriet Girardeau of Monticello reported that she had put Long's suggestion for a Centennial association to be formed in that town to "some of our public-spirited ladies but no inclination whatever to form such an association was evinced."[118] Another correspondent, Joseph Browne of Key West, was equally unhelpful, attributing lack of interest in what he called Long's "centennial scheme" not to "indiffere[nce] . . . but the changes in the condition of society . . . in the last few years."[119] The changes referenced here were, of course, around the place of African Americans in southern society and politics. Browne's reply also stressed the connection between discussion of the Centennial and the politics of Reconstruction when he mused about "the great party [Democratic] which has so valiantly vindicated our much abused country."[120] In spite of his pessimism, Browne was able to report to Long a little over a year later that his wife had managed to get "all the patriotic ladies" of Key West interested in the Centennial, resulting in a "Grand Calico Ball." Browne explained that had the costs of the ball not been so great, it would have raised more than the $155 that it did.[121] Harking back to the memory of a "Founding Mother" and slave owner, a "Martha Washington Tea" in Jacksonville, Florida, held in conjunction with the Mount Vernon Ladies' Association, raised $450 toward the Women's Building in Philadelphia. A correspondent described it to Long as a "very elegant entertainment" with one woman dressed as Martha Washington and "ladies and gentlemen in costume . . . as in olden times."[122]

Long occasionally authored pieces for the *Semi-Tropical*, a local journal published by former Republican Florida governor Harrison Reed. In December 1875, Reed, worried that Florida would not "occupy the conspicuous place she should" at Philadelphia, commissioned Long to write a piece plugging the upcoming Centennial. Reflecting gendered ideas of separate spheres for men and women, Reed specified that Long should "give us one of your stirring appeals solely in behalf of the Ladies' Dept., leaving me to fill out with an article on the general subject."[123] Long herself , for all her perennial activism, clearly also had well-defined notions of women's proper sphere. In self-congratulatory notes she made on the founding of the Tallahassee Ladies' Memorial Association, Long noted that through their contributions as "angels of charity and . . . labor *proper to their sphere* . . . the women of the South deserve to take rank with the highest heroes of Antiquity."[124] And while at the exhibition in Philadelphia, she suggested a gender specific legacy when sending her niece "a complete copy of the Women's Centennial Paper—which in fifty or a hundred years from now will be interesting and valuable so you can bequeath it to your eldest grandson."[125]

Ellen Long's vigorous promotion of the Centennial as a means of sectional reconciliation was likely an extension of her politics: the Floridian was a vocal proponent of the New South and raised hackles in Tallahassee when, in the 1880s, she supported the nomination of a Black man for the position of postmaster in that city.[126]

In Texas, newspapers across the state carried an appeal from Mrs. M. Jennie Young, who announced that she been enlisted by the National Women's Committee in Philadelphia to "hold . . . tea parties, international assemblies and other entertainments" in order to raise money for the construction of a women's pavilion at Fairmount Park. Mrs. Young reported that she was "authorized to form sub-committees" and listed the names of appointed ladies in various Texas towns. She concluded, in a call for Centennial commemoration that was both reconciliatory and distinctly Texan, that "the children of the Alamo . . . should do honor to their revolutionary sires and crossing the ugly chasm that yawns between the two place our flag of rejoicing upon the old [Bunker] hill and say 'this is also my heritage.'"[127] When the Democratic *Dallas Herald* published her pitch to the women of the Lone Star State, it endorsed her to its "fair readers" with a ringing confirmation of her Confederate credentials: "Mrs. Young was as true a rebel as lived south of the Potomac, yet she justly claims our full share in all the glories connected with American independence. We trust the ladies of Dallas will enter into the matter with their accustomed liberality."[128] The use of the word *yet* in this context made clear the problematic

connection between "rebeldom" and the celebration of American independence. In correspondence with the National Women's Committee,
Young attributed her "deepest interest" in the success of the Centennial not only to a patriotic interest in the past but to her hopes for
a peaceful future. She conceded that Texas might be perceived as a
"Mexican step-daughter" by other states and alluded to secession and
war by remarking that, like the biblical Naomi, Texas "went down for
a time into the land of strangers" but returned "a true and lovely Ruth,
fully instructed in the ways of Israel."[129] Lest any readers miss Young's
analogy, she inserted the phrase "patriots of '76" in brackets after her
reference to the "ways of Israel."[130]

Young's and Long's counterpart in Tennessee was Cynthia Brown,
widow of a Tennessee governor, sister of Confederate general Gideon
Pillow, and in her own right, a vice regent of the Mount Vernon Ladies'
Association. Brown sought assistance from her state's Democratic governor, James Porter, to ensure representation at the exhibition, only to
be politely refused. Porter replied that he had previously organized a
commission "for the purpose of having the Great State of Tennessee
properly represented at the Philadelphia Exposition . . . next to nothing has been accomplished and I believe any effort in this direction
would be attended with a like result."[131] Porter provided no elucida-
tion on the specific reasons for this failure, but the *Chattanooga Daily
Times* encouraged Brown to plow ahead. Describing the existing state
Centennial commission as "played out," it exhorted: "Now ladies, God
bless you, *go it alone.* You who are blessed with means and leisure,
Mrs. Brown, Mrs. [James K.] Polk . . . start the ball, call your sisters
throughout the Volunteer State to lend a hand, and we'll be bound you
will make your sluggish husbands, brothers and sons ashamed of their
inertia on the Centennial subject . . . But time is short."[132] Time *was*
too short, and Tennessee had no official presence at the exhibition, but
this raises an interesting question: was historical memory the province
of those "blessed with means and leisure," namely, women? Michael
Kammen has commented on the "special role of women as patrons

of the past" and "custodians of tradition," and some women, notably Ellen Call Long, clearly saw themselves in this role.[133] The Centennial represented a collision and a melding between memory and politics, and in discourse around the exhibition, those women who did engage tended to focus on the Centennial as a site of memory, even if political considerations were never far from the surface.

When the appeal from the National Women's Committee reached the ladies of Alcorn County, Mississippi, their response reflected wartime loss and residual bitterness: "Ladies of the North . . . one of this committee lost a father, and another lost two brothers, all killed in battle in the late war . . . Our politics and yours have not been calculated to allay the prejudices long matured and nourished between the two sections."[134] However, it also recognized the Centennial as a path to reconciliation and invoked the same sort of sisterhood that Long had called for in her appeal to Florida's women: "We regard [the Centennial] as calculated to unite us all in a national enterprise . . . lay a foundation for a permanent peace."[135] Caroline Janney, in highlighting the recalcitrance and bitterness of white southern women, remarks that "I have only been able to find one reference—tellingly, by a Union woman—claiming that the bonds of widowhood and bereaved mothers might help foster national healing."[136] However, the response by the women of Alcorn County suggests just that. They also acknowledged a sisterhood of sorts with their northern counterparts: "Though we heartily joined our husbands, fathers and brothers in the late hostilities, we can now . . . unite with you . . . lay a foundation for a permanent peace . . . and show the world what we women of America are capable of."[137] In a similar vein, Kate Minor of Natchez wrote that she was "earnestly at work, praying fervently that God will bless our undertaking . . . and in witnessing the fruits of toil from the hands of Northern and Southern women side by side, we may feel that they are united in their hearts in 1876."[138] It should be noted, however, that although a former slaveholder, Minor was notorious in Natchez for her Unionist sympathies and not "accepted among the Confederate elite society of Natchez."[139]

In Memphis, discussion of the "First Centennial Tea Party" in August 1875 led the *Memphis Daily Appeal* to predict that the city's Centennial efforts would be "both brilliant and successful. How could it be otherwise when our fair and cultured ladies are its guiding genius?"[140] The *Appeal's* account obliquely stressed the primacy of state identity by emphasizing that the outcome of the "patriotic" efforts of Memphis women would result in a "representation" at the Centennial of which Tennesseans could be "proud."[141] Similarly, Ellen Long's work in Florida also reflected the localized motivations that underpinned so much of the white South's enthusiasm for the Centennial. Much effort went into gathering exhibits that would promote tourism and/or economic stimulus for the Sunshine State. One of Long's correspondents described, happily, the "lovely native grasses and mosses" that she felt would make "striking decorations" for a Florida Centennial exhibit, going on to point out the profit realized in the state from "the sale of these beautiful grasses, collected and dried in the spring and summer for winter sales to visitors."[142]

When the Women's Executive Committee issued its final report in 1877, it noted what these women considered a bond that transcended sectional bitterness. Acknowledging the general inability of southern women to provide material or financial aid to the endeavor, the Philadelphians nonetheless acknowledged that "the hands of the women of the North were strengthened by the sympathy of their Southern sisters and their efforts were redoubled."[143] It would be quite a stretch to argue that white southern women were less influenced by partisan and sectional prejudices than were men. Indeed, Union general William Sherman observed that "the deep and bitter enmity of the women of the South" was unparalleled in history and that "no one who sees them and hears them but must feel the intensity of their hate."[144] While Sherman's march to the sea in 1864 had earned him a particularly prominent spot in the pantheon of despised Yankees, his experience of southern women's enmity was far from unique.[145] Janney, in her recent work on postwar reconciliation, stresses white southern women's resistance:

"Southern white women proved to be even more recalcitrant than their husbands and fathers in resisting the reconciliationist gush."[146] It's also useful to note that several southern states went entirely unrepresented on the Women's Executive Committee.[147]

Nonetheless, the rhetoric employed by some of these women in Centennial discourse was at once more open about the scars of war and, arguably, more genuinely reconciliatory than the utilitarian and/or recalcitrant positions held by white southern men. This difference was acknowledged by Republican Florida governor Marcellus Lovejoy Stearns when he admonished his state's legislature for failing to fund Centennial representation. After expressing the standard regret that Florida would miss out on the opportunity to show the world and potential investors its economic potential, Stearns commended Ellen Call Long and her organization, commenting that he "sincerely trust[ed] that the *men* of Florida would not be long behind them in seeking to uphold the dignity and advance the fame of their beautiful state."[148] However, it is perhaps useful to consider the venues in which these Centennial sentiments were aired. The white men arguing against Centennial engagement or advocating it for economic reasons were largely doing so in public spaces—particularly in the pages of newspapers—while the majority of female opinion on the exhibition discussed here was in private correspondence. The relative lack of a performative political aspect to these female viewpoints may be a factor in the arguably more nuanced approach to Centennial engagement taken by white southern women. It is also necessary to realize that when we look at these white southern women, we are looking at an elite stratum of society. Governor's daughter Ellen Long, for example, and those she corresponded with, generally wives of judges, politicians, and businessmen, were people with the means and the leisure to engage with the Centennial and the systemic privilege of having their correspondence preserved. One indication of this privilege is the fact that the homes of three of Long's correspondents quoted earlier, as well as that of Long herself, are preserved and listed on the National Register of Historic Places.

AFRICAN AMERICANS AND THE CENTENNIAL

In contrast to the ambivalence with which white southerners viewed the Centennial celebrations, African Americans saw the commemoration as an opportunity to express their essential Americanism. From the time of the initial planning stages of the Centennial, Black Americans planned and debated the form that their participation should take. Unlike white southerners, the advantages that African Americans saw in Centennial participation had as much to do with laying claim to American identity as with economic or political gain; the objectives were not mutually exclusive. A passage from the *Savannah Tribune*, a Black Georgia newspaper, exemplifies African American attitudes toward the Centennial on a number of levels. It invokes the nation's birth and lays claim to Black presence and participation at the founding. It also utilizes the past to serve the present: African Americans were using the commemorations of 1776 to claim their place and help secure their standing in 1876: "Would it not be as well for us to inform some of our patriotic friends who are so gloriously celebrating the 100th anniversary of American Independence, that the first blood that was shed for American liberty was that of a negro, Crispus Attucks, who fell while nobly defending the city of Boston March 5th, 1770? And yet our Democratic friends say this is a white man's country."[149] The excerpt also makes explicit the political polarization that characterized the United States in the election year of 1876, with its identification of the Democratic Party with the desire to exclude African Americans from the benefits of citizenship.

Black efforts to establish symbolic connections with the founding were not new: in 1858, African Americans in Boston had organized a celebration of Black Revolutionary hero Crispus Attucks that became an annual fixture in the city. Attucks was celebrated, in the words of historian Craig Bruce Smith, as a link through which Black Bostonians could "claim [their] symbolic inheritance of the spirit of the Revolution."[150] The Centennial, however, provided a larger, nationwide, canvas for Black Americans' use of Revolutionary memory and considerable effort was made to take advantage of it.

A contributor to the *Christian Recorder,* the organ of the Black African Methodist Episcopal (AME) Church asked rhetorically in March 1872 if the "colored people had any share in the work of bringing this country to its present status? . . . We have . . . Let us be up and doing . . . Let us claim that our labor of the past has added something to the glory of the country."[151] Here we see Black Americans referencing their participation and their presence throughout the history of the United States and insisting that it meant something. There is also recognition that the commemoration of the hundredth anniversary of independence was an opportunity to articulate this claim to citizenship and belonging. In this spirit, the Convention of Colored Newspaper Men proposed the publication of an eighteen-volume "Centennial Tribute to the Negro" intended to "let the coming generations know our true history." Demonstrating the way in which African Americans already saw the importance of commemoration and the usability of history as a statement of identity and belonging, this set was projected to include volumes on "One Hundred Years with the Negro in Battle," "One Hundred Years with the Negro in Business," "One Hundred Years with the Negro in the Pulpit," "One Hundred Years with Negro Lawyers & Doctors," and so on.[152] Lack of funding kept this ambitious project from getting off the ground.

There was one official Black contribution to the Philadelphia exhibition, and its rocky history can perhaps serve as a metaphor for the Black experience of the Centennial. *Christian Recorder* editor Benjamin Tanner was the moving force behind a drive to honor AME founder Richard Allen (1760–1831) with a statue on the Centennial grounds. The *Recorder* pleaded in an 1874 editorial: "Why can't we do it? Do what? Why can't we . . . have a hand in the great Centennial? Indications are that we as a distinct yet integral portion of the American people are not going to do anything. At the inception of the movement, here in Philadelphia, we were invited to take part, in common with others, but the sequel proved that while they invited us in common, they treated us in particular, which, you know, never answers."[153] This is likely a reference to the imbroglio over the sidelining of the Black women's committee in Philadelphia (which I will discuss later in this chapter) but was also indicative of the general status of Black Americans everywhere. The editorial continues, with some bigoted rhetoric that might be seen as a qualifying attribute of the Americanism that was being claimed: "As a people we are surely to be credited with as much common sense and as much patriotism as are alien Romanists, who are not and cannot be truly American . . . What then, can we do? LET THE A.M.E. CHURCH REPORT A MONUMENT IN FAIRMOUNT PARK, DEDICATED TO RELIGIOUS LIBERTY and have it crowned with a statue of Allen."[154] This assertion was followed with claims about what such a monument would accomplish, evoking comparisons with the opportunistic entreaties of pro-Centennial white southerners but coveting recognition and pride rather than economic benefit: "It would be a grand thing, a thing that would tell mightily in the interests not only of our church but of our whole race. And it can be done . . . It would pay, one of its first fruits would be recognition . . . As the thousands who visit the Centennial and look upon the bronzed face of the old Christian hero, they would be led to enquire, who is this? And by whom was it erected? The replies given would be altogether to our advantage."[155]

Five months later, the *Recorder* was still pushing for the monument, citing the prestige it would bring to the church and claiming it would be the "grandest thing the American Negro ever did."[156] Here was an attempt to use commemoration to bolster the standing of African Americans by memorializing a high-achieving former slave, and it was taken up with some enthusiasm across the AME denomination, which was growing rapidly in this period. The growth was largely through evangelization of southern freedmen and women: total church membership would reach 300,000 by 1876, and 400,000 in 1880, concentrated mostly in the South.[157] The Arkansas chapter was especially active, with Bishop John Brown and Secretary Andrew Chambers both writing letters to the *Recorder*.[158] There was some dissent within the church: the denomination's business manager, William Hunter, dismissed any gains to be had through representation at the Centennial as "intangible."[159] In responding to Hunter, Chambers linked the proposed statue with African Americans' status as citizens, crediting it with almost mystical powers: "It shall be a stepping stone to the colored men of America to rise higher in self-esteem and the esteem of all nations. We intend to leave Philadelphia in 1876 as did the heroes in 1776, with a fixed resolve to achieve noble results; and in 1976 we expect our progeny to gather around the Monument in question, shed tears of gratitude . . . and call us blessed."[160] As we shall see in chapter 5, though, these hopes were destined to remain unfulfilled.

Another significant and telling episode in the story of African American Centennial engagement was the attempt by the Philadelphia subcommittee of Elizabeth Gillespie's Women's National Centennial Committee to involve local Black women in their efforts. This biracial endeavor proved unsuccessful. As the *Springfield (MA) Republican* stated, in an editorial republished verbatim in the *Christian Recorder* a few weeks later:

> The ladies of the Centennial Commission very properly invited some of the wealthy and cultivated colored ladies of the city to meet them . . . talk over the work that needed to be done . . . very unfortunately . . . the task of explaining the views and wishes of the Commission was entrusted to a doubtless well-meaning but maladroit member who discharged it in such a way as to outrage the susceptibilities of every colored lady present and utterly frustrate the purposes of the consultation. It is certainly a great pity if such an anniversary as this, the hundredth birthday of the common country in which black and white have an equal right, is to be marred by this miserable prejudice of color.[161]

What the maladroit member said that so offended the "wealthy and cultivated ladies of color" was that they were not permitted to solicit funds from among white people but were restricted to working within their own community. The ladies resigned from the committee. In response to the dispute, the *New York Tribune* counseled Black Americans to "make a special separate effort . . . for the Centennial, rather than be merged and herded with the indiscriminate mass of foreigners and natives," but the *Christian Recorder* rejoined that the nation, of which they emphatically claimed membership, should "come together as one great national family."[162]

This expression of national unity is from the same *Christian Recorder* that went to such lengths to promote the Allen Monument as a commemorative touchstone for a particular segment of the population. It is perhaps useful to remember that the *Tribune's* advocacy of a "special, separate" effort was coming from a white source, one not likely to embrace the idea of integrated efforts. The *Recorder* would have seen their monument efforts not so much as a claim to distinction but as staking their distinct claim to membership in that "great national family." Philip Foner has quoted the *Philadelphia Press* as reporting that the Women's Committee retorted that the disgruntled "ladies of color" could "emigrate to Africa" if they were not happy with the racial status quo in Philadelphia.[163] The *Camden Democrat,* in New Jersey, reported condescendingly that "the duties assigned them brought the colored sisters in too close proximity to the whites. Silk refused to herd with calico—cologne couldn't stand musk—and a teapot tempest was the consequence."[164] This journal linked the Centennial both to Radical Republicanism and to mercantile interests, echoing much southern sentiment concerning the exhibition. Remarking upon the "fastidious taste [of] the matrons and daughters of the radical merchant princes," the *Democrat* asserted that "these frequent snubs ought to satisfy colored people that the professions of those who prate of 'equality' between the two races is nothing but the quintescence of hypocrisy [sic]. The prejudice against 'race and 'color' is just as strong with their pretended friends as with those who are falsely charged with being their enemies."[165]

The fact that the *Democrat* was a northern paper demonstrated again the overlapping political and regional fissures that characterized the 1870s. This could also be seen in the West, where the *San Francisco Weekly Alta* criticized California's Democratic-controlled legislature for failing to fund that state's presence at the Centennial. The paper went on to suggest that the state Republican Party incorporate state support for a Centennial presence into its platform.[166] This schism along party lines was further reflected in the pages of the Democratic *Los Angeles Herald*. It counseled that when "such men [Centennial organizers] begin to babble patriotism, it is a pretty sure sign somebody is about to be robbed . . . this centennial celebration, if it ever comes off, will pour millions of dollars into the pockets of Quaker City residents. They will squeeze the American people, and fleece the civilized world."[167] Meanwhile, a report in the *Springfield (MA) Republican* highlighted another division in American society: class. The *Republican*'s comment that the African American women approached by the Philadelphia committee had been "some of the wealthy and cultivated colored ladies of the city" further serves as a reminder that only the middle and upper classes, in either race, would have had the time and the means to work for, write about, or perhaps even spend much time thinking about the Centennial Exhibition.

In 1874, as Congress considered an ultimately unsuccessful appropriation of three million dollars for the Philadelphia exhibition, Representative Josiah Walls of Florida, an African American Republican, addressed the House about the proposed bill. Replying to those (largely southern) critics who dismissed the Centennial as a moneymaking exercise, he declared that "the exposition has been sneeringly alluded to as 'The Philadelphia Job' as though it were an evident attempt to . . . foist upon an indifferent and unwilling people a scheme foreign to their interests and in opposition to their wishes . . . all for the petty gains . . . [for] the local benefit of a particular section."[168] Walls fell into line with the rhetoric of those promoting the Centennial by recounting the economic wonders that would follow Centennial participation: "The general interests of the nation as a whole, as well as the particular interests of each State and section, will be surely and so largely promoted by the intimate intermingling of citizens from every corner of our own country."[169]

The congressman went on to put the exhibition in its commemorative, nation-defining context, seeing in it the power to "blot out" the divisions of war and Reconstruction:

> I allude to the tendency of such a gathering . . . to revive invigorate and stir to vigorous life that feeling of national patriotism in our land which recent occurrences have somewhat weakened . . . I believe that when from every corner of this broad land . . . thousands and millions of the free citizens of a free government shall assemble in the very cradle and place of birth of all that they politically hold dear . . . there will be aroused in the bosoms of all a higher and purer sense . . . of the free institutions [of the United States]. . . and kindle a blaze of patriotic feeling in whose dazzling light all questions of minor differences and . . . past disagreements will be blotted out.[170]

Walls had a special point to make, though, as a Black American commending the Centennial as a commemorative and defining moment. He concluded his remarks by reiterating that the Centennial could serve to heal the wounds of Civil War and bind the nation together by reminding North and South, Black and white, of their common revolutionary heritage: "For myself and at least four millions of the new freemen of this land of liberty, I will hope that . . . I may on the 4th of July 1876 stand in the very shadow of Independence Hall and with glowing heart read the undying words of Webster: 'Liberty and Union, now and forever, one and inseparable.'"[171]

Other African Americans made similar rhetorical recourse to the founding but in a more pessimistic context. A correspondent signing him- or herself "Civis" wrote to a Black New Orleans paper, laying claim to Americanness: "I regard the battle of Bunker Hill and the signing of the Declaration of Independence as constituting [the birth of] our national life." But Civis qualified that remark with the statement that "we are not yet a nation in the proper sense of the term." Civis went on to fault the founders themselves: "The founders of our government in making the Black man an exception to what they deemed a self-evident truth not only falsified the principles upon which their theory of government wholly rests but they poisoned the very fountain of national life."[172] Taking a pessimistic view of the state of American nationhood, this Louisianan then presciently concluded that only "restraint" by the federal government would enable Black equality: "Persistent indulgence in the vices which slavery generates has demented the entire white population of the South and rendered it morally irresponsible. Impervious to remonstrance, it is amenable only to restraint. That it will be restrained, I have no doubt, but how it will be restrained is as far beyond the reach of human ken or now as the method of the emancipation of our race was before the Rebellion."[173] These observations offered a sobering and bleak assessment of the relationship between the races of the American nation as it celebrated its centennial and a grim portent of race relations in the century to follow. They also give an indication of just what was at stake in that year's presidential election, as a Democratic victory would likely spell the end of federal "restraint."

The Centennial and the Politics of Representation

"There are thousands of Democrats up North who are first rate fellows and if they desire to see Texas at the Centennial we would like to gratify them . . . [but] it is not to be expected that a respectable lady like Texas would enter the festivities on the arm of a satyr like Parsons."[1] This was the acerbic reaction of one Democratic Texas newspaper, the *Brenham Banner*, to the presence of a Republican politician, William Henry Parsons, on the National Centennial Commission. The passage reflects not only the often emotive and angry responses some white southerners had to the Centennial Exhibition but also the way in which the exhibition served as a proxy for the political battles of the Reconstruction era. This chapter provides some case studies of these Centennial-related political struggles, looking in particular at Texas—a state that, uniquely, ended up with two competing sets of National Centennial commissioners, nominated by consecutive governors who were bitter political rivals. The furor over these commissionerships provided the impetus for widespread public discussion of the Centennial and the part, if any, that these southern states should play in it. These struggles mirrored the wider political battle over Reconstruction politics and the place of both white southerners and African Americans in the reunited States.

The Republican "satyr," William Parsons, was appointed by Republican Texas governor Edmund Davis, along with Democrat John Chew, to represent the state on the National Centennial Commission. After

Davis was defeated by Democrat Richard Coke in December 1873, the new governor attempted to replace Parsons and Chew with two Democrats, Alfred Hobby and J. W. Jennings. Parsons and Chew fought a months-long battle to retain their positions. This struggle provides a sharp vignette not only of the partisan divide around an ostensibly national and reconciliatory commemoration but also of the ways in which language about "representative men" was used to shore up the political supremacy of white former Confederates in Texas and the South.

WILLIAM HENRY PARSONS

The central figure in this story, Republican appointee William Henry Parsons, was born in New Jersey and raised in Alabama but settled in Texas in his midtwenties, after seeing service in the war with Mexico. At that time still affiliated with the Democratic Party, he published a secessionist newspaper, the *Southwest*, in Waco, and when the Civil War broke out, he led a variety of Texas companies over the course of the conflict, most notably the Twelfth Texas Cavalry, also known as Parsons's Brigade.[2] He was named an acting brigadier general in 1862 and, though the promotion was never made permanent, was known as General Parsons from that point on.[3] In 1865, Parsons joined those diehard Confederates who preferred exile to surrender and fled to British Honduras in a futile attempt to set up a Confederate colony there.[4] Back in Texas a few years later, Parsons, in January 1868, joined with other prominent Lone Star Democrats, including future governor Richard Coke, as a delegate to a "Conservative State Convention," which based its platform around opposition to the Republican Party and what it called the "Africanization of the state."[5]

In the late 1860s and early 1870s, Texas was under the control of a Republican Party whose Radical wing, headed by Edmund J. Davis, had gained ascendency. Elected governor in 1869, Davis was a former Southern Unionist and had commanded the First Texas Calvary in its battles with Confederate forces for the city of Galveston, among other campaigns.[6] Davis's particular brand of Radical Republicanism promoted publicly funded education, Black citizenship rights, and commercial development. White Democrats, as elsewhere in the South, generally opposed these aims, and throughout the early 1870s, the Democratic Party in Texas put all its efforts into "redeeming" the state and reversing Republican policies. At an Austin political meeting in July 1870, Democrats attacked Davis "in almost hysterical tones . . . for assuming despotic powers." These men felt that things had been turned upside down: "They saw their world in turmoil and viewed Republicans as radicals who had betrayed their community and the white race."[7] The central unifying feature of Texas Democracy was abhorrence of the Radicals and all they stood for. These Democrats were determined to undo Reconstruction: the centralization, the taxation, and most of all the racial upending that characterized it.

In the midst of this bitterly divided political landscape, William Henry Parsons proceeded to do the unthinkable: in a rather startling metamorphosis in 1869, he earned the lasting enmity of white Democratic Texas by running successfully for the Texas Senate as a Radical Republican.[8] In the words of one disgruntled Texan: "He was a rampant, unreconstructed rebel . . . but all at once, in a twinkling of an eye, [he] flopped over. Without notice to or conference with any old friend, he suddenly became the radical candidate for the state senate and by the niggers was duly elected."[9] Looking back on Parsons's switch during the Centennial controversy, the *Waco Register* provided a Republican interpretation, claiming that "while in the foreign city of Rio de Janeiro, alone, sick and a stranger, he saw a power to befriend and protect in the United States flag borne over the seas . . . the scales fell from his eyes and he resolved to return and labor henceforth for a united rather than a divided country."[10] Historian Carl Moneyhon has characterized Parsons's conversion to Republicanism as being based on the belief that the Republican economic plan was better for Texas than that of the Democrats, writing that Parsons "was convinced that the Democratic

Party offered no hope for the successful reconstruction of the state and particularly for its future development." Parsons himself described the switch as being designed to enable him to "act upon convictions of individual duty to self, family and State."[11]

Another possible factor in Parsons's "flip" was his much younger brother, Albert. Despite having served in the Confederate army, like his brother, Albert began publishing a Radical Republican newspaper, the *Spectator,* in 1867 in Waco.[12] He became involved in socialist, and later anarchist, politics and was hanged for his involvement in the 1886 Haymarket Riot in Chicago. William Parsons remained close to and supportive of his brother over the years and described Albert's wife, Lucy Parsons, a mixed-race woman who had likely been born a slave and who fought for Albert's radical agenda into the 1940s, as a woman of "youth, beauty and genius."[13] Historian Paul Avrich has posited that Albert was influenced by William Parsons's renunciation of secession and support for the rights of freedmen.[14] Given that Albert launched the *Spectator* more than a year before William's switch, it seems more plausible to suggest that the older brother's views were influenced by the younger's. But whatever the true reasons for Parsons's change of party, reaction to it indicates clearly how deeply questions of political identity resonated with many Reconstruction-era white southerners.

The former Confederate general was a key figure in Reconstruction Texas. One contemporary report stated that a "Parsons clique filled every position of honor under Davis's administration."[15] Parsons resigned his legislative seat in December 1871, when Governor Davis appointed him to serve as an immigration agent, based in New York City, for the State of Texas.[16] A month later, Davis also named Parsons as Texas's representative on the National Centennial Commission. Sharing office space with Parsons in New York was the man who would be Governor Davis's second appointment to the National Centennial Commission: Democrat, Confederate veteran, Mississippi native, and former slave owner John Calhoun Chew. Chew was residing in New York City as an agent and correspondent for several Texas newspapers.

POLITICAL STRUGGLES IN RECONSTRUCTION-ERA TEXAS

Parsons's resignation of his Senate seat had been well timed: the first stage of Democratic "redemption" of the state came with that party's assumption of legislative control after the 1872 elections.[17] Then in the gubernatorial contest of December 1873, Edmund Davis faced Democrat Richard Coke. Coke, a native Virginian, had been in Texas since 1850, voted for disunion in the state's secession convention, and served in the Confederate Fifteenth Texas Infantry throughout the Civil War.[18] Coke defeated Davis by a margin of two to one in an election that was rife with fraud and intimidation on both sides. The *Dallas Herald*'s response was jubilant, proclaiming that "the tyrant's chains have fallen from [our] limbs!"[19] But a farcical imbroglio ensued when the state's supreme court ruled the election results invalid. Davis refused to vacate his office and barricaded the state capitol, and Coke's supporters had to use ladders to access the building's second floor. In defiance of the court's ruling, Coke was sworn in as governor after President Grant declined to intervene with military support for Davis. When Davis left, he took the key to the locked governor's office with him, and Coke's supporters used axes to gain admittance.[20] Before leaving, Davis's wife put her "shapely foot" through a portrait of the president who had failed to back up her husband, and after arriving at the governor's residence, Coke is said to have trampled the flower beds that the Davises had planted.[21]

Historian James Marten has remarked that with Coke's assumption of the gubernatorial chair, "Reconstruction in Texas finally ended."[22] This is arguable; the state continued to be governed under the Reconstruction constitution of 1869 until a new document was drafted in 1875–76, albeit largely by Democrats with Confederate backgrounds who, in the words of historian Alwyn Barr, "saw their task as basically the prevention of any repetition of what they believed to be administrative and financial excesses by the Republican administration of 1870–1874."[23] It is also evident, through the discourse that would surround William Henry Parsons's place on the Centennial commission, that the divisive politics of Reconstruction did not end with redemption and that the Centennial Exhibition served as potent proxy for ongoing sectional and political animus.

CENTENNIAL COMMISSION CONTROVERSY

William Henry Parsons and John Chew served on the National Centennial Commission for a few years without much notice in the press. In 1875, however, as the Centennial drew nearer, Parsons began to attract opposition from the other side of the political and sectional fence. In August, the *Galveston Daily News* declared that "the appointment of Parsons is neither creditable nor satisfactory to the people of the Commonwealth . . . It is not at all improbable that [Coke] could secure the removal of Gen. Parsons and the appointment of a representative man by a simple request and presentation of the facts in the proper quarter."[24]

The idea that Parsons was somehow not "representative" would crop up repeatedly throughout 1875 and 1876, highlighting the exclusivity with which many white Texans defined themselves, and revealed tensions around the question of who could be a true Texan. At a July 1875 meeting in Houston to discuss plans for the Centennial, one man suggested that the fact that Parsons was "to all practical intents and purposes not a citizen of Texas" might furnish grounds for the governor to ask President Grant to replace him.[25] Gideon Strother, a Texan who was himself resident, interestingly enough, in New York, wrote to President Grant about the inappropriateness of his state being represented by someone living outside its borders: "The present commissioner, a resident of N.Y., is obnoxious to the people of our State and our legislature will never appropriate one dollar while he remains in that position as he is a non-resident . . . I understand that should your excellency commission another, our legislature will make an appropriation from thirty to forty thousand dollars."[26]

Closer to home, another detractor identified only as "White River" wrote to a Dallas newspaper, reminding Texans of Parsons's recent past: "As a senator in the infamous 12th legislature . . . with its unholy outrages on the people of Texas . . . its villainous registration and election laws, its bribed subsidies to railroads and a multitude of other infamies, the people of Texas honestly believed and yet believe that Mr. Parsons was a master spirit, and these are the reasons that Texans have for refusing to join in the Centennial, while he is a chief commissioner from the state."[27] At the July meeting in Houston, charges of corruption had also been made, with one speaker insistent that it was Parsons's corruption, and not his political affiliation, that was the real issue. This was also the main theme of White River's letter to the *Dallas Herald:* "Where did this man, poor to penury all his life, get the money to, as he now boasts, pay his own expenses for three years in Philadelphia? As he has been in no business since his somersault in 1869 . . . the question in the mind of every Texan who knows his antecedents, is 'where did the money come from?'"[28] But some critics were frank that it was Parsons's Republicanism that was the stumbling block to Texans' acceptance of him as their Centennial commissioner: "Several prominent gentlemen addressed the meeting and all agreed on one point, viz., that not one dollar could be raised by subscription or appropriation to have the state represented at the Centennial as long as Gen. William H. Parsons remained the Centennial Commissioner for Texas, he having been appointed by Gov. Davis to that position and being a block in the way whom it was desirable to remove before Texas would take any stock in the exhibition."[29]

The widespread reluctance to allow Parsons to be seen as representative of the state was symptomatic of the era's sectional and political divisions and was echoed repeatedly in the state's Democratic press. The *Dallas Herald* conceded that while Parsons was not, technically, a carpetbagger, he was so "utterly base and contemptible" that Texans could not muster any enthusiasm for the Centennial under his commissionership and implied a connection between this and the fact that he had been nominated by the "Radical governor" and not Governor Coke.[30] The *Brenham Banner*, appropriating the mantle of patriotism for those who objected to Parsons's representation of Texas, implicitly linked patriotic feeling with state rather than nation. The Democratic newspaper recommended that "the application of a number seventeen boot to the part [of Parsons's anatomy] where it will do the most good . . . the boot should be well-filled with foot and be made to swing rapidly from a patriotic leg."[31]

The reaction to Parsons in Texas triggered some concern with the National Centennial Commission in Philadelphia. On 4 August 1875, John Welsh, chairman of the Centennial Board of Finance, wrote to prominent Texas Democrat Ashbel Smith expressing fears that because Parsons was "not agreeable to the people of Texas," the state might boycott the exhibition. Welsh pointed out that while concern over Parsons's character might be "a proper subject for criticism," it should not "retard . . . a great national movement . . . in which the honor of the Country is involved."[32] The letter concluded with a plea that summed up the conciliatory aims of the Centennial: "I am very anxious that the men of the South should show as much interest in our great work as the men of the North, the East, and the West and it would be a great misfortune for the Country, if when all Country, if when all the rest of the world is here our whole people are not here to meet them."[33]

A month later, John Chew made reference to Governor Coke's "sudden suspension of correspondence with this office."[34] In fact, Coke had, more than a full year after becoming governor, decided to remove both Parsons and Chew and replace them with Democrats of his own choosing. On 31 August 1875, Coke wrote to Alfred Goshorn, the director general of the Centennial Exhibition: "Representative men of the State shall have charge of her interests there. Messrs. Chew and Parsons, heretofore appointed Commissioners on recommendation of my predecessor, Governor Davis, are not such men. If the State must be represented by them or not at all, the latter alternative will be preferred, and no appropriation will be made by the Legislature for the purpose."[35] He continued that Chew and Parsons had left Texas and moved to New

York and thus, as far as he was concerned, were no longer citizens, thereby annulling their appointment and creating vacancies.

Coke's claim that Parsons and Chew were not "representative" of the state was more than an obfuscation of a desire to have his state represented at the Centennial by politically congenial Democrats of his own choosing. It also signals a concern with representation that was echoed repeatedly throughout the mid-1870s. The *Marshall Tri-Weekly Herald,* for instance, editorialized against Democratic congressman John Hancock's election to the U.S. Senate on the grounds of his wartime Unionism and lack of Confederate service. The *Herald* argued that "a representative man, as we understand the term, is one who reflects the position, politically and morally, of the people he represents."[36] This indicates that one definition of *representative* in this context was having Confederate, as well as Democratic, credentials. The *Herald* continued that it wished to see such a representative man sent to the Senate, where "the Democratic statesmen of the North . . . can clasp fraternal hands with him as a representative man." The newspaper went on to insist, rather unconvincingly, considering their definition of *representative* and their restriction of fraternal sentiment to Democratic northerners, that the "prejudices and hates of the past have no existence in Texas since the close of the war."[37] The *Austin Evening News* unpacked what was meant when Parsons was called "unrepresentative": "We make an objection . . . not on the ground that he is an appointee of Gov. Davis, or that he is not a true Southerner . . . our objection is that he is a man whose interests are not closely enough allied to Texas so that he can be said to represent this state in every sense. He has spent too much time away . . . He cannot know every foot of the soil, or her capacity as a man should. The . . . commissioner should know Texas thoroughly and we believe sincerely that Gen. Parsons does not possess these qualifications."[38] Despite the attestation of "sincere" belief that a representative man should be familiar with every square foot of Texan soil, the salient point here appears to be the requirement for "allied interests," or an interest in restoring and maintaining the power of the white, property owning and conservative elements served by the Democratic Party.

Coke's vow that Texas would have nothing to do with the Centennial unless the unrepresentative Parsons and Chew were replaced was reiterated frequently through the state's Democratic press and indicates that the Centennial served as much as an arena for political point scoring as of a national celebration or commemoration.

COMPETING COMMISSIONERS

Three days after Coke's letter to Goshorn, on 2 September 1875, the *Galveston Daily News* reported that Democrat and "eminent Galvestonian" Colonel Alfred Marmaduke Hobby had been appointed to the National Centennial Commission by Governor Coke. The *News* repeated the by now familiar mantra that "no state [had] more to gain from presence at the Exhibition than Texas," and no city more than Galveston, and exhorted its readers to attend a meeting at which "we could all unite in requesting Col. Hobby to accept the position."[39] Hobby was a native Georgian who had been in Texas since the 1850s, served in the Confederate army, and authored such patriotic Confederate–themed poetry as "The Sentinel's Dream of Home."[40] Coke selected J. W. Jennings, a Missouri Democrat residing in Texas since only 1872, to replace Chew as alternate commissioner.

Although Parsons's absence from the state in the 1870s was attributable to his position as the state's immigration agent in New York City and then to his appointment as Centennial commissioner and Chew's to his work as a newspaper correspondent and immigration agent, Coke stuck to nonresidence in Texas as his ostensible reason for replacing them. Judge James Hall Bell, a Republican (though not Radical) Texas jurist wrote to President Grant in defense of Parsons and Chew in August 1875, stating that the law "in reference to the Centennial Exhibition . . . did not intend that Your Excellency should be made the instrument of injustice or political prejudice" on the part of Governor Coke and requested an interview with Grant to provide him with the "full facts" of the case.[41] Whether or not he received an audience with the president, the matter dragged on a further eight months. U.S. secretary of state Hamilton Fish recorded his own conversation with Grant about the issue in March 1876, noting that he informed the president that "Parsons . . . had been a Confederate who at the close of the war went to Brazil and was subsequently brought home in one of our public vessels; that he was a member of a disloyal and disreputable organization . . . had made a considerable amount of money in some very questionable operations and . . . had not resided [in Texas] for several years."[42]

Coke's nominated commissioners, Hobby and Jennings, set off for Philadelphia in April 1876 to present their credentials to the National Centennial Commission and see what progress had been made by the "former commissioners," as the Galveston News referred to them, though Parsons and Chew were still in place.[43] Hobby courted the press upon his arrival in the Centennial city. The New York Graphic ran a glowing piece, reprinted widely throughout Texas, which called him one of the "great men of the state he represents . . . a man of culture with an understanding singularly comprehensive . . . esteemed for virtues of courage, generosity and public spirit . . . conspicuous for social qualities, he is abstemiously temperate, having never tasted or touched tobacco, wine or cards."[44]

Ten days later, the Galveston Daily News published a gushing report that described Hobby's welcome by his new colleagues and his "intelligent answers to questions about the resources of Texas and the sentiments of her people."[45] Hobby told the News that he was received with "distinguished courtesy" by the rest of the commission and, appealing to state pride, noted that the word Texas was "the open sesame to every door" in Philadelphia. He went on to stress the economic advantages of representation at the Centennial. The apparently well-primed reporter then asked, "If Texas is represented, will it not aid us in obtaining appropriations from the national government?" Hobby responded that "the impression is that it will place Texas in a more graceful attitude to ask favors by thus manifesting her appreciation and interest in the exhibition in which the other states have taken so lively an interest."[46]

It is perhaps significant that Hobby made no reference to patriotism or the Revolution of 1776 in his interview. Indeed, the only references to reunion were in the context of emphasizing outsiders' high regard for his state. This was likely designed to neutralize any Texan touchiness about the Civil War's outcome that might detract from his argument that the state would benefit economically from a presence at Philadelphia. Stressing the welcome he received in Philadelphia also served to bolster his own credentials in the face of controversy surrounding his appointment. Hobby reported to the press that he hurried to the exhibition grounds, where he met Centennial officials and discussed the situation. A dedicated building would cost the state around fifteen thousand dollars, while renting space in an existing building would amount to half that figure. Hobby urged formal support, reiterating the point he had already made to the *Galveston Daily News* about the linkage between Centennial participation and federal largesse: "The non-appearance of Texas may appear ungenerous and operate prejudicially when appropriations are hereafter asked for her benefit."[47]

In the summer of 1875, as Coke schemed to replace him, Parsons had written to the *New York Herald* in a spirit of reunification: "The most august spectacle of . . . the century, will be the complete and voluntary extinguishment of the embers of war during the Centennial celebrations . . . the men of the blue and the gray will renew the olden bonds of amity and re-consecrate the original spirit of liberty and union."[48] Parsons managed to integrate this statement of the key Centennial theme of reconciliation with an apparently calculated appeal to Confederate sensibilities. Writing to the *Herald* to refute its claim that Robert E. Lee had done nothing to encourage sectional reunion in the years after Appomattox, Parsons quoted from a letter in which Lee pointed out the wisdom of "submission to authority" and proceeded to claim that he carried a copy of Lee's letter "in a memorandum book on my person, as I have treasured it in my heart."[49]

In August 1875, the *Waco Register* published a letter from Parsons in which he decried the "cormorants" who were trying to drive him from office and pointed out that he had been working on the National Centennial Commission for three years without pay, had been a proud Texan for thirty years, and plaintively pointed out in response to charges that he was no longer a Texan, "My work is here and not in Texas."[50] Two months later, the Republican and pro-Centennial *San Antonio Express* reported on a ten-page letter that Parsons, obviously stung by the abuse he had been receiving, had released to the press. The *Express* described the letter as being "conceived in a temper and couched in a style" that would do Parsons no favors were they to publish it in full.[51] Parsons's main point was an important distinction: that his role was as a national commissioner from Texas, not a Texas commissioner, and that, as paraphrased by the *Express*, "ever since his appointment . . . he [had] ignored party politics" and worked to make the Centennial a success. The *Express* backed Parsons, arguing for his "legal and moral right" to retain his position.

Statements from J. W. Jennings in the Texas media were scarcer than those of his fellow commissioners, but he did contribute to the public dialogue. Addressing the readers of the *Waco Daily Examiner,* this *alternate* alternate commissioner stressed the shortcomings of Parsons and Chew even as he reiterated their message concerning the potential benefits of the Centennial to the state: "[Parsons and Chew] have done nothing towards securing our state even space enough to show a pair of longhorns . . . The importance of the Centennial Exhibition to the future of our state cannot be estimated in dollars and cents . . . we must be prepared to surprise even the most skeptical of our greatness by exhibiting the fertility of our soil . . . the capitalists of the old world and the Eastern states are looking for some point to invest this surplus wealth."[52]

It is interesting to note that the rhetoric of Chew, Hobby, and Jennings on the importance to Texas of Centennial engagement is virtually indistinguishable. All three men urged participation for the same reason: the benefit of Texas. With no discernible differences in their approach to the exhibition, it seems clear that the rancor was all about politics and that service on the National Centennial Commission in Texas's name was symbolic of much more than the planning of a fair. The only Texas commissioner who had much to say about the importance of the Centennial in furthering sectional reconciliation was the widely detested Republican general William Henry Parsons, reinforcing the argument that debates around the Centennial were much more about power and politics than they were about celebrating a reunited nation.

Six months into the Parsons-Chew controversy, an editorial from an Austin paper neatly exhibited the interconnectedness of partisan politics and the Centennial. The piece also demonstrates the way these politics were personalized to the extent that the people of Texas—or at least the ones for whom this writer claimed to speak—could not abide participation in the fair because of the involvement of one man. Other recurrent themes were expressed here, including the idea that the fair was a northern scam but one that held out economic potential for its participants (but only if the fair was untainted by Parsons):

> The appointment of A. M. Hobby and J. W. Jennings . . . gives per-
> fect satisfaction to the people . . . and since we may now have proper
> agents the people should evince a share of practical interest in having
> the products and industry of Texas properly presented. The wonders
> of nature in the vegetable and animal kingdom should be gathered as
> rapidly as possible. The legislature's . . . first action will have reference
> to the ways and means for the perfect illustration in Philadelphia of the
> riches and resources of this commonwealth. The world will be there to
> see . . . even though selfish spoilsmen make personal profit the aim of
> the Centennial . . . if *Messrs* Hobby and Jennings accept the position[s]
> . . . then the aversion of the people to participation in the great Phila-
> delphia Exposition will be remedied.[53]

As the controversy raged, Chew remarked, with some justification, that the "idea that the avenue to Texan representation [at the Centennial] should be permitted to be blocked by [opposition to] General Parsons struck me as . . . supremely ridiculous."[54] To the oft-repeated claim that he was no longer a Texan, Chew stated: "Of all the compound fluid extracts of villainy that has flowed from a scribbler's pen,

that which emanated from some devil who objected to me as a representative Texan on the ground of non-citizenship, certainly deserves
a premium. If he will come to Philadelphia next year I will see to it
that he is decked with a crimson rosette and labelled the champion
slanderer of the Lone Star State!"[55]

In an ironic echo of the charges against Parsons, the *Austin Weekly
Statesman* now questioned Jennings's qualifications, with a correspondent claiming that while Hobby was universally admired, former
Missourian Jennings was in "no sense a resident of Texas."[56] Lone Star
residents seem to have placed a rather strict construction on their definition of just who was and who was not a true Texan. It seems plausible
to suggest that some would have found fault with anyone chosen to represent their state on the National Centennial Commission. Moreover,
it demonstrates that this always had more to do with resentment of
Republicans and the Union, illustrating the shaky state of reconciliation
and reunion in 1870s Texas and the South as a whole.

On 27 March 1876, after having vigorously defended their positions
in the press, Parsons and Chew wrote to President Grant explaining the
practical reasons behind their out-of-state residences: "We state the
question fairly when we say that the allegations of our removal from
our state was only a pretext made to subserve the purposes of partisans
who wished to accomplish our removal because we were the nominees
of a Republican governor."[57] The *Washington (DC) National Republican*
concurred, declaring that "Gov. Coke and the Texas Bourbons were
determined to remove [Parsons]."[58]

At a meeting on 26 April, the National Centennial Commission decided not to recognize the credentials of Hobby and Jennings. Secretary
of State Fish had concluded that commissioners could be removed only
with their own consent, and so Parsons and Chew remained in their
posts, despite Coke's crowing, prematurely, in a letter to Hobby that
"Parsons and Chew have been superseded. I am much gratified that I
have succeeded in prying them out."[59] The political motivation behind
Governor Coke's attempted reshuffle of the Centennial commission
seems clear. The *National Republican*'s description of it as "the most

petty display of Bourbonism that has yet been made by him or any of that set" appears to be suggestive of the Bourbon–New Departure split within the Democratic Party that affected attitudes toward the Centennial.[60] In this case, however, such a reading may be too simplistic. The evidence indicates that the postbellum political landscape in Texas was too fractured and fluid to be able to discern any such overarching pattern in Democratic Centennial discourse during 1875–76. Because some counties were more overwhelmingly white than others, local Democrats had differing priorities at the local level, making it difficult for the party to exercise control at the state level. Because of these differing priorities, as historian Patrick Williams has stated, "the sides Texans took in one debate didn't necessarily carry over to the next." Williams has described a pattern of shifting coalitions rather than enduring alliances, which means that it is difficult to differentiate between an agrarian-Bourbon or Whiggish New South faction.[61] This is demonstrated by the way that the Centennial was used as a cudgel against Governor Coke by a Democratic paper, the *Denison Daily News:* "Gov. Coke claims credit for prying Parsons and Chew out of their positions as Centennial Commissioners for Texas. We happen to know that he had no influence whatever on that transaction. The truth of the matter is that Centennial Commissioners [were] almost unanimous by asking the President to make the change for reasons satisfactory to themselves. It is stated on good authority that Gen. Parsons had become very obnoxious to his brother commissioners."[62]

In the end, Texas had no official presence at the exhibition. John Chew laid the blame for the state's absence squarely with "Gov. Coke, Mr. R. Q. Mills [Coke's congressional correspondent] and their coadjutors. It was their pleasure to pursue the 'rule or ruin' policy and they did it with a persistence and a venom rarely equalled."[63] Although Coke did evince some interest in Texas being represented at Philadelphia, it is clear that for him, as for many others, having what he saw as representative Texans as the state's commissioners trumped any desire to use the exhibition as either commemoration or platform for economic boosterism.

REPRESENTATIVE MEN?

The Parsons affair had parallels elsewhere. Republican commissioner William Gurney of South Carolina drew condemnation that was, if anything, even more vociferous than that directed at Parsons. Gurney was a New Yorker who, after being stationed in occupied Charleston in the closing days of the Civil War, chose to remain in the South and established himself in business and in Republican politics in Charleston.[64] Gurney was an appointee of Republican governor Franklin Moses, reviled in his native state as a scalawag who vigorously championed equal rights for African Americans.[65] Even a Republican paper, the *Hartford (CT) Courant*, observed that Gurney was "said to be one of the corrupt leeches which have sucked the blood of [South Carolina]."[66] A Boston newspaper made the point that Gurney was considered one of the "worst class" of carpetbaggers and, though abstaining from making any judgment on Gurney's conduct or character itself, commented that he would prove himself a "better man than he is represented to be" if he were to step aside as Centennial commissioner.[67]

A South Carolina judge, T. J. Mackey, wrote to the president of that state's Agricultural and Mechanical Society, citing the importance of the opportunity the Centennial presented to "advance . . . the prosperity" of all South Carolinians and recommended simply ignoring Gurney and liaising directly with the national commission. The society's president, one Major T. W. Woodward, responded that such dispassion and pragmatism was beyond him. Indeed, Woodward explained, Gurney's appointment "render[ed] it impossible for me to have any lot or part in the centennial celebration . . . [Gurney] is the fit representative of South Carolina carpetbaggers and not of the descendants of Revolutionary patriots . . . could no native born citizen be found to represent South Carolina, one of the original thirteen?"[68] Woodward here raised the familiar question of just who could be representative of a people, disqualifying the outlander Gurney by citing South Carolina's heritage as one of the original thirteen colonies. He asserted that no "true South Carolinian" would take part in the Centennial "under the auspices of the present commissioner." He went on to strike another common theme, that of the fragility of white southern honor: "The insult . . . must have been designed to degrade . . . we cannot, without unmanly humiliation, meet the true men of the North at Philadelphia and thus remember . . . that we are all descendants of the heroic rebels of the glorious revolution of 1776."[69]

The *Weekly Telegraph,* of Macon, Georgia, provided a bit more nuance to the politics of this episode by characterizing Judge Mackey, who made the proposal that Woodward was rejecting, as a "notorious scalawag" and by suggesting that Woodward's rejection of the possibility of South Carolinian Centennial participation while Gurney was representing the state would have made "even Mackey's brazen cheek burn with shame."[70] A letter published in a Charleston newspaper argued that the Palmetto State could not engage with the Centennial without incurring shame, due to the state's "degradation." In the case of South Carolina, this was defined as "a government not of our own formation or choice, put upon us by force and fastened upon us as with a rivet by peculiar circumstances made available; for the purpose through unnatural laws."[71] The writer made clear here the link between what this Carolinian considered "self-rule"—governance by a white, Democratic Party—and "home rule." He went on to warn that engaging in Centennial celebrations could dull the sense of outrage and purpose necessary to return South Carolina to home rule: "Now, to rejoice is to signify satisfaction and to become or even appear to be, satisfied under such circumstances is just our danger, for from satisfaction proceeds impassive indifference. It is important to our restoration to our proper degree that our people never lose sight of this fact of degradation . . . If South Carolina can be wheedled and flattered into playing the part of an equal, many a troubled conscience among those who substituted moral degradation for physical punishment, will rejoice in the excuse for shaking of the reproach of such an act."[72]

Another paper, also Democratic, took an opposing view of the contretemps: "Major Woodward seems to think . . . there was a set purpose to degrade the state. Were such the case, we would fully support his

actions. But we cannot believe that there exists any want of appreciation for our state abroad, or any desire to exclude us for an equal
and fair representation in the proposed Centennial celebration."[73] The
Fairfield Herald saw the 1876 celebrations as an opportunity to "bury all
disappointments, all our bitterness . . . and . . . once more appear clad
as full brethren at the Centennial feast."[74] On the same page, however,
the *Herald* declared that Gurney was a "fine specimen of the genus
carpet-bagger" and had acted as Moses's "coadjutor in his many infamous schemes."[75] The account was vague as to what these schemes
entailed, but it is plausible to infer that they involved Black suffrage
and civil rights. The national administration didn't escape blame either:
because the president made Gurney's appointment official at Moses's
recommendation, the *Herald* continued, "the people of our state . . .
[felt] supreme disgust at Grant's folly . . . and a determination to take no
part in the Exposition, except as individuals."[76] Again, here was a blithe
assumption of who the "people" were—white Democrats—and what
they wanted. The writer went on to express regret that South Carolina
would forfeit the economic benefits of Centennial participation and
condemned the "blind partisan which render[ed] it impossible" for the
state to be represented at the exhibition.

Franklin Moses's successor in the governor's chair, Daniel Chamberlain, was also a Republican but sought to replace Gurney. The governor wrote to President Grant that Gurney was "personally so obnoxious to the white people of the state that we are unable to do anything
towards having our state represented at Phila. under his auspices."[77]
Chamberlain's explanation of the need to replace Gurney served, in
contradiction to a literal interpretation of his words, to highlight the
extent to which the political and the personal were conflated in the
Reconstruction-era South. The governor told President Grant that "it
is perhaps not necessary to indicate the grounds of objection to him.
They are not political, at least not wholly . . . whether well founded
or not, the objections are so serious as to make it impossible to accomplish anything while he holds this office."[78] As he had in the case
of Parsons and Chew, Grant referred the matter to Secretary of State

Fish, who could find no grounds for removing the commissioner. Gurney remained on the commission, and South Carolina had no official presence at the Centennial.

In Mississippi, Ohio-born Republican governor Ridgely Powers appointed a fellow transplant from the Buckeye State, Obidiah C. French, to the national commission. French was a Republican legislator and a close political ally of Adelbert Ames, who succeeded Powers in the governor's chair. French was routinely excoriated in the state's conservative Democratic press, apparently not without justification; historian William C. Harris has referred to French as a "shady Carpetbagger" whose questionable dealings had raised concern even among other Republicans.[79] The federal government at one point sued French for a six thousand–dollar shortfall in the accounts of a Freedmen's Bureau branch that he had managed in the late 1860s.[80] In 1871, one Democratic legislative colleague, Z. P. Landrum, posted cards around Jackson denouncing French as "a coward, a poltroon . . . a scoundrel . . . a low-bred carpet bag cur."[81] In May 1876, the Bourbon-leaning *Hinds County Gazette* cited an item about the Centennial in the *Jackson Clarion* that referred to French. The *Gazette* pointedly put quotation marks around French's name and title, "Col. O. C. French, Centennial Commissioner from Mississippi, and went on to comment: "This is the same French, if we are not mistaken, who swindled the people of Mississippi out of the swamp lands and the same man who got a bill through the negro legislature granting him 450 able-bodied convicts from the Mississippi Penitentiary, free of charge, 200 of which he instantly transferred to Col. Ed. Richardson for the handsome sum of $15,000, which he pocketed. But 'O.C. French' is no doubt worthy of the position he holds—a representative to one of the grandest humbugs and frauds of the age."[82]

Meanwhile, in Louisiana there were criticisms of U.S. congressman John Roy Lynch, appointed to the national commission by Republican governor William Kellogg. Lynch had previously faced accusations in the Democratic press of election fraud favoring Radical Republican candidates, and vague, unsubstantiated potshots continued throughout the Centennial years: "'Honest' John Lynch, having arranged his little speculation locating the Agricultural and Mechanical College upon his estate . . . has gone on to Philadelphia to have a pow-wow with the commissioners about the Centennial Exhibition matter."[83] On the exhibition's opening day, one Democratic journal, after reporting that "Grant and his dead-heads will be in force at the Centennial to-day" went on to describe the twenty-nine-year-old Lynch as the "old fraud . . . who misrepresent[s] Louisiana on this occasion."[84] Implicit again here was the assumption that this Black Republican could only misrepresent true Louisianans. Six months later, the *New Orleans Times* took the opportunity to take a jab at Lynch, ignoring the fact that seats on the commission were unpaid: "The Centennial has closed, the show is over, and many anxious enquiries are made as to what Honest John Lynch, Centennial Commissioner for Louisiana, did to earn his money."[85]

In February 1876, a North Carolina congressman delivered a speech from the floor of the U.S. House of Representatives on the hoped-for sectional healing to be brought about by the Centennial Exhibition: "I would go to Philadelphia and shake by the hand the brave men I used to meet on the field . . . We hope to see such a greeting of the patriots of the North and the South as will show to the whole Union that the flood tide of sectional hatred has ebbed forever."[86] The speech was reprinted, approvingly, in the *Austin Weekly Democratic Statesman*, the same newspaper that just a few weeks earlier had sneeringly referred to the Centennial as a "money-catching device for the City of Brotherly Love."[87] In Texas and throughout the white South, reunion rhetoric, when indulged in at all, appears to have been just that: rhetoric. The Democratic *San Antonio Herald*, reporting on the exhibition's opening, remarked that "once more in the Union, we are with them heart and hand and in this Centennial year and its appropriate celebration, we are with them." They were with them to the extent that in the same article, the *Herald*'s editor had commented, "The great Centennial about which there has been so much gas . . . opens today . . . on one pretext or another, they [Centennial organizers] have got their hands into the Nation's treasury."[88]

In 1873, William Parsons had addressed his fellow Texans on the importance of Centennial engagement; that message had been based on the assumption that the Centennial would be "neither a sectional nor a party question."[89] At that early stage, Parsons had still been able to portray his Republican affiliation as a virtue in promoting the Centennial, emblematic of a bipartisan approach to celebrating a reconstructed and reunified United States. Parsons's outlook, however, proved optimistic, if not naive, given the tumultuous state of Texas politics in the 1870s. By 1876, it was quite clear that Parsons had been wrong.

The *Austin Weekly Statesman* complained in 1875 that Republican rule left white Texan men in a state of "degradation" and that submission to Radical control was at the cost of loss of self-respect and personal dignity, exacerbated by the negation of white votes by those of "apes."[90] This statement was not made in reference to Parsons or the Centennial, but a connection can be inferred. William Parsons personified Radical rule and hence, to many white Texans, it would seem, their own lack of control during the years of Reconstruction. A Republican Centennial commissioner thus served as a convenient proxy for the anger, humiliation, and resentment that still festered after both "redemption" and a decade of "peace." (Democrat John Chew was collateral damage, victim of his pairing with the despised Parsons.) Discourse around the Centennial provided a platform for white southerners to express these feelings as well as their determination that Texas (or South Carolina or fill in the blank) was a white, Democratic state and could not be legitimately represented by one such as Parsons or Gurney or French. The Centennial Exhibition in Philadelphia provided an opportunity for Americans to commemorate the anniversary of their founding and a space in which to declare and display a new postwar identity. But it was more than a physical space. The Centennial served as a rhetorical arena as well. The obsession with selecting "representative men" to represent their state underscored the determination of many former Confederates to exercise power in what they saw as *their* state(s). The sense of Confederate identity spawned by the Civil War did not disappear or transmute smoothly into a renewed American nationalism. It was channeled into that fierce sense of state and partisan identity that made carpetbagger or Republican representation on the National Centennial Commission simply intolerable.

The white southerners opposed to Parsons, Gurney, and others were also concerned with degradation, humiliation, and emasculation. Confederate general Jubal Early had written to Robert E. Lee in 1868, "We lost nearly everything but honor and that should be religiously guarded." Indeed, the story of the political struggle in the South during Reconstruction is in one sense also the tale of southern honor being avenged, due to the Democratic Party's success at conflating their own party with the Confederacy and, later, the Lost Cause, leaving no room for legitimate political opposition. In the words of one journalist in 1866: "Southerners, you have lost that Confederacy, but you still have its honor to sustain . . . you have to battle against being reduced to vassalage by the Radicals of the North . . . They have triumphed and conquered over you in the field, but they have not lowered your proud spirit yet."[91] In this context, political rapprochement, or even recognition of Republican political legitimacy, was construed as a twisting of the knife, a further humiliation.

Already dealing with these feelings as a result of military defeat and a loss of political control, southern white men saw the Centennial as an arena in which their manhood and honor were further threatened. It's impossible, though, to divorce concerns about honor from the question of power. Republican appointees of Republican governors were not responsive to the will of men who saw themselves as the legitimate rulers of their respective states and thus were simply not acceptable to these men as any sort of representative.

The Centennial was not, for many white southerners, something that transcended politics or sectionalism. For them, the Centennial *was* politics: something to be shunned if associated in any way with appointees of a Republican governor, something to be considered alongside ratification of a new constitution. It was a blank slate, a vessel to serve as rhetorical proxy for a wide array of political and social discussions. Issues around southern engagement with the Centennial would be further contested once the great fair opened to the public on 10 May 1876.

5

White Southerners and African Americans at the 1876 Centennial

"A Yankee never eats anything that he can sell, and a Southern man never sells anything that he can eat."[1] This aphorism, appearing in a small-town Mississippi newspaper, captured the way many white southerners saw themselves in the Centennial year of 1876 and the way in which their self-definition was bound up in their perceived differences from their northern counterparts. Michael Kammen has argued that a repudiation of or disinterest in the past had, for nineteenth-century Americans, led to the lack of "a firm foundation on which to base a shared sense of their social selves."[2] Kammen was focusing on a slightly earlier generation here, but this notion is relevant to white southerners of the Civil War era. The foundations of southern identity were largely based on sectionalism and the fleeting existence of the Confederate States. This made for a white South that was primed to react to the Centennial of the United States adversarially, or at best through the lens of their southernness. The exhibition in Philadelphia served as a catalyst for white southern reflection about sectional distinctiveness, while African American experiences of the Centennial, in contrast, centered largely around frustrated hopes of using the exhibition as a platform to lay claim to full American citizenship.

The fierce debate over the extent of southern participation in the commemoration described in chapter 3 continued into the Centennial year but began, once the exhibition had opened, to be overshadowed by descriptions of the great fair that were sometimes as politically and sociologically loaded as the debates around participation had been.

THE INESCAPABLE CENTENNIAL

The exhibition's significance and power to both confirm and challenge American identities were ratified by its sheer reach: the Centennial grounds hosted a staggering 20 percent of the American population, and virtually every literate person among the remaining 80 percent would have been exposed to discussion and descriptions of the fair. Put simply, the Centennial was inescapable in 1876. Newspapers across the South regularly listed the names of local citizens who had "Gone to the Centennial" and ran prominently displayed advertisements from railroad companies offering special excursion fares to and from Philadelphia. In Pulaski, Tennessee, the local newspaper published a letter signed by dozens of local citizens requesting that Captain C. P. Jones, recently returned from Philadelphia, deliver a lecture on "The World's Great Show" for Pulaski residents unable to see it for themselves. Jones's acceptance was also published, along with the caveat that he was incapable of "convey[ing] any adequate conception of the Great Show at Philadelphia."[3] In Columbia, Tennessee, the *Herald and Mail* reported that "Reverend Stoddert, who . . . gives interest to every subject upon which he speaks, is expected to lecture . . . on the Centennial. Having devoted sometime [sic] to the examination of all subjects of interest at this grand Exposition of the world's curiosities, he will be able with his great powers of delineation to present a panoramic view of the whole scene which will be more perfect and far better than nine tenths of the visitors will ever see amid the hurly-burly and wild rush of the excited crowds."[4] In the view of this Tennessee editor, then, there was no need for anyone to actually travel to Philadelphia when they could instead rely upon the delineative powers of a local minister to experience what was more an exhibition of curiosities than a commemoration.

Elsewhere in the same edition, the paper noted that "several of our handsomest and most prominent young bachelors are making their arrangements to start to the Centennial. While we believe it is money badly laid out, yet it is theirs. They can very conveniently spare it and if they choose to use it in this way, no one has a right to object."[5] The newspaper seemed more sympathetic to "Bob Frierson," who, it observed, was going to "stay at home, smoke Centennial cigars, and wait for the next hundred years to roll around."[6] This was typical of the surfeit of often labored humor, much of it focused on the ubiquity of Centennial talk. An Arkansas newspaper editor joked that "Centennial fever is worse than measles; it's bigger."[7] The *Richmond Enquirer* noted that "the advocates of phonetic spelling have neglected to avail themselves of every public writer's weariness over the words 'Centennial Exhibition' as a plea with which to get their theories into favour. Every newspaper writer . . . would look with favour upon a proposition to write 'Cen1oyl' or '1oc.yl.' or ANY other abbreviation of the word, which must be used so many times in every newspaper."[8] The *Dallas Herald,* meanwhile, defined a "Declaration of Independence" as "refusing to take your mother-in-law to the Centennial Exhibition."[9] But the extent of Centennial fever was perhaps best embodied by George Washington Americus Vespucci Snodgrass, of Ripon, Wisconsin, who provided the *Chicago Tribune* with details of his plan to push a wheelbarrow across the country to the exhibition in Philadelphia. The newspaper's report on Snodgrass's pilgrimage demonstrated the extremities of patriotic fervor that the anniversary brought out in some Americans as well as the fact that cynicism about Centennial overkill was not confined to the South. The *Tribune* remarked that Snodgrass was

> about to set out for the Centennial with his patriotic contribution to the
> horrors of that Exhibition. He will, he says, be attired in a Continental
> suit of clothes, made of the Stars and Stripes pattern, his wheelbarrow
> is similarly painted and decorated with the star-spangled banner, and
> its contents are 37 enamaled [sic] bricks, each bearing the name and
> coat-of-arms of one of the states. Mr. Snodgrass will carry the 38th

brick in his hat until he hears that Colorado has been admitted to the Union, when it will be added to his load. A hand-organ attached by a crank to the wheel of the barrow will grind out patriotic airs as he progresses on his wheeling way. Mr. Snodgrass sends the *Chicago Tribune* an elaborate time-table, giving the day and hour at which he will be due at a variety of given points. This time-table will be of great convenience to the Vigilantes, who will thus be enabled to make their arrangements for lynching or tarring and feathering him, as humanity may dictate, with the smallest possible waste of time.[10]

THE CENTENNIAL AS SPECTACLE AND SYMBOL

Most southern visitors to the exhibition arrived by train rather than wheelbarrow, and many sent back breathless accounts of its wonders. A Virginia woman, writing to a relative, explained: "When I first got there I felt bewildered and my eyes hurt me from looking so much. I hardly know where to begin to tell you of what I saw." She continued that she felt that those who avoided the exhibition would feel "very blank" in twenty years' time.[11] The *Atlanta Constitution,* meanwhile, informed its readers that the Centennial was an opportunity no man "who can command the necessary time and money should neglect. Two weeks are needed, although one busy week is better than none at all." The paper also advised potential visitors to travel during the summer, "before the hordes of Northern farmers get there."[12] The *Richmond Enquirer*'s report was typical:

A more magnificent scheme was never gotten up in any city in these modern times . . . To describe all or even a part of what is to be seen there in even slight detail would take days, weeks, even months. There is such a variety of every conceivable product, from all parts of the world, that the mind becomes confused in attempting . . . to enumerate them. It is almost futile to attempt even a formal description of what's to be seen . . . All I have to say is come, see and be satisfied. If you've got the money, alright, come. If not, borrow it, it will pay you to go into debt and pay fifty per cent interest, rather than not see the Arabian Nights of modern times. If worst comes to worst, buy a walking excursion ticket and start up the railroad track. At any rate, come, for you may live a hundred years and still never see anything like it.[13]

The Arabian Nights theme was reiterated by a young North Carolina lawyer, John Henderson, who wrote to his mother: "In going through the different buildings one is utterly bewildered by the displays. It reminds me more of the Arabian Nights than anything else . . . People think of nothing else here except the Centennial. Nobody talks politics. You read about that in the papers."[14] Henderson's assertion about politics is not supported, though, by the evidence. While the Centennial Exhibition itself bedazzled and made some forget politics, the Centennial in abstract, the idea of the exhibition and what it represented, was *all* politics, and people's reactions to it seemed to exist independently of the actual exhibition.

A contentious subject throughout the years of planning, the exhibition continued to serve as a lightning rod for partisan discourse when it opened its gates to the public on 10 May 1876. In contrast to the *Richmond Enquirer*'s awestruck descriptions of Centennial wonder, reporter Harry Moss, writing in the *New Orleans Daily Picayune,* was eager to downplay the success of the exhibition: "Never since the world began has any city so overcropped herself as Philadelphia has in her Centennial expectations." Moss painted a picture of empty hotel rooms and desperate vendors, describing "oceans and oceans of lager which has never been tapped, regiment after regiment of white-aproned waiters who have never served a customer, battalions upon battalions of snappish hotel clerks with scarcely anybody to snap at."[15] Ten days after the fair opened, the *Mobile Register* gloated about "over-grasping" Philadelphia's "disastrous financial failure."[16] The *Register* counseled Alabamians to avoid "Centenniadelphia" and played down both the appeal and the success of the Centennial, remarking that "the Centennial rush from the South has dwindled into almost nothingness . . . our people are too poor to go northward this year . . . especially when they reflect that it will be one of universal extortion and cheating, with the mighty Yankee Nation 'on the make' as one man."[17] Here the *Register* employed the familiar trope that the exhibition was a moneymaking scam devised by a people more commercial, and more avaricious, than were southerners. This had been a consistent theme of those southerners arguing against Centennial engagement during 1873–75 and remained popular after the fair opened.

These descriptions are at odds with most other accounts, but taken with the jaundiced views expressed in Bourbon-leaning papers such as the *Hinds County Gazette,* they seem to illustrate the ways in which the Centennial served a purpose beyond amusement and beyond commemoration of an anniversary. The exhibition sparked strong feelings, and its relevance and meaning were evident in the efforts of those determined to tear it down and dismiss its importance. Commenting on a report that very few residents of the Magnolia State had visited the exhibition in its first month, the *Gazette* remarked simply, "Sensible Mississippians."[18] And when discussing Mississippi's Centennial headquarters, the *Gazette* pointed out the state's economic dependence on northern manufacturing when it sneered that the "close-fisted Yankees no doubt shake with laughter as they pass by the house erected at the expense of the exhausted Treasury of impoverished Mississippi out of 68 varieties of wood gathered from forests that did not supply the handles for the axes that provided the 68 varieties."[19] In contrast, the relatively pro-Centennial *Clarion* of Jackson saw the matter differently, demonstrating how much of the southern discourse around the exhibition centered on state pride: "Our rustic cottage at Fairmount Park, displaying the great variety of timber grown in Mississippi, is attracting very general attention . . . several large contractors and builders have been around, looking at and admiring our fine specimens of yellow pine, etc. . . . a great many ladies who have visited the building have carried off pieces of the bark as curiosities."[20]

North Carolinian John Henderson had commented to his wife (before they knew they would be attending the exhibition) about a relative who harbored ill feeling toward the commemoration: "Yr uncle Tom Ruffin has conceived a violent hatred of the Centennial and all connected with it or who patronize it or who speak of patronizing it. I told him you and I would fail to patronize [it] for no other reason than because we were too poor to do so and that I wished exceedingly that that obstacle could be removed. That statement however did not make him view the subject any more leniently. If anything, he now looks upon us with much less favour than ever, on account of our weakness for the Centennial."[21] Tom Ruffin's reaction was typical of the strong reactions the Centennial could elicit. While the precise source of Ruffin's animus is unknown, it is likely safe to infer that it was grounded in sectional resentment, like much of the anti-Centennial rhetoric that had echoed through southern legislative halls and across editorial pages in the months and years of buildup to the exhibition.

A strong sense of sectional identity is evident in much white southern discussion of, and reaction to, the Centennial; for those white southerners who did go, the Centennial Exhibition appears to have engendered a good deal of self-conscious southernism for a commemoration that was intended to promote sectional amity and postbellum healing. One Mississippian described their emotions upon coming across that state's Centennial headquarters as "kindred to the feelings which is [sic] awakened when one catches a sight of the flag of his own country waving among the pennons of other nations in a strange port."[22]

Another southerner described an incident that occurred as she and a companion traveled to Philadelphia for the Centennial: "An Irishman was in the seat behind us . . . [he] was a highly educated man, he got to talking to a gentleman next to him who was quite deaf, in the course of his remarks it came out that the Irishman was a Southern sympathizer and the deaf man was a Republican. He quite horrified the Rep[ublican] by saying if the thing was to be done over again he would come over and help the South, and paid the Southern people compliment—for which Bettie turned around and thanked him."[23] "Bettie" was typical of the southern visitor, male and female, to Philadelphia:

they seldom seemed to lose consciousness of their difference and their status as outsiders, or "foreigners," at the Centennial. The same correspondent, in describing some objects on display at the exhibition that she "suppose[d] . . . came over on the May flower [sic]," declared herself unimpressed: "Not that I admire it on that account, for I wish she had sunk in mid ocean."[24] This violent reaction to the seventeenth-century voyage that resulted in the settlement of New England serves to emphasize a white southern sense of apartness, harking back to the old belief that New Englanders descended from Puritan Roundheads and southerners from the Cavaliers.

REPRESENTATION OF SLAVERY AND CIVIL WAR AT THE CENTENNIAL

Puritan relics were not the only items on view at the exhibition that aroused strong regional feelings. Particular sensitivity was also shown to any artistic representation of slavery or emancipation. The Republican *Knoxville Chronicle,* commenting on disappointing attendance during the Centennial's first few weeks, predicted that while the exhibition would end up losing money, the fair would succeed on an aesthetic and artistic level. The Democratic *News,* of Bristol, Virginia, seized on this assumption of "failure" to proclaim that "the fact that it is being made a sectional parade for flaunting the bloody plumes of the late war and the laurel wreaths of northern heroes will cause it, not only to lose much patronage it would otherwise have had, but cease to be regarded as a national affair."[25] The *News* concluded with a sentiment that encapsulates the delicacy of white southern sensibilities in any matter concerning the war and its outcome: "There ought not to be anything there which revives the unpleasant memories of the late bloody struggle inside the nation."[26] The newspaper's reference to "the nation," while allowing that there was *a* nation, serves to point up the shaky state of reconciliation. The difference in attitude between these Republican and Democratic southern newspapers toward the Centennial is just one indicator of how deep the partisan and sectional split was in 1876 and of how discourse around the Centennial reflected these divisions.

The *Petersburg Post* of Virginia described one southerner's reaction to a painting on display entitled *Emancipation,* which depicted Abraham Lincoln using a sledgehammer to break the chains on a "heavily shackled" Black man while hovering angels smiled their approval: "The gentleman who saw this disgusting picture at once turned on his heels and left the Centennial grounds and a few hours after was on the train speeding homewards. He now advises every Southerner to keep away from the Centennial, or if they care to be insulted, to go by all means."[27] Another Virginia paper, in recounting this anecdote, dismissed the Centennial as a "bigoted sectarian show for the humiliation of the conquered South."[28]

A reporter for the *Richmond Enquirer* took offense from another work: "One very objectionable thing I did see. It was a bronze in the United States department, wherein a negro is represented struggling with a mammoth bloodhound who has him by the throat. A brazen slander on the Southern people."[29] Commenting on a different bronze, probably Francesco Pezzicar's *The Abolition of Slavery* (1873), a correspondent for the *New Orleans Daily Picayune* conveyed their disgust at "the malicious insolence of the idiots who are running the Centennial."[30] Describing a piece of "abolitionist scarecrow," "Cousin Nourma" continued that "placed thus conspicuously by some malicious and spiteful persons, with no other design but to flaunt an insult in the eyes of Southern visitors . . . the thing is a frightful caricature of the subject it represents." Unable or unwilling to recognize any motive beyond a desire to insult southerners, Nourma concluded that the piece "frightens children, shocks ladies, alarms girls and is sneered on by men. So the artist has found his reward in failure."[31] A correspondent for a Galveston paper concurred, describing for readers "a brassy looking bronze figure, representing the negro set free, which the Yankees think very fine but which looks like a dancing dervish to me."[32] Susanna Gold has recounted other negative reactions to the work, noting that the image of a muscular, seemingly powerful Black man, with the implication of entitlement to "social and political authority," was deeply problematic for most white Americans.[33] Notions of Black masculinity were especially threatening to the rigidly gendered white South, and the widely hostile and dismissive reactions to Pezzicar's work provide an uncomfortable foreshadowing of the rape scares that would characterize the early Jim Crow South a generation later.

Unsurprisingly, the Civil War itself was another sore spot for southern visitors to the exhibition. The largest of over thirteen hundred paintings in the American Gallery at Fairmount Park was Philadelphia artist Peter Rothermel's *Battle of Gettysburg.* Measuring sixteen by thirty-two feet, it was, according to the *New York Tribune,* the "central showpiece at the Centennial."[34] Besides commemorating a decisive Confederate defeat, arguably the turning point of the war, the picture, according to Gold, "celebrates Northern efforts by depicting the beginnings of the Southern demise." Gold contrasts the painting's depiction of brave, triumphant Union forces with "fearful, helpless and ungainly Confederates."[35] The painting was only the most notable of several works of art depicting the war and prompted one Texan to comment, "I do not much admire the American paintings (at the Centennial) and there is one—the largest in all the collections—that should never have been hung." The Texan remarked on the painting's prominent position and, noting the large crowds that gathered around it discussing the war, quoted a fellow southerner as having said, "That picture will make trouble yet, you had better take it down." This observer was particularly galled because the painting's presence there seemed to fly in the face of the Centennial's goal of selective commemoration: "I believe it was understood there was to be no reminders of the 'late unpleasantness.'"[36] The *Mobile Register* used Rothermel's work and the prominent position it was given to demonstrate the "glaring . . . [lack of] common decency and taste" in what it dismissively referred to as "this love-feast of the centuries."[37] In Bristol, Virginia, the local newspaper's correspondent referred to the "thousands" of works of art on display at the exhibition but only commented on Rothermel's, pronouncing it a "daub" noteworthy only for its gargantuan size and the "bloody memories it revives."[38] The *Richmond Enquirer*'s correspondent, adopting a milder tone, reassured his readers that "there is little to be found that will offend Southern sentiment. I do not think the mammoth picture of the battle of Gettysburg is so very objectionable as it has been made out to be, except that it has a strong tendency to revive the memories which had better be left buried."[39]

In these reactions, we see a touchiness on the part of the white southerner, a wary concern with how the South was represented on this national and international stage. In another example of white southern sensitivity, an Augusta cotton broker wrote to Georgia Centennial commissioner George Hillyer, enclosing a newspaper clipping purporting that a portrait of Robert E. Lee had been refused a place in the American gallery by Centennial officials and was being kept "in a dark corner among the works of Norway."[40] Hillyer relayed the report of this offense to southern sensibilities to the national commission, testily requesting it locate the reporter responsible, ascertain the facts, and allow him to publish the truth, as he was "heartily sick of these scurrilous squibs" and wished to reassure his constituents "how little cause there is for persons who sided with the Confederacy . . . to feel that anything has been done, or would be done . . . to wound their feelings."[41] John Sartain, who was in charge of art exhibitions at the Centennial, responded to Hillyer's query by explaining that the painting was indeed on display and "well-placed" in the American Gallery. Sartain admitted that it was not in the center but went on to point out that it had been received after the deadline for inclusion and, in his words, had "only been accepted because it was from the South and was a portrait of Gen. Lee." Sartain conceded that "pictures from Norway and Sweden have overflowed into this gallery but it is an American room nonetheless and a sign in large gilt letters makes it known as such."[42] Interestingly, Susanna Gold has pointed out that Sartain took pains to ensure that Rothermel's *Battle of Gettysburg*, in contrast to the Lee painting, was center stage in the gallery, quoting the curator as proposing that "Rothermel's great picture form the centre of the wall in the American portion of the great . . . hall."[43]

Here the American gallery serves as a microcosm of the sectional divides and tensions besetting 1876 America. White southerners took offense at a work of art seen as representing *them* apparently being relegated to a less desirable, non-American position in the gallery. John Sartain, in correcting that misapprehension, made the point that only special consideration of and sensitivity to southern feeling allowed the tardily received portrait to be on display at all. The same John Sartain had, however, ensured that a painting bound to provoke southern ire and resentment was given pride of place in an exhibition explicitly designed to heal the wounds of Civil War.

AFRICAN AMERICANS AND THE CENTENNIAL

It was not just white southerners who were sensitive to the Centennial Exhibition's value as an arena for asserting and contesting identity and the symbolic importance of the objects on view there. African Americans hoped to utilize the Centennial to bolster and reinforce their new status as American citizens. The bust of Bishop Richard Allen, founder of the AME church, which had been the focus of a major fundraising effort, can perhaps serve as a useful exemplar for Black experience of the Centennial Exhibition. After successfully raising funds to pay for the statue and winning agreement from the Centennial Commission for its inclusion on the fairgrounds (for the duration of the fair only, unlike Catholic and Jewish monuments, which were intended as permanent), the statue was commissioned.[44] A Cincinnati monument maker created the twenty-two-foot base for the statue, a "marble gazebo-like structure with columns, arches, and decorative cherubim and angels."[45] The *Philadelphia Press* described it: "On the pedestal are four Gothic columns, each one of which bears an ideal bas-relief representing the high state of civilization to which the African race had attained many years ago. Above the column is a Gothic pavilion, in the center of which will be placed a bust of Bishop [Allen] carved by the artist Alfred White of Cincinnati."[46]

The site on the Centennial grounds where the statue would be situated was the scene of a dedication ceremony on 12 June, with unveiling of the monument scheduled for 4 July. Andrew Chambers wrote to exposition director general Alfred Goshorn on 8 June, about the "unostatious [sic] ceremonies contemplated by the colored people Monday next at the laying of the Base of the Allen Monument . . . hoping there may be no objection to the delivery of fifteen minute speeches of . . . eminent men of our race."[47] This was the only occasion during the Centennial in which Black people delivered any kind of official speeches. Frederick Douglass, the most prominent Black citizen of the day, had been invited to sit on the main platform with President Grant and other dignitaries during the Centennial's opening ceremonies, on 10 May 1876, but was not among the speakers. Historian Philip Foner has recounted the humiliating scene that ensued when "the police of Philadelphia . . . refused him admittance, unable to conceive that a Negro—they used a more pejorative term—would be allowed entrance to this august company on this august occasion."[48]

Chambers had to write again to Goshorn when the bust was not ready in time for the July Fourth holiday, and dedication of the statue was then rescheduled for 22 September, the anniversary of Lincoln's preliminary Emancipation Proclamation. On 7 September, the *Christian Recorder* announced the apparent success of the endeavor: "With unbounded gratitude to God and rapturous pleasure . . . I announce to you the success of our grand Centennial Enterprise: inaugurated for the sublime object of representing the four millions of American Negroes at the Banquet of Nations. On the 22nd Day of September 1876 in the presence of all civilizations and nations on earth, amidst stirring strains of music, kindlings of the loftiest sentiments of manhood, patriotic enthusiasm, chanting of children and the ecstatic joy of the rising sons of Africa, the Allen Monument . . . will be dedicated."[49]

The monument was viewed as a symbolic representation of African American claims to citizenship; it was even referred to as "The Negro's Bunker Hill, Independence Hall, and Liberty Bell."[50] This claim was then twinned with African Americans' own particular legacy: "Let the Anniversary of Emancipation Proclamation be to us the counterpart of the Anniversary of the Declaration of Independence . . . Come in cars, steamers and carts. Come young and old, maid and matron. Thousands are daily visiting the Centennial, let tens of thousands of our race be present and demand a recognition which is not accorded until demanded."[51] But Chambers's grandiloquent rhetoric and talk of "demands" were in stark contrast to the meek and subservient tone he took in writing to Director General Goshorn, a contrast that points up the sad reality behind his dreams of what such a statue might accomplish for Black Americans.

The day of 22 September came and went with no statue and not a peep from Chambers or the *Recorder.* Then, on 5 October, the *Recorder* conveyed the sad news of the "Destruction of the Allen Monument."[52] On its way to Philadelphia, the sixteen cars of the train carrying the monument had plunged off a bridge and into the Chemung River in Pennsylvania and the sculpture, columns, arches, cherubim and all, was destroyed.[53] The bust of Allen however, was in another car, and survived. Finally, on 2 November 1876, a week before the exposition closed forever, the bust of Richard Allen, on a pedestal made of granite blocks, was dedicated in Fairmount Park. At this point, Chambers and the AME made another request for the bust to remain in Fairmount permanently. This was turned down by the Centennial commission in a curt letter citing park standards.[54] The bust, largely forgotten, spent the next century in storage at Wilberforce College in Ohio, before being returned to AME headquarters in Philadelphia in 2010, a sad metaphor for African Americans' experience of the Centennial.

Disappointment in the way the Centennial turned out for Black Americans is also evident in a letter to the *People's Advocate,* a Black newspaper in Alexandria, Virginia, signed "Red Cloud." The letter writer first described himself as an American, then expressed his sense of alienation at the exposition:

> Standing amidst her accumulated ideas and flower garden of thought at the Centennial grounds I tried to form . . . some plausible excuse for the absence of any one of my own race in any responsible place; I said to myself that we are all Americans now and as such nothing is

lost from the general progress and acceptance of the homogeneity of our advancement, but another thought came rising up and knocked the bottom right out of that two [sic] thin excuse which could not stand scrutiny . . . when . . . I could not discover among all that mass of people one single Negro in the discharge of any duty save as restaurant waiters and barbers . . . I came fully to the conclusion that it was [because] of American prejudice.[55]

Red Cloud's letter sparked an outpouring of comment, with some writers in agreement and others arguing that there was no need for any special recognition of the "Negro" at the Centennial, that "it was [not] the duty of the Centennial managers to give any more of a special invitation to the colored people of this country than that given other citizens. There is a class of men in our midst constantly contending for the obliteration of the color line . . . and yet those same men are as much out of their element as a fish out of sea unless they are specially named as colored men before they can take part in any enterprise."[56]

Another correspondent to the *People's Advocate*, identified only as "P.H.M.," agreed with Red Cloud, but only to a point. After remarking that attempting to convey an adequate description of Centennial wonders would be a task "of which even a Hercules would not have dreamed," P.H.M. conceded that "you need be a patient searcher, and one especially bent upon the purpose of finding out the Negro, to discover any creditable product of his hand or brain."[57] The results of P.H.M.'s patient search, as relayed to the *People's Advocate*, were a collection of West African jewelry, Lewis's *Death of Cleopatra* (the Black sculptor Edmonia Lewis being commended for "bringing out the voluptuousness of Egypt's amorous queen"), and an American-educated African, representing a "fair sample of . . . [the] finish" of the (Black) Hampton Institute, "a live Negro, his tongue still thick with African lingo."[58] As the Centennial served as a proxy for other issues facing white southerners, it similarly served to demonstrate tensions around Black identity and Americanism as seen in the discussion of Black identity and assimilation sparked by Red Cloud and in the distinction implied by P.H.M. between African Americans and the "thick-tongued" African "Negro."

White southern newspapers paid little if any attention to the question of Black representation at Philadelphia, but the (white) *Atlanta Constitution* did pose this question: "The radical party in its malignity and insanity, has made the Negro an equal citizen and sharer in the blessings of this republic . . . if [the centennial] is to celebrate the hundredth anniversary of liberty in this country why should the beneficiaries of its most recent expansion be ignored? If the exposition is the memorial of human emancipation from . . . subjugation . . . why are [African Americans] put aside as unworthy of a place in the festival?"[59] The *Constitution*'s argument was not, on the surface, dissimilar to the heated complaints about Black exclusion in Philadelphia that appeared in the columns of the *People's Advocate* and other African American papers. But the *Atlanta* paper had a different point to make: "The matter is of no particular concern to us. It is only a queer exhibition of the hypocrisy and duplicity of those who projected this grand farce."[60] The *Constitution* here conflated the Centennial organizers with the Radical Republicans and claimed a double standard between the civil rights extended to African Americans during Reconstruction and the role allowed Black people in the planning and running of the Centennial Exhibition. The notion that African American voters were merely dupes and pawns of corrupt white Republicans is also implicit in the *Constitution*'s argument (this trope of Black gullibility and lack of agency would persist through the Red Scares and civil rights movement of the next century). Following the actual Centennial Fourth, the *Constitution* played down the exhibition's success, claiming that "attendance has thus far been a disappointment" and that "speculators . . . have already come to grief."[61]

SECTIONALISM AT THE CENTENNIAL

Running in tandem with the Centennial theme of reunion was an attempt to accommodate southern distinctiveness and identity within

American nationalism. One attempt to woo the former Confederacy took the form of a guidebook especially for southern visitors to the fair, apparently the only one of myriad Centennial guidebooks that was produced for a specific segment of the American population. This little book, written by North Carolinian Democrat Theodore Bryant Kingsbury, exhorted its readers: "By all means, whether or not your state has contributed money and material, let all go who can afford to do so, for it is *our* Centennial as well as the Centennial of the Northern people. We are a part of the Union. This country is *our* country . . . it is now more than eleven years since the last Confederate gun was fired . . . Let the dead past bury the dead. Let all bitter memories be forgotten."[62] The book went on to offer some helpful advice to its southern readers: "In travelling, keep off the platform of cars, and do not put your arms or head out of the window [of a moving train]."[63]

This promotional effort for the Centennial offered a microcosm of the paradigm that would define American-southern relations for the next half-century, with southern distinctiveness being affirmed rather than challenged. An example of this, touted in the guide for southern visitors, was the Restaurant of the South, or Grand Southern Restaurant, which illustrated "Southern plantation scenes" and featured entertainment by what was described as an "Old Plantation Darky Band" who would "sing their quaint melodies and strum the banjo before visitors from every clime." The *Guide* offered its view of how this would represent the South to the rest of the world: "Imagine the phlegmatic German . . . with his frau and kinder, gazing with astonishment at the . . . essence of ole Virginny."[64] Meanwhile, writer James Dabney Mc-Cabe's widely distributed guide to the exhibition assured its readers that the Grand Southern Restaurant's proprietor hailed from Atlanta, Georgia, and that "the waiters were all colored men."[65] In describing "[American] nationalism's deliberate acquiescence to Southern sectionalism," Christopher Hayashida-Knight has ably demonstrated the lengths to which Centennial organizers and backers went to accommodate white southern sentiment at the exhibition. As he has observed, "At no point in these Centennial promotions are southerners asked to 'give up' their sectional prejudices for the sake of reunion; on the contrary, their political and cultural biases are stroked and celebrated."[66]

There was, though, some strong northern and Republican reaction to southern sensitivity. Furthermore, as will be demonstrated, much northern press coverage of the Centennial was not conducive to inculcating reunion or unity.[67] In an article headlined "Absurd Manifestations of Tenderness for the Feelings of Unconverted Rebels," the white and Republican *Chicago Inter-Ocean* recounted a contretemps over Black employment at the exhibition. The newspaper, noting the controversy over Rothermel's *Gettysburg*, commented that "the commission has been assailed because they let the canvas have a space in the art gallery. It tended to revive the animosities of the war, they said, and therefore it ought to be kept out. So steadily has this prating of reconciliation been kept up, that one might have believed that the Southerns are really converted, that they had given up the doctrine of states' rights . . . that they were only too willing to accord to the colored men all the rights and privileges to which they are entitled. But it seems this is all a mistake."[68]

The *Inter-Ocean* related that a Centennial commissioner from Iowa had proposed a resolution that the commission authorize the employment of Black men on the Centennial police and guard forces. As the newspaper put it, "Nearly every one of the Southern members was on his feet, canes and umbrellas were flourished . . . these howlers for reconciliation demanded that the offensive resolution be withdrawn." The motion passed, but barely. The *Inter-Ocean* published the vote tally—the majority of the southern commissioners had voted against the resolution, including, interestingly, John Lynch, Louisiana's Black commissioner. The paper summed up what it saw as the Centennial management's priorities in pandering to the hypersensitivity of a sulking South at the expense of Black Americans: "The fear of offending some over-scrupulous visitors from a section of the country that contributes almost nothing to the Exhibition is a sentiment that will meet no favour with the great multitude of the North . . . simply the resurrection of that morbid sentiment which has so long disgraced our civilization."[69] The *Inter-Ocean* reported that as of 27 May, no African Americans had been hired and attributed failure of the Centennial's reconciliatory aims to southern recalcitrance and racism: "It is time to stop talking about reconciliation. The Southerns do not want it and will not have it if it involves any concessions. This is to be a great Centennial year of jubilee but according to the Confederate notion, white men only are allowed . . . the black men are to be left to peek through the knot-holes. That the colored people feel the slight . . . is apparent. Your correspondent, among the hundreds of thousands of visitors he has noticed . . . has not seen a dozen negroes of any age or sex."[70]

If Centennial organizers were not particularly interested in racial inclusivity, they did encourage state pride and allegiance. One method of doing this, while simultaneously boosting attendance, was to hold "State Days," encouraging residents from specific states to attend the exhibition on a given date, designated to salute that state. "Pennsylvania Day" set a daily attendance record of 275,000, unmatched not only for the Centennial but for any world's fair to that date. "Ohio Day" drew 125,000 visitors. The *Cincinnati Daily Times*'s account described both the "immense crowds" and, with the speech, introduced by Centennial commission president Joseph Hawley, of that state's governor and Republican presidential nominee Rutherford Hayes, the utilization of the exhibition as a political space. At the speech's conclusion, cheers were given for "the next President of the United States."[71]

There were no days set aside for specific southern states, although several southern governors made speeches in Philadelphia. On 12 September, for example, Texas governor Richard Hubbard delivered a platitude-laden speech that was ostensibly about sectional reunion but sounded more like an advertisement for the benefits of settling and/or investing in the Lone Star State. The *Galveston Daily News* reported that the "eloquent orator was greeted by a large crowd . . . including more than a hundred Texans."[72] The account went on to describe Hubbard's speech as "a description of the resources and capabilities of the state."[73]

There were plans for a day to celebrate Virginia, but the state's Democratic governor, James L. Kemper, issued a well-publicized explanation for his refusal to sanction or participate in "Virginia Day." Kemper, grounding his statement in the Old Dominion's dire financial situation, noted that the commonwealth had already "declined to incur the cost of taking part in the Centennial because her poverty, not her will, forbade the diversion of any portion of her revenues to that object."[74] The governor went on, with reference to Virginians' personal fiscal responsibilities, that he "would not, if I could, attract to Philadelphia those who, in view of their necessities at home, ought not to go at all."[75] Kemper managed to embed within this homily on frugality an acknowledgment that while Virginia was of course only interested in reconciliation, others were using the exhibition as a vehicle for expressing sectional and antagonistic sentiment: "With regretful composure, without abating her known spirit of conciliation, she beholds the untimely sectional animosities and reproaches which, provoked by no act of hers, tend to mar the noblest design of the Centennial celebration."[76]

Kemper's refusal garnered some criticism in the northern press. A New Hampshire newspaper, paying scant heed to the governor's claims of financial concern, zeroed in instead on Kemper's remarks on "sectional animosities," terming them "very unpatriotic." The newspaper then quoted, disapprovingly, the *Richmond Dispatch*'s claim that the Centennial may have been "a fine exhibition of art and artifice, but as a celebration of things that live not in the American heart, an abomination."[77] The *New York Tribune* also took Kemper to task over the decision, saying that, in effect, the South needed to get over the war: "The world moves, it cares little for ancient prestige or prejudices. The individual or state which stands indifferently or sulkily aloof will soon find itself thrust to one side and forgotten."[78] Clearly demonstrating the ways the Centennial could spark divisive rhetoric, a New Orleans paper described the *Tribune* piece as a failed attempt to "fire Northern hearts" and as "petty sectionalism that we might have expected to find in a back-woods weekly."[79]

In response, then, to what the *Cincinnati Daily Gazette* called "the refusal of Gov. Kemper to appoint a day for that state at the Centennial," 19 October was designated as "Southern Day" in joint honor of Virginia,

Delaware, and Maryland.[80] With a turnout of 170,000, second only to Pennsylvania Day, the highlight of the day was a jousting tournament. It featured fifteen "knights," representing each of the original thirteen states plus two bonus gallants, one personifying "the Union" and the other "the Centennial." The knights were garbed inconsistently—some in tinsel and velvet, others in sashes, plumed hats or sombreros, and brightly hued scarves. The actual sport, "so popular in the South," according to one newspaper, involved attempting to collect two-inch rings (suspended from three fifteen-foot-high arches) on a spear or lance while galloping at full tilt.[81] Most of the knights were, according to the *New York Times,* "gentlemen of the South, experienced in the art [of jousting]," whose skills caused the thousands of spectators to "gape in wonderment."[82] Delaware's "knight" emerged victorious and, in post-tournament festivities that evening, had the honor of crowning a "beautiful brunette from Rockingham County, Va." as "the Queen of Love and Beauty."[83] Following this coronation, "a band of plantation darkies rendered a song in true southern style in salutation to the Queen, after which the audience paid their respects to Her Majesty."[84]

While those in southern newspapers tended to adopt a matter-of-fact tone, accounts in northern journals of Southern Day at the Centennial seemed to emphasize the distinctiveness and the exoticness of the South, with its velvet-clad cavaliers and serenading "darkies."[85] An often mocking tone further underscores the sense of regional alienation discernible in southern accounts of the exhibition. The *New York Herald* commented on the "different shades of peculiar Southern dialect" that could be heard at the exhibition and, in a less than gracious dig at the almost desperate importance many southerners attached to the concept of honor, remarked facetiously that "a brick thrown in the air would be sure to fall on the head of a 'Kernel' or a Major . . . who had lost 'all but . . . honnah, in the late wah, sah!'"[86]

Historian K. Stephen Prince has outlined what he calls a "ruin discourse" in northern views of the postwar South, citing the ubiquity of tropes of southern ruin and devastation in northern media. He attributes this to voyeurism, genuine concern, and jingoism but above all to "the metaphorical value of those ruins."[87] Prince argues that southern ruin was a "potent cultural symbol . . . invaluable in helping northerners conceptualize the character of the defeated South and articulate the challenges and possibilities of the postwar period."[88] This argument is clearly borne out in northern reaction to white southerners at the Centennial. The *New York Graphic,* perhaps working on the assumption that southern visitors would be gaunt, starving, and incapable of appreciating the Yankee ingenuity on show, stated that "Reconstructed rebeldom was out in force. The contrast between the representative visitors of the two sections was plain enough, but the Southern visitors appeared well and were profoundly interested in what they saw."[89] At this point, the *Graphic's* tone became even more patronizing: "The Exhibition probably made a deeper impression on them than on those of the North who are familiar with mechanical inventions and products and works of art. It showed these Southern visitors what the real deficiencies of their section are and the lines on which their activities must move to win wealth and material success."[90] The New York paper concluded with lines that simultaneously pointed up the reconciliatory and nation-building aims of the exhibition and the wide chasm that still existed between the sections: "It [the exhibition] must have taught them that the contentions of politics and the antagonisms of races are directly in the way of industrial prosperity and material power. Really, could all Southerners spend a week in the Exhibition it would do more to extinguish their old war passions, and give them a new conception of their true interests and duties and make them thoroughly loyal and united in their efforts to promote order and industry and education and art."[91]

Massachusetts novelist and journalist William Dean Howells's description of Mississippi's Centennial headquarters, while gentler in tone, still stressed the exotic qualities of that state's representation in Philadelphia:

Wholly built of Mississippi wood, the rough bark logs showing without and the gables and porch decked with gray streamers of Spanish Moss. A typical Mississippian, young in years but venerable in alligator-like calm, sits on the porch . . . with his boots on the railing and his hat drawn over his eyes and sheltering his slowly moving jaws as they ruminate the Virginian weed . . . he answered all queries without looking up or betraying the smallest curiosity as to the age, sex or condition of the questioner. Being tormented (I will not reveal the sex of his tormentress) concerning the use of a little hole or pouch (it was for letters, really) in the wall near the door, he said that it was to receive contributions for a poor orphan. "I," he added, "am the orphan." And then at last he looked up, with a faint gleam in his lazy eye which instantly won the heart.[92]

Howells pointed out that "this Mississippian" was white, and that "another, black, showed us civilly and intelligently through the house which was very creditable in every way to the state and told us that it was built of 70 different kinds of Mississippi wood."[93]

The idea that the white South had something to learn from the Centennial and the North was acknowledged, with a strong sense of sectional alienation, by "Traveler," a correspondent for a Macon, Georgia, paper, who provided an impression of the exhibition: "The most striking feature of this whole Centennial business is the . . . 'get up and git' you see about everything and everybody . . . There is no 'Sleepy Hollow,' 'wait for the wagon' or 'hang 'round the corner' schedule run here . . . Move! Go! You catch it from the peanut and popcorn sellers on the sidewalk. You hear and see it and feel it in the jostling, wrestling crowd . . . you begin to shudder at your own insignificance and involuntarily feel a desire to 'get up and git.' And you do get, and everybody around you gets . . . the only question is, how much of it can you stand . . . ? Everybody is centennializing." This account also endeavors to point out that the South should acquire some "get up and git": "What a pity it is that some of this energetic 'matter' can't be taken from these live Doodles and punched into the arms and feet and legs of our sleepy-headed men and boys of the South."[94] This southerner's account of the hustle and bustle, the commerciality, the "get up and git" of the North, highlights the alleged lack of these attributes in the "sleepy-headed" South and gives us a sense of what proponents of an economically revitalized New South hoped to achieve by their program of industrialization and boosterism. This report shows the Centennial as a vehicle for confirming identity, through the sense of cultural alienation the reporter describes and the realization that, to paraphrase, "we are not like that."

A Centennial visitor from New Orleans, identified only as W.E.S. Jr., also found inspiration for southern improvement. Commenting, somewhat facetiously, that the only evidence of the South that he could find at Fairmount Park was "a box or two of chewing tobacco from Virginia and Kentucky," this correspondent decried the dearth of fine art in the region. Issuing a "call to action," he continued: "Unless we would be forgotten we must cultivate the fine arts, nay we must excel in them . . . To the people of the South I say that oblivion is threatening them. What part do they play in the literature of America? Go into any Southern household and take up the first book you can lay your hands on. It is published at the North and the chances are a thousand to one that it is written by a Northerner. The North makes our literature—makes it to suit itself."[95] After remarking that northern literature tended to stereotype southerners as "rascals," W.E.S. Jr. concluded that the South must "bestir herself . . . make and publish her own books, paint her own pictures, sculpt her own figures . . . For the sake of our individuality we must preserve whatever of devotion, of self-sacrifice, of bravery and heroism that the war called forth."[96] Here we see a white southerner whose sense of sectional identity was stirred by the exhibition, more specifically by the lack of southern presence and engagement there, and who sensed in the northern version of the United States on display in Philadelphia a threat to that southern distinctiveness that was so clearly important to him.

POLITICAL IDENTITY AND THE CENTENNIAL

Running in tandem with the great fair was one of the most bitterly partisan, and ultimately fraudulent, presidential elections in U.S. history. Ulysses Grant, his administration besmirched by scandal, was approaching the end of his second term in office. When Grant's most likely successor for the Republican nomination, James Blaine, became embroiled in scandals of his own, the Republicans went for a compromise candidate, the personally honest but colorless Rutherford B. Hayes.[97] The Democrats nominated New York governor Samuel J. Tilden. There was a dearth of any real difference between the two parties' platforms, with both agreed on the desirability of withdrawing federal troops from the South and the need for civil service reform. Still, the campaign was rancorous and in some ways seemed to embody a proxy continuation of the war.

Sectional and political identity were closely linked and frequently conflated during the Reconstruction era; exacerbated by the election, this connection was borne out in much of the discourse surrounding the Philadelphia exhibition. One example can be found in the account of the Georgian who styled himself Traveler. He described the headquarters of Philadelphia's Union League (a Republican men's club) as being festooned with gas jets forming the words virtue, liberty, and independence. He also quoted a bystander who remarked, after the wind had blown out the first two words: "How emblematic of the Republican Party! There's 'virtue' gone, and 'liberty' gone, and but d——d little of 'Independence' left."[98] In Tennessee the *Fayetteville Observer's* report on the Centennial's opening highlighted President Grant's reference to his "countrymen" by placing it in inverted commas, seemingly indicating that they did not fall into that grouping.[99] The same paper quoted another local visitor as saying that he "couldn't turn around" for the Radicals in Philadelphia.[100] As a majority of white southerners saw Democratic affiliation as more or less synonymous with *being* white southerners, this would give an impression of Philadelphia as an uncomfortably foreign place. The Centennial correspondent of the *Cleveland (TN) Herald* felt the need to describe in detail a Democratic Party rally he attended at Bristol, Virginia, en route to Philadelphia. He struck up an acquaintance with a South Carolinian visiting the fair, and in the alien landscape of the North, they "swore by Old Father

George [Washington] that we would stick to each other like brothers until separated by fate."[101]

A Centennial correspondent for a small-town Georgia newspaper included in his reportage an account of a Republican rally, or what he described as "an amusing entertainment," that he witnessed in that election year of 1876. The purpose of the meeting was to ratify and endorse the nomination of the Republican ticket of Hayes and Wheeler, but "not once was the name of R. B. Hayes . . . mentioned . . . poor Hayes was left out in the dark."[102] The reporter listed a series of speakers who castigated the "Southern Rebs" to the approbation of the Philadelphia audience, quoting one who declared that "Southerners were the most ignorant set of people on the globe, that they had no schools or colleges and that there wasn't a Southern man, who when the war broke out was six years old, who could now read and write." Describing his reaction to this diatribe, the correspondent continued: "This struck me like a thunderbolt. I scratched my head to feel if it was really on my body. I pulled out pencil and paper to try if I had forgotten how to write . . . I only restrained myself from openly calling [the speaker] a prevaricator by the thought that he was a Republican and therefore not to be blamed for falsehoods."[103]

A reporter from Bristol, Virginia, meanwhile, drew a connection between the Gatling gun on display in Machinery Hall and the federal forces at that time still in control of the state of Louisiana. In the midst of descriptions of "silk fibres" and "rustic Terra Cotta vases," he editorialized that the gun "brought up memories of the death of civil liberties in Louisiana at the hands of men trained to war and unwisely placed in charge of such unspeakable heritages as Magna Carta and Habeas Corpus."[104] Analogous to wartime claims that the Confederacy was the true embodiment of the Founding Fathers' ideals, a remark like this extended the sense of southern proprietorship of liberty even further back while incorporating a dig at federal suspension of habeas corpus during war and Reconstruction.

The *Mobile Register* also used the Centennial to make political points. Musing upon the changes seen since 1776, the *Register* reflected that "in precisely the same ratio as today is ahead of that day in steamboats and telegraphs and Gatling guns, it is also ahead in demagoguery, demoralization and Blaineism, and in this latter is the ugliest and worst of the progress we have made."[105] The *Register* complained that Republican James Blaine, who had spoken in Congress against extending amnesty to Jefferson Davis and was widely accused in the South of "waving the bloody shirt," had "stifled much of the fraternal gush, without which the Centennial Exposition is only a Mechanic's Institute." Striking a note of injured righteousness, the paper claimed that the South had been prepared to "gush as spontaneously as any Brotherly Lover" until Blaine's words in Congress "fiendish[ly] rend[ed] open nearly healed scars."[106]

These angry digressions in generally positive accounts of the Centennial Exhibition serve to emphasize the overlapping sectional and political divisions in the centennial year as well as the strength of these partisan sentiments. Feelings were running so high that one southern visitor observed that "there is more excitement than there has been since 1861, and really it looks more like war than it did then."[107] Resumption of war, then, was not an unheard-of idea in 1876, and the Centennial "exhibited" a federation of states that was far from united. This was the same year in which the Centennial Exhibition was meant to provide a setting for Americans "from every corner of this broad land . . . [to] gather by land and by sea to the City of Brotherly Love and with kindly and loving hearts exchange the warm grasp of common brotherhood under one and the same nationality."[108] Yet as one Republican, stumping for Hayes, declaimed: "Every man that endeavoured to tear the old flag from the heavens that it enriches was a Democrat. Every man that tried to destroy this nation was a Democrat . . . the man that assassinated Abraham Lincoln was a Democrat . . . Soldiers, every scar you have on your heroic bodies was given you by a Democrat!"[109] This type of rhetoric, known as "waving the bloody shirt," ensured that the war was never far removed from public discourse.

In October 1876, just before the presidential election, the *Christian Recorder* warned: "We stand today face to face with a crisis involving the life of the nation. We confront in the contest an enemy bolder, a more adroit, and far better matured than in 1860. Then, as now, there was a 'solid South.' But now murder, violence, and fraud are more persistent and studied."[110] Here the *Recorder* acknowledged a white South made more militant, more cohesive, and more determined to define citizenship on its own terms by the events of war and Reconstruction. The piece conflated the two sides in the Civil War with the two main political parties and warned that if the choice between Republican Hayes and Democrat Tilden fell to the electoral votes of South Carolina or Mississippi, "scoured to the Democratic juggernaut by violence and fraud," resumption of war could be necessary: "Only this, Americans: war or abject, cowardly craven submission to a more wicked and diabolical plot than that of 1860–61 . . . the only patriotic . . . way out is to elect Hayes . . . by a majority so crushing that the embodiment of all the crimes in the Decalogue will not dare question the result. 'Up guards, and at them!'"[111] The *People's Advocate* also commented on white southern determination to ensure Democratic control, citing white terrorist groups and warning of the sectional alienation that would result from that party's victory: "The Louisiana Leaguers, the Mississippi murderers and the Baltimore 'Bloods' are as ready as minute men to take the matter in hand and if necessary to make a united Democratic South they will wade knee-deep in Republican blood at the polls . . . Virginia, North Carolina, South Carolina and Louisiana are Republican states, and if under fire, they are driven into the Confederate Democracy the status will be fixed and we shall have a Southern grey Democracy and Northern blue Republicanism . . . with little or no affiliation between the sections."[112]

White southerners were similarly invested in the outcome of the election; though if anything, they were even more concerned with regaining control at the state level. The fiancé of a young South Carolina woman wrote to her about the victory in that state's gubernatorial election of Democrat and Confederate general Wade Hampton: "Great excitement have prevailed . . . since the Election, all were anxious to hear that Hampton and Tilden were Elected, some nights last week one of [my] Bro[ther]s. would be in Columbia until near two o'clock to get the latest despatches, Hampton's friends have been almost wild with enthusiasm. Bro. said that when the flag was put through the window of the Democratic Hall with Hampton's portrait on it, and the words 'Our Governor' written above the crowd appeared almost wild."[113] This emotionalism over the election of a Democrat demonstrates the strength of feeling among white southerners that their sense of participation in the American nation was dependent on the success of this party. The *Christian Recorder*'s warning about the "Solid South" seems to make clear that Black Americans likewise invested their hopes and aspirations in the success of the Republican Party.

That assumption is borne out by this supposedly humorous snippet from the Democratic *Galveston News*. In ostensibly reporting remarks made by a Black member of Virginia's state assembly arguing against a Centennial appropriation, the *News* quoted the legislator: "Wherefor is it, and why I'm axin', never, no sah. What? Ten thousand dollars fur to be giv away to Philadelphia? . . . Look at de Treasury, look at de money de Governor hov spent in postage stamps a fixin' fur dis occasion."[114] When not lampooning and infantilizing African Americans, mainstream Democratic commentators deprived them of agency, seeing them as dupes and pawns of the Radical Republicans. The *Richmond Enquirer* noted: "We are sincerely sorry for the colored population of the Southern states. This is the time of year when it becomes part of the necessities of the Radical policy that riots between the races should be instigated and that the Northern mind should be fired by reports of bloody massacres of negroes by the cruel Ku-klux. Already from Louisiana and Mississippi there come up blood-curdling and hair-erecting stories, which are published in the Radical journals . . . setting forth that the innocent negroes, for no provocation except their color and their politics have been waylaid and assassinated by the masked and murderous White Leaguers."[115] The *Enquirer* concluded that racial turmoil was fomented deliberately by the Radical Republicans "for the coolly calculated purpose of creating a feeling of bitterness against this section" in the North. Reminiscent of southern attribution of the civil rights movement almost a century later to outside agitators and Communists, this position relegates African Americans to dupes of the Republicans and shrugs off widespread atrocities as the Radicals' fault.[116]

And yet, as Mitch Kachun has pointed out, "African Americans were hardly monolithic in their views"; some even supported the Democrats.[117] South Carolinian W. A. Leaphart wrote to his fiancée: "We have just heard that a riot is expected at my Uncle's in the upper part of Orangeburg Co., a colord [sic] Democrat was severely beaten and had his house burnt by a colord [sic] rad[ical Republican]."[118]

This anecdotal evidence of political dissent within the Black community can be further explored by looking at the 1876 "Negro Declaration of Independence." Philip Foner, in his 1978 examination of Black involvement with the Centennial, cites a "Negro Declaration of Independence" that was read out in Washington, DC, on 4 July 1876. Foner correctly points out that this document was modeled, as other expressions of Black citizenship were, upon the original Declaration of Independence and asserts that this "Declaration" was ignored in the white press, attributing this lapse to white "blindness" toward Black grievances in the Centennial year.[119] Foner says that "rather than George III, the target of specific grievances . . . was the American government." An inspection of the original document, however, reveals it to be both more and less than Foner represents it to be. Foner does not identify its authors, but it was the product of a group calling itself the "National Independent Political Union," headed by one Garland H. White. Formerly enslaved by Robert Toombs of Georgia, who served as secretary of state to both James Buchanan and Confederate president Davis, White had escaped to Canada and later returned to the United States during the war and helped raise a Black infantry regiment in Indiana, for which he served as chaplain.[120]

The document is, in fact, a sharp critique of the Republican Party, its subtitle being "Republican Faithlessness and Corruptions Exposed and Scathingly Denounced by Colored Men." Foner quotes the document in a way that makes it seem like a generic plea for full citizenship and rights rather that a purely political broadside: "For these and other reasons too numerous for enumeration, we feel justified in declaring our independence of all existing political parties and we hereby pledge to each other . . . that we will . . . support only those parties whose fidelity to the original Declaration of Independence is unquestioned."[121] The original document, published on 28 February 1876 (not 4 July), was, though, starkly partisan:

> We, colored men, representing nearly all the States and Territories of the United States, believing with the fathers, that the happiness of the people is the sole end of government, . . . do hereby denounce it [Republican Party] as being the primary cause of all the wrongs committed against us . . .
>
> For these and other reasons too numerous for enumeration, we feel justified in severing all connection with this profligate party . . . and deeming the time auspicious when past differences should be buried, and reconciliation and good feeling between the races pervade the land . . . we ask nothing but FULL AND EQUAL JUSTICE BEFORE THE LAW, PROTECTION FOR OUR LIVES AND PROPERTY AGAINST LAWLESSNESS AND MOB VIOLENCE, AND EQUITABLE RECOGNITION IN THE SEVERAL DEPARTMENTS OF THE GOVERNMENT, BASED UPON OUR INTELLIGENCE AND INTEGRITY.[122]

Further details of the partisan nature of this group can be gleaned from clippings kept in a scrapbook by Virginia's Centennial commissioner and future governor Frederick Holliday, a Democrat who obviously approved the anti-Republican sentiments they expressed. One clipping is a letter from Garland White, detailing the harassment and abuse he received as a Black Democrat in the South: "A few weeks ago, while from home in the canvass for Tilden and Hendricks and the Democratic state ticket, they (Republicans) failed to follow me to a single place of public speaking, but went to my church and urged my dismissal as pastor upon the ground that I was an enemy to my race because I was a Democrat. That . . . got up a stampede among my flock, which resulted in my dismissal."[123] White enumerates further instances of intimidation and harassment and concludes: "We are all still slaves and will ever be as long as one portion of us submit to the Republican party lash . . . Live or die, sink or swim, I will do all in my power to elect Tilden . . . unless Mr. Tilden is elected, the country is gone."[124] In another of Holliday's clippings, W.H.L. Coombs, the Black president of a "Tilden and Hendricks Club," writes to a Richmond newspaper stating that "the sensible free-thinking colored people are tired of the radical [Republican)] yoke and its injustice to us and its insult to our brave and well-disposed fellow citizens of the South."[125]

It is difficult to credit the sincerity of the reference to well-disposed southern whites, but perhaps some southern Blacks felt that a degree of appeasement toward their white neighbors and former enslavers was necessary and made more palatable by the flexibility and agency that came with freedom from strict party loyalty. As the paper that printed Coombs's remarks editorialized: "In dividing their vote between the two parties the colored men are wise and are doing the very best thing they could do to advance their own interests . . . in a few years they will be cared for and protected by both parties."[126]

Black southerners who supported the Democratic Party may have been pragmatically attempting to maintain good relations with their white neighbors or merely reacting to bullying by local Republicans, but they were still engaging with the American polity and expressing themselves as Americans—and dealing with divisions and a rancorous sectarianism that was typical of the recently recombined nation as a whole.

It was against this bitterly divided (both politically and racially) landscape that the Centennial Exhibition aimed to commemorate one hundred years of American nationhood. Clearly, the timing was far from auspicious. Reinforcing the sectional divide that overshadowed the fair, Cincinnati's *Daily Gazette* categorized the Centennial Exhibition as a northern venture and went on to link southern attitudes to the Centennial to a possible recurrence of civil war: "Several of the Southern states have always regarded the Centennial with disfavour . . . [they have never] concealed their dissatisfaction with an exhibition which has so signally demonstrated the superiority of the North in most of the essential elements of civilization." The *Gazette* then castigated "untaught and unteachable Southern Bourbons" and, in a reference to the 1876 elections, warned that "the evidence is indisputable that the same spirit of disorder and rebellion that brought on the Civil War now animates the Democrats' rank and file and that they are better armed than ever."[127] As white southerners staked their status as Americans on Democratic electoral success in 1876, so Black Americans saw Republican victory as guaranteeing their own American future, and the Centennial Exhibition provided a backdrop for this deeply contested election. In the end, Democrat Tilden won the popular vote but remained one electoral vote shy of victory. The electoral votes of South Carolina, Florida, and Louisiana were in dispute, and each state submitted multiple sets of returns. The outcome was decided by an Electoral Commission set up by Congress and in the "Compromise of 1877," Democrats acquiesced in Hayes taking all the electoral votes of the disputed states, in return for the withdrawal of all federal troops from the South. Hayes was proclaimed the winner two days before Inauguration Day 1877. This was the "end" of Reconstruction, and although Democrats failed to take the national prize, their control of the South was solidified.

CENTENNIAL AFTERMATH

When the Centennial Exhibition closed its gates to visitors on 10 November 1876, it was generally celebrated as a rousing success, with the *Los Angeles Daily Star,* for example, proclaiming that the "future historian . . . would pronounce it the grandest event of the decade and the greatest exhibit to the gaze of mankind yet made."[128] The African American *Savannah Tribune,* notwithstanding Black Americans' largely unfulfilled hopes for the celebration, declared the exhibition a "grand affair" and argued that Centennial president Joseph Hawley deserved the nation's thanks for the exhibition's success. In Arkansas, one of the two southern states (with Mississippi) to fund a presence at the exhibition, there was satisfaction at the state's involvement. In an account that exemplified the primacy of economic opportunism as the chief motivation behind Centennial engagement, one newspaper praised the "wisdom of our legislature" for appropriating money for the exhibition and went on to state that the Centennial had "afforded an opportunity to make a display of the resources of Arkansas which has never been presented . . . the world has been given a peep into our treasure house . . . and Arkansas will hereafter be indorsed as a place to move to instead of from."[129]

This report also echoes many others in manifesting state, rather than national, pride.[130] In Mississippi, the governor, Democrat John Stone, reported to his legislature, in seemingly grudging fashion, that he had been informed "by many visitors" that the Mississippi House was "one of the most attractive in the Park" and that the state had mounted a "creditable display."[131] In other southern states, there was some remorse at an opportunity lost and continued, if posthumous, use of the Centennial as a political proxy. A Georgia correspondent reflected that the Peach State had lost out by not participating and pointed the finger of blame at the conservative Bourbons: "Voluntarily waiving all rights to the immense advantages to have been derived from a participation in it. We have come here in scores and hundreds and wasted in an indefinite, aimless sort of way more money than would have presented us as a state in a better style than either Ohio or New York. And what excuse do we have to offer for this stupidity? None under heaven but the sulky prejudices of a surly executive or the extreme Bourbonistic tendencies of a very small legislature."[132]

While many white southerners did travel to "Centenniadelphia" (with most accounts enthusiastic) the proportion of southern visitors, both as percentages of fair attendees and of the overall southern population, must have been relatively low. Mississippi's state building on the Centennial grounds, for example, recorded 3,800 visitors from the

Magnolia State over the course of the exhibition, out of a total population of about 830,000.[133] If the Philadelphia exhibition served to both reflect and in some ways amplify the sectional and political divisions of an unreconstructed nation, it must be remembered that the Centennial Fourth was also celebrated beyond Philadelphia, on a nationwide scale.

6

July Fourth 1876 in the South

In 1875, the Fourth of July had been, for the *New Orleans Daily Picayune,* "The Day We Do Not Celebrate."[1] A year later, on the eve of the Centennial Fourth, the same paper alerted its readers that "the observance of the great national holiday is an invariable custom with the *Picayune.* Therefore there will be no evening edition issued from this office on the 4th."[2] As this volte-face indicates, the anti-Fourth arguments still being voiced in many southern quarters in 1875 seem to have largely dried up by 1876, which saw local commemorations entered into more or less enthusiastically across the states of the former Confederacy. Indeed, the centennial Fourth was observed in New Orleans with "business houses closed . . . the streets . . . gay with flags and brilliant bunting and the air resounding with the strains of music and the rattle of the inevitable fire-crackers."[3] It is probably safe to extrapolate from one newspaper's remark that "the observance of the Fourth was more general throughout Virginia than at any time since 1860" that the piecemeal re-embracing of Independence Day seen across the white South in 1875 reached a tipping point in the centennial year.[4] This appears to hold true throughout the South without discernible regional variation.

There was likewise little deviation from the way that the politics of Reconstruction consistently underpinned and informed these celebrations, though we do see shifts in tone and emphasis along partisan and racial lines. What's most striking is the consistency of the political conditionality seen across the white South in its return to the Fourth. Looming over these observations was the much-anticipated overthrow of sixteen years of Republican rule at the national level, and the commemorations reflect these political concerns. As we have seen, Democrats had been gradually regaining control of local and state governments for a few years, but the perceived likelihood of the reviled Republicans losing their grip on national power had a clear influence on white southerners and their attitude toward reconciliation and re-union. This is seen both generally in the movement back to Independence Day and specifically in the type and tone of the rhetoric around these celebrations. Meanwhile, African Americans continued to use the Fourth to both display and claim their own American identity with celebrations frequently, but not always, held alongside white Republicans.

In Memphis, the *Daily Appeal* attributed the reemergence of July Fourth spirit to the commemorative activity of 1875: "If since the termination of the war the southern states have not been disposed to gush, the celebrations at Concord and Lexington, Bunker Hill, Charleston and Mecklenburg did much to revive the old love for the Fourth of July." This Democratic paper reminded readers that although the Stars and Stripes had been "a sign and token of social disorder, a violated constitution . . . a mockery of freedom . . . time has produced a change." The nature of that change went unspecified, but a clue might be found in the name of a cannon used in the Memphis celebrations:

> The city was alive with fluttering flags and streamers . . . the firing of cannons made the usual noise so charming to the heart and soul of every American citizen. Col. T. O. Sullivan's gun squad and artillery "Little Democrat" have been very active during the celebration of the great centennial anniversary. The little gun barked sharp and loud all over the city, amusing a majority of the people and making a few angry, but those few were unpatriotic people who could not appreciate the musical notes made by a cannon . . . The "Little Democrat" will celebrate a Democratic county victory in August, and a Democratic Presidential victory in November.[5]

A (presumably) different "Little Democrat" boomed in Rocky Mount, North Carolina, for that town's Centennial Fourth. A "goodly number of patriots" rolled into the town from surrounding areas to, in the words of the *Tarboro Southerner,* "celebrate the Centennial Fourth and raise the Tilden and Hendricks flagpole."[6] After the Little Democrat ceased booming, human Democrats took over, delivering partisan orations under a ninety-eight-foot-high flagpole bearing a United Sates flag emblazoned with the names of Samuel Tilden and Thomas Hendricks, the Democratic nominees for president and vice president that year. The *Southerner,* easily conflating partisanship and patriotism, went on: "The speeches abounded in words of lofty patriotism. [The speakers] hurled hot shot into radical ranks in a way that was amusing to Democrats and excoriating to their opponents."

In Bainbridge, Georgia, the local newspaper remarked that the Fourth had been generally shunned in the region since "the bold and intrepid South broke asunder" the Union. Democrats had regained control of the Peach State four years previously, and with Democrat Tilden widely tipped to take the White House that November, the paper recognized that white southerners were now ready to re-embrace the holiday, coyly referencing the "reasons of a sensitive nature" that had impeded celebration and could now be discarded.[7]

In Perry County, Arkansas, the Centennial Fourth was marked with a "grand barbecue" for which "every horse, mule and wagon" in the vicinity was required to transport the celebrants. The paragraph following the description of the commemoration in a local paper commented that the "political outlook at present is very promising." Democrats had regained control of the state the previous year, and the paper went on to portray the local population as "jubilant" over the prospect of a Democratic victory in that year's presidential election which, the report prophesized, would lead to "a free and independent nation, instead of a mockery and tyranny."[8]

In Nashville, the *Daily American* congratulated the nation on its Centennial celebrations, noting (falsely) that "at Philadelphia nothing was said or done to wound the tenderest feeling, nothing even to recall the dreary past few years."[9] The paper went on to frame southern reengagement with Independence Day as genuinely felt patriotism and an aversion to hypocrisy:

> In the South and especially in Tennessee, for the first time since the war, the people by a spontaneous outburst burst over all reserve, fused into the old Fourth of July feeling, and neither led nor driven by politicians or prudence, paid in every village and in almost every county reverential and patriotic respect. Prudential leaders have often before tried to create Fourth of July sentiment . . . and celebrations, but our people are incapable of hypocritical outward observance, and long indifferent—not hostile—they only moved when the real spirit of recovered patriotism and national feeling moved them.
>
> With aroused hope and a feeling of pride in country they begin to feel is theirs they have turned with the change in their own feelings and paid the tribute none could compel or buy. It is the dawn of hope and harbinger of peace, prosperity, national feeling, fraternal relations and benign government.[10]

One might read between the lines here and posit that the "change in their own feelings" was inextricably linked to the certitude expressed in the first line on that particular page of the *Daily American:* "The election of Uncle Samuel Tilden is an assured thing."[11]

In Marshall, Texas, the locals, white and Black, went all out in celebrating the day. The local *Tri-Weekly Herald* reported that "all idea of business was forgotten. Stores and workshops were closed and men, women and children surrendered themselves to a day of enjoyment."[12] The *Herald* devoted thousands of words to a breathless recounting of the day's activities, with detailed descriptions of the numerous floats in the town's procession and listing by name many of the participating townsfolk: "The triumphal car of Columbia 'twas a chariot of rare beauty decorated with taste by Mrs. Matthews and other ladies. The character of Columbia was well sustained by the beautiful Miss Laura Marsh, seated on an elevated throne, and protected from the sun by an airy canopy."[13] This sort of account, with descriptions of the parts played by people most readers would have been acquainted with, lent an immediacy to the local celebrations that no account of goings-on in Philadelphia could match. The *Herald* went on to describe an apparently racially inclusive celebration: "The greased pig on the public square . . . the sack race, and the climbing of greased pole, in which the colored boys took part. Immense hilarity among all and many a hearty laugh."[14] As with antebellum Fourths, these southern observances didn't vary much in form from those of their northern counterparts, with northern newspapers including similar accounts of processions, picnics, and greased pigs.[15] The difference lay in the rhetoric and orations delivered on the day.

While the *Herald*'s account was focused on the activities of the day rather than any analysis of its significance or meaning, its account of the day's orations provided a momentary distraction from greasy pigs and poles. A local reverend gave an invocation that offered thanks for "a new era in our history, with the dark and threatening clouds of anarchy dispersing. And we pray that this may be the dawn of soul liberty, when all tyranny shall disappear from the earth." Clearly, with the "dark clouds" of Reconstruction lifting, these white Texans anticipated release from the "tyranny" they had been subject to for the past decade and thus proved more amenable to celebrating the national holiday. In a more secular vein, a Mr. James Turner told the Marshall assemblage that the Fourth was a day "not of strife but of reconciliation." Turner went on, saying that of the two sides in the war, one had "fought, as they believed, for freedom, the other had fought for the union . . . and in peace they were once more friends, claiming a common history and common heritage."[16]

A similar story was unfolding 265 miles south, in Brenham, Texas. The conditionality of postwar nationalism in the white South, and the extent to which this was contingent upon hopes of Democratic Party primacy, can be gleaned from a report of the Centennial Independence Day celebrations in that town. The local newspaper described processions, speeches, and "streets thronged with people in holiday attire" and pronounced the commemoration a success, concluding that "everyone was perfectly satisfied and reconstructed. We are now fairly launched on the second century of the Republic, with flattering prospects for an honest Democratic administration of national affairs."[17] Further, it implicitly highlighted the way Republican rule was seen by many Texans and underscored the feelings behind Texans' reluctance to be represented at the national Centennial commemoration by a Republican appointee of a Republican governor.

Similarly, a description of the Fourth at the other end of the South, in Danville, Virginia, made clear the connection many southerners made between re-embracing their Americanism and the electoral success of the Democratic Party: "The Fourth was generally observed as a holiday. Stores were closed and there were picnic excursions . . . Tonight there will be a grand ratification of the nomination of Tilden and Hendricks."[18]

Meanwhile, in a "beautiful and inviting grove" near Carrollton, Georgia, a crowd gathered to celebrate the Fourth with songs, psalms, and orations. Rhetorically posing the question of why the day should be celebrated, one speaker emphasized the theme, so prominent in discourse leading up to the Centennial, of the South's inherited right to the legacy of 1776: "We are descendants of those illustrious sons of liberty . . . in assembling ourselves thus, we prove to the world that we still hold in grateful remembrance, the deeds and virtues of the soldiers of the Revolution."[19] Implicit here is the argument that secession and war did not disqualify the South from claiming this legacy, a theme that had featured prominently in white southern discourse in the early days of the war and resurfaced in debates around both Centennial engagement and Independence Day. After recitation of a poem called "The American Flag," "everybody was ready for the onslaught to the table."

This account went on to make clear the gendered assignation of roles in these commemorations: "The ladies, God bless them, had made everything prepared and in readiness for the repast. I always feel thankful that though Eden was lost, woman—dear woman—was saved. The ladies had spread out . . . on a commodious table . . . [a]

most inviting and sumptuous feast . . . pies, custards, fried chicken, ham and Miss Ludie's pickles vanished like snow before the morning sun."[20] This lengthy account, notwithstanding its detailed itemization of the "tasty, elegant and sumptuous" victuals on offer, nonetheless made clear the political context that underpinned the consumption of fried chicken and Miss Ludie's pickles: "Everyone present seemed to have due respect for the stars and stripes as their ample folds were unfurled to the breeze. It was indeed an enjoyable occasion and reminded us of the brighter and better days of the Republic . . . as it was not convenient for us to be at Philadelphia it was very pleasant for us to be at Waddell's store, and we hope the 'Old Flag' will be carefully folded away and pre-served for a similar occasion on July 4, 1877, at which time Samuel J. Tilden will be President of these United States."

The gendered nature of these celebrations could also be seen in Anderson, South Carolina, where the local Democratic Club "ear-nestly requested" the cooperation of the "ladies" in ensuring the suc-cess of a "basket-dinner" celebrating the Centennial Fourth. In what can be construed as a subtle reference to the November elections in that still Republican-controlled state, the club expressed hope that it was a "happy augury of the future [that] the Fourth of July is to be re-established in this Centennial year as a day of rejoicing and Thanks-giving among our people."[21]

As it had in 1875, the *Montgomery Advertiser* devoted a significant amount of column inches to promoting Fourth celebrations in that city. One reader wrote that "as a lady admirer of your paper, I can't help but feel proud that you have taken the matter in hand . . . don't stop writing about the Fourth, Messrs. Editors, but keep the ball rolling."[22] The ball did roll, and Montgomery's Centennial Fourth saw an oration delivered by Alabama's wartime governor, Thomas Watts. Stating the obvious, he began by noting that "suspension" of the southern Fourth observances had been because of the war. Then, using commemoration to shape memory and history, he invoked the idea, heard so frequently during the Confederacy's infancy, that the Confederate States of America had been the true embodiment of the founders' legacy. Watts declared that the war had been generally misunderstood; that "it was never the purpose of the South . . . to destroy the principles . . . embodied in the Constitution. Quite the reverse was the purpose. It was not to destroy but to preserve this great charter of liberty . . . that the South commenced that contest . . . The South was not the less a lover of liberty because she sought to separate from the North."[23] Watts went on to acknowledge the "fortitude and dignity" with which the South had acquiesced in Union victory and attributed renewed embrace of Independence Day to "the mellowing influences of time." Time's mellowing influence having been hastened along by the fact that Democrats had regained control of Alabama's state house in 1874, the *Advertiser* reported that Watts's speech was well received and noted that "nearly every store was closed" and that "hilarity and joy ruled the hour."[24]

Watts's juxtaposition of memory and commemoration was echoed in Memphis. In that riverfront city, a "Centennial Picnic" at St. James Park on July Fourth raised several hundred dollars for a monument to *Confederate* war dead. These white southerners were shaping their commemorative activity as well as their ideas about nationalism and identity to fit around their unique and distinct position within the reformed Union.[25]

As was the case with earlier Fourths, and indeed with the Centennial itself, African Americans operated in parallel with and sometimes in opposition to white southern Democrats, using and commemorating the same day but to different ends. In Orangeburg, South Carolina, a newspaper description of a July Fourth barbecue stressed that the celebration, attended by about twenty-five hundred people, was not a "partisan or one-sided affair. The crowd here could elect any ticket put into the field." This is doubtful: the affair was billed as a "Republican Barbecue." Orations delivered included passages such as this "We enter fully into the spirit and sentiment of Freedom which today pervades this Government and believe that we, as Republicans, have as much right to glorify it as any other party."[26] The gathering, chaired by Orangeburg County's Black Republican sheriff, also passed a resolution endorsing the nomination of Rutherford Hayes as the Republican presidential nominee. Meanwhile, in Black-majority Aiken, South Carolina, celebrants were treated to a recitation that would likely have resulted in a riot at some other celebrations. In Aiken, Connecticut-born white Republican Frederick Palmer delivered a Centennial poem that, while invoking the ideals of the founders, acknowledged their hypocrisy:

> But while they threw their own chains off, they bound in binds more
>   strong
> the bands that held the colored man in misery and wrong
> but soon or late all wrong comes right for such is God's decree
> and in His own good time He set the black man free.[27]

Joint celebrations with African Americans and white Republicans continued in 1876 but were becoming less common than they had been in the first years of Reconstruction. Racial divisions within the party became apparent as Democrats solidified their control across the South, and the Radical Republican influence nationwide waned. Kathleen Clark has described a mixed Republican Fourth in Charleston that saw a white Republican insist that "[the Fourth] did not belong to them [African Americans]. They had nothing to do with it."[28] This scene had occurred in 1874; by 1876, and in subsequent years, there was a "gradual and uneven . . . shift towards segregated celebrations."[29]

African Americans stressed Black citizenship and social uplift in their own celebrations. Observations of the Centennial Fourth in a Texas Sunday school were linked with the "elevation" of the Black race. A local man provided a report to the national journal of the African Methodist Episcopal Church, the *Christian Recorder:*

> Knowing the great interest you take in the elevation of our race, no matter where located, I will send you a few lines as to our progress in Texas. The A.M.E. Sunday Schools of Columbia and Green Hill met, and a courteous repast was spread by the parents and friends in St. Paul's Church, to which the youngsters did ample justice. It done the heart of your correspondent good to see the cake and chicken, raisins,

candy and other good things disappear, and to see the faces of the little ones light up . . . The recitations were of a fine order. We had a good time. Trusting all the race will be elevated everywhere, and the African banner will yet float over the "Lone Star State."[30]

It is unclear how literally the notion of an "African banner" over Texas was meant to be taken, but it seems certain that these Black Texans were utilizing the Fourth as a means of teaching children about their American citizenship, and that citizenship, linked with their religion, was seen as a means of "elevating" them. In Portsmouth, Virginia, African Americans gathered at the AME church, "crowded to its utmost capacity," where a choir sang "My Country" and a pastor offered a "brief and most patriotic prayer."[31] This was followed by a reading of the Declaration of Independence and an oration by Black educator and former abolitionist John Mercer Langston. The account of Langston's speech in the *People's Advocate* described his focus on the Declaration of Independence and the Constitution, "showing at once how those great papers had declared the freedom of the Negro from the day they were written." He also stressed African *American* identity, with references to Crispus Attucks's Revolutionary sacrifice and the "not insignificant . . . part which the colored citizen took in this American anniversary."[32]

So, as they had in previous years, African Americans used the Fourth to display and claim their American identity and to establish their place in the memory of the founding and development of the nation. And as they had in the years since 1865, white southerners dismissed these efforts. The white newspaper in Newberry, South Carolina, stressed the poverty of African Americans celebrating the Fourth in that town: "Before the pic-nic of the colored people on the 4th of July a procession was formed which marched through the town accompanied by the inevitable brass band and U.S. flag. Fully one hundred were in the procession, representing all the different degrees and stages of impecuniosity. Altogether it was a unique affair. Not much enthusiasm manifested."[33]

The same tone prevailed in the paper's account of a larger gathering of Black Americans in Charleston, describing a procession in which one of the horseback Black participants, "little eyes fairly swimming in a sea of greasy perspiration," rode on a horse whose lively prancing brought "intense and undisguised delight [to] the old maumas who could be heard blessing "de lord" and clapping their hands." This account also highlighted the relative poverty of the African American celebrants: "A perfect sea of humanity . . . of the darkest description, but an impecunious one . . . iced lemonade grew warm in pitchers, ice cream relapsed to its original form, flies settled on sliced cake, watermelons wilted, for buyers were few, no doubt the crowd was hungry and appreciative but the ability to indulge was lacking."[34] This sort of attitude, most charitably described as patronizing, signals the inevitable tensions aroused as southern whites reclaimed the Fourth. The extent of these tensions can be gauged by the violence that occurred at Hamburg, South Carolina. This town was, in Eric Foner's words, a "center of Reconstruction black power," with a majority Black population and numerous Blacks holding local office, and events there on the Centennial Fourth proved to be flashpoint, highlighting how high the stakes were for those involved in contestations over the Fourth.[35] The episode both illustrated and inflamed the racial and political battleground of July Fourth.

As the local Black militia under the command of Dock Adams celebrated the Centennial Fourth, two white men, son and son-in-law of a local farmer, took offense at being held up on a road by the parade. After a tense exchange, Adams ordered his men to move aside and let them pass. The next day, however, the father/father-in-law of the two white men filed a complaint with Black magistrate Prince Rivers against Adams for obstructing the road. Adams was set to be tried on the eighth, and over the next few days, racial tensions in the area escalated, with armed whites flocking into the town from the surrounding countryside. A prominent local Democrat, General Matthew Butler, was set to prosecute Adams. As tensions mounted, Butler (sans any actual authority) ordered the militia to disarm. They refused but, outnumbered and outgunned, took shelter in their headquarters and were quickly surrounded by the white posse. Gunfire soon broke out, and a white man outside was killed. Butler afterward released a self-serving statement to the press, stressing his own innocence in the whole affair ("I was not the leader of this body of infuriated men"). He described the dead white man as "most estimable" and remarked that the whites "under the leadership of no one," soon made use of a cannon, forcing the militia to surrender. Nonetheless, several Black men were rounded up and murdered in cold blood by the white mob. Ninety-four men were indicted but never prosecuted for these deaths.

The Hamburg episode, grounded in Black observation of the Fourth, proved a rallying point for aggrieved whites and a key development in South Carolina's Democratic "redemption" later that year.[36] Contemporary reaction to Hamburg reveals very sharply the racial and political divides in the Centennial year. Butler's lengthy account was largely focused on stressing his own innocence in the whole affair but toward its close placed the onus squarely on assertions of Black rights: "This collision was the culmination of the system of insulting and outraging of white people, which the negroes had adopted there for several years. Many things were done on this terrible night which of course cannot be justified but the negroes sowed the wind and reaped the whirlwind."[37] The *Augusta Chronicle and Sentinel* noted that because "two negroes" were among the ninety-four accused, it proved conclusively that "the unfortunate occurrence of July 8 had nothing to do with race or politics." It then, however, went on to echo Butler's point, arguing that Hamburg was "one of the inevitable fruits of negro rule."[38]

The arguments around Hamburg didn't divide neatly into two camps, illustrating perhaps the inchoate nature and overall messiness of Reconstruction politics. One Democratic South Carolina journal defended Butler's actions in using force to disarm Adams's militia but drew the line at the murder of the surrendered men: "The shooting of those defenceless prisoners is the essence of the Hamburg affair; the provocation goes for nothing. That brutal murder excites the North and makes them think that we are Reconstructed on our lips but not in our hearts. Those men who shot those defenceless prisoners should be punished."[39] The same paper went on to once again make clear the importance of Democratic victory in the 1876 election as well as how much weight was given to appearances and outward shows of reconstruction: "Those who endeavour to cover up the criminality of the act are electioneering for Hayes and Wheeler and gin for them 10,000 votes in the Northern states where they gain one in South Carolina for Tilden."[40]

Meanwhile, an African American paper in Savannah reinforced the link between violence and Democratic electoral success when it remarked: "A Democratic contemporary calls the Alabama election 'the first gun for the Democracy.' It is just possible that he did not hear the guns at Hamburg, so we must excuse his ignorance."[41]

South Carolina's Republican governor Daniel Chamberlain wrote to President Grant about the matter, requesting federal assistance in protecting the rights and lives of freed people. Chamberlain pointed out that the demands for the company to disarm "would seem to indicate a purpose to deprive the militia of their rights on account of their race or political opinions . . . the effect of this massacre has been to cause widespread terror and apprehension among the colored race and the Republicans of the state. There is little doubt, on the other hand, that a feeling of triumph and political elation has been caused by the massacre in the minds of many of the white people and Democrats."[42] Grant's response fell short of offering any practical aid but made clear that he recognized Hamburg for what it was, characterizing it as a "barbarous massacre" and linking the "cruel, blood-thirsty, wanton and unprovoked" events in South Carolina with the violence and fraud behind recent Democratic victories in Mississippi and Louisiana.[43]

The *Huntsville Weekly Democrat,* in Alabama, characterized Grant's response to Hamburg as a "malicious, vindictive libel . . . designed for partisan purposes . . . [to] rekindle sectional animosity and encourage white and black Southern radicals in their incendiary work against the white Southern race . . . The Radical Party of the North and Radical Government of the United States have been persistent in their efforts to humiliate the South . . . Does His Excellency [Grant] expect men of the Caucasian race . . . to yield to the vulgar tyranny of black barbarians? . . . never can the white race thus submit to the African."[44] This kind of rhetoric highlights not only the response to a local, if violent, difficulty arising out of an attempt to commemorate Independence Day but also the near impossibility of achieving any kind of real reunion when recognition of any Black political agency was perceived as submission to "the African." Hamburg had ramifications far beyond a dispute over a blocked road on Independence Day. The tensions it both exposed and exacerbated led to a hardening of political lines in the state; there had been some momentum behind a fusionist movement bringing together Republicans and more moderate Democrats, but Hamburg led to a polarization that made that impossible. Enshrined in white memory, as massacres tend to be, as a "riot" that needed to be put down, the events that followed that Centennial Fourth had repercussions for years afterward. Matthew Butler went on to serve in the United States Senate, as did another of the ninety-four who were indicted and never prosecuted, Ben Tillman, who later became an influential force in South Carolina and was instrumental in the establishment of Jim Crow and Black disenfranchisement.

The centrality of commemoration and historical memory runs through the sorry tale of Hamburg: it was sparked by white anger at a group of African Americans parading to celebrate the Fourth of July, and it was used to shore up white supremacy not only through Tillman's later use of the massacre for political capital but through a monument erected in 1916 to McKie Merriwether, the "estimable young man" whose death was used as justification for the massacre. A Dunningesque 1955 history of Aiken County, South Carolina, drew parallels between the massacre and 1776, noting that "the beginning of the revolution to overthrow Reconstruction in South Carolina took place on the 4th of July, 1876 . . . Thus, South Carolina lying prostrate the day of the Hamburg Riot, hopeless and desperate, had risen, gloriously alive to join her sister States and to fight for many years to overcome the wounds of Reconstruction."[45] Here we see the memory of what one widely reproduced African American pamphlet sarcastically called *A Centennial Fourth of July Democratic Celebration . . . Massacre* being invoked generations later to shore up a Democratic, partisan, and racist version of Reconstruction.[46]

In contrast to the racist vitriol that Hamburg engendered, some white southerners made use of the Centennial Fourth to perpetuate stereotypes of the docile and content Black American; an acquaintance of former Confederate vice president Alexander Stephens published an account of a Fourth of July visit to the ailing statesman that did just that. This narrative referenced the events at Hamburg by noting that trouble had been predictable due to the nature of its African American inhabitants, with white visitors there "often subjected to annoyances and insults by colored men." However, the correspondent swiftly moved on to a more congenial subject: the loyalty that Blacks in his hometown of Crawfordsville, Georgia, felt toward Alexander Stephens: "Mr. Stephens was rolled in his chair out into the long piazza as the vast crowds [of African American Sunday school delegations] advanced up the lawn . . . perhaps you have never heard a Georgia negro sing. At all events I am confident that you have never heard twenty-five hundred of them sing in chorus as they did on that afternoon . . . for the entertainment of the invalid statesman whom of all men they love and honor the most . . . their neat and orderly appearance, with their Sunday clothes and simple banners, not only gratified Mr. Stephens . . . but enraptured him."[47] The enraptured Stephens, who in 1861 had declared slavery the cornerstone of the new Confederate nation, commented later that he almost "wished he could have died" while enjoying this serenade and then spoke of "the generally good condition of the negroes in that section, where many of them own snug little farms and other properties and between whom and their white neighbors the most friendly relations obtain."[48] Available accounts do not, unfortunately, provide us with the perspective of the Black Georgians who sang to Stephens.

The Centennial Fourth in Chattanooga, Tennessee, threw into sharp relief the continuing political gulf and issues surrounding the reconciliation of southern and American identities. A women's group "intertwined" the U.S. flag and the Confederate battle flag, flying the two together as part of a Centennial July Fourth celebration. The move was criticized by a local Republican paper, the Commercial, which described the pairing of flags as "repulsive" and the southern banner as "dead . . . its meaningless colors dragged from the grave . . . to excite the smoldering prejudices of those who followed it."[49] The paper continued, likely with deliberate naïveté, that the flags represented opposing political systems but not any personal animosity: "These men did not hate each other or fight each other like brutes to inflict bodily harm. Hence there is and has been no need of personal reconciliation." From this Republican perspective, the war was over, the question of American versus southern nationhood was decided, and it was time to put away "the flag of the dead . . . [and] love, cherish and obey the living flag of the living nation which protects the rights of all and remembers harshly the errors of none of its citizens."[50]

Naturally, these sentiments were not shared by other Chattanoogans. The *Daily Times,* acknowledging military defeat and the death of the Confederate nation, expressed a sarcastic "envy for that flexible patriotism that can always rally with blatant enthusiasm to the side of victory."[51] While stating "we are all Americans," the *Times* castigated those southern Republicans who had "cast off the principles of their fathers and for the love of gain or political preferment joined in with the jackals who for years have been preying upon the panting, dying institutions of that crushed republic."[52] There is no explicit mention of African Americans in this journalistic exchange, although the Republican *Commercial*'s reference to "rights for all" was no doubt a reference to the wider debate over the role of Black people in American life. Finally, the exchange highlights again the central, if "delicate," role of women in these struggles. It was a women's group who raised the Confederate standard on July Fourth, and the male writer in the *Daily Times* framed his argument around "Southern women . . . who will not have another opportunity of expressing their admiration for the flag of their country in so delicate a manner."[53] For this particular commemoration, with women engaged in action more substantive than merely provisioning picnic tables, we are still reliant on a male voice informing us that the Confederate banner was for these women the "flag of their country." Without sources to tell us what these women intended, we can only look to their actions, and while raising the Stars and Stripes at this local Fourth indicates a recognition of renewed Americanness, the pairing of flags reinforces the presence of a Confederate identity that remained potent in 1876.

Celebration of the Fourth was not yet universal in the white South; however, even when not celebrated, it was marked. A letter published in the *Augusta Chronicle* noted that the centennial Fourth in Oglethorpe County, Georgia, "passed off as quietly as if it had been no more than any other day in the calendar. There was no demonstration, no firing of guns, no spread-eagle speeches, no suspension of business, and no old-time country barbecue."[54] In Tallapoosa, Alabama, the lack of Independence Day observation was tied in with Reconstruction politics. A resident of the town reported to the *Montgomery Advertiser* that Tilden's selection as the Democratic presidential nominee was a popular one in his town and, after a lengthy review of the New Yorker's merits, remarked that the Fourth was going unobserved in his town, due only to "hard times" (in itself, perhaps an implicit criticism of the Republican administration). He held out the hope that "another Fourth of July will find us under Democratic rule, both state and national, and in that event will be prepared to celebrate the glorious day that brought liberty and independence to this country." In this writer's mind, only Democratic rule would allow white southerners to "forget the oppressive laws and shackles of the past few years" and wholeheartedly re-embrace the Fourth.[55]

But in the nearly "redeemed" South of 1876, these examples proved the exception. Local commemorations were less of an abstraction for these southerners than the exhibition in Philadelphia so while the local activities also served as arenas for assertions of political and national identities, the appeal of greased pigs, firecrackers, barbecues, and pickles, in commemoration of a struggle far removed from the more recent one, helped overcome, at the local level, white southern antipathy to Independence Day. It seems clear, however, that white Democratic control, or in some cases just the prospect of redemption, was the key element in white southern celebration of the Fourth in 1876. African Americans used the day, sometimes, but less frequently than a few years earlier, in conjunction with white Republican allies, to assert their own American past, present, and future. Overall, in 1876, July Fourth celebrations in the South, underneath the picnics and firecrackers, were as politically charged as the great exhibition in Philadelphia.

Conclusion

David Goldfield has aptly described the Civil War as a ghost haunting the American memoryscape, one that "has not yet made its peace and roams the land seeking solace, retribution or vindication."[1] In the 1870s, however, it was no ghost and much more than a memory. Northern journalist Whitelaw Reid traveled extensively throughout the South in the years immediately after the war and noted that to "talk of genuine Union sentiment, any affection for the Union, any intention to go one step further out of the old paths that led to the rebellion than they are forced to is preposterous. They admit that they are whipped; but the honest ones make no pretense of loving the power that whipped them."[2] Anne Sarah Rubin, more recently, has highlighted the degree to which white southerners nursed bitterness while outwardly expressing capitulation. She quotes an Alabama colonel: "Let us keep a pleasant equanimity of mind . . . we have well learned the lessons of toleration and will we not profit from it? Yes, and when we can stand on our own two feet, will we forget the law 'an eye for an eye'?"[3] This discomfort was negotiated by some white southerners in a more flexible, pragmatic way that did not, however, necessarily imply lesser attachment to the South or greater affinity for the Union. There are clear indications that the split between utilitarian and disdainful approaches to white southern engagement with the exhibition can be linked, broadly, to the accommodationist New Departure and the more recalcitrant Bourbon wings of the Democratic Party, respectively. In general, we see in the embittered rhetoric of those who wanted nothing to do with the Centennial, who saw in it nothing but "Yankee humbug," a reflection of the old planter class, resistant to change. Indeed, Nashville's *Republican Banner,* in describing the vociferous and cantankerous Centennial critic Raphael Semmes, referred to him as "die-in-the-last-ditch anti-Centennial gentry."[4]

Meanwhile, it seems likely that New Departure white Democrats, the more liberal wing of the party that favored a more cooperative relationship with the federal government and were resigned to some element of Black citizenship, were the element more likely to push for Centennial participation. New South proponent Henry Grady's *Atlanta Daily Herald* applied this "utilitarian" philosophy to the Centennial, taking to task a sister journal that apparently fit the Bourbon mold: "We are not surprised that the editor of the *Savannah News* is opposed to the Centennial. He will continue to oppose it . . . even while everybody else has gone to the Centennial and are sounding Georgia's glories to the world he will remain at home, raking among the ashes in a garb of sackcloth . . . there is a utilitarian view of the subject that will bear presenting . . . nothing but bad blood and childishness can keep the South out of the jubilee. We shall have a show of which every Georgian will be proud."[5]

Although these hopes for the state's participation remained unfulfilled, Georgia, and the South, would have further opportunities to market itself. The Centennial of 1876 was America's first world's fair but far from its last. An even grander affair was held in Chicago in 1893 to mark the four hundredth anniversary of Columbus's voyages. As with the Philadelphia exhibition seventeen years earlier, the World's Columbian Exposition was perceived in the South as a chance to benefit economically as well as to iterate a distinct identity. Perusal of southern newspapers in the run-up to the Chicago exhibition provides a sense of Centennial déjà vu in that one sees repeated admonishments that Georgia or South Carolina or Alabama *must* be represented properly at the Columbian Exposition. For example, it was suggested that

Georgia's headquarters, which apparently combined "beauty, dignity and strength," would, as an advertisement of the state's resources, be "worth thrice its price."[6] Generally absent from southern discussion of the Chicago fair, however, was sectional animus, although a distinct sense of sectional identity and pride was evident in white southerners' desire to be represented at the fair. The African American experience of Chicago was, though, depressingly reminiscent of Philadelphia. No Black persons were appointed to any position of authority with the exposition, and there was division within the Black community over issues such as whether or not there should be a dedicated "Colored People's Day." Black journalist Ida B. Wells argued that the gesture was condescending, while Frederick Douglass saw it as an opportunity to educate whites on Black progress.[7]

The financial success of the 1876 Centennial also inspired southern world's fairs in New Orleans (1885), Atlanta (1895), and Nashville (1897), among others. Robert Rydell has highlighted the linkage between these fairs and the idea of a New South, arguing that "each fair presented an image of a New South imbued with the spirit of progress and patriotism."[8] These exhibitions achieved, to a degree, what the Centennial could not: they served as canvases to project an image of a distinct and economically viable South within a reunited nation. In these years in which the white South was being left to order society as it saw fit, it was keen to demonstrate to the world that the "problem" of race had been solved and made use of these exhibitions to demonstrate this purported achievement to potential investors. The fairs included Black exhibitions—Atlanta's "Negro Department," in particular, was central to that fair's thematic presence. Although the intent of those African Americans who worked on the exhibit was to demonstrate capability and progress, the most significant impact of Black involvement with the fair came with Booker T. Washington's famous "Atlanta Compromise" speech, delivered on its opening day. As historian Bruce Harvey has pointed out, the white press focused on what it saw as Washington's message of letting the South handle race relations free of northern influence and largely ignored his focus on Black education and uplift.[9]

These fairs, most particularly the one in Atlanta, framed and defined a new order in the South, a racist and "redeemed" society existing within a reunited States. In the words of Robert Rydell, southern fairs "forged a link between race and progress that prepared the way for national acceptance of *Plessy v Ferguson*."[10]

In debates around the origins of Jim Crow segregation in the South, historian Howard Rabinowitz has argued that African Americans played an active role in the development of this hierarchical society, seeing segregation as a lesser evil than the alternative: exclusion.[11] The Centennial and subsequent exhibitions might be said to reflect that development. The African American role in the Centennial story provided a poignant counterpoint to the narrative of white southern ambivalence: eager to use the exhibition to claim and demonstrate their status as American citizens, their efforts met with obstruction, ill fortune, and indifference. Endeavoring to lay claim to a part both in America's Revolutionary heritage and its industrialized future, Black Americans found themselves as marginalized on the fairgrounds as they were becoming in American society. The later fairs, while more inclusive of Black Americans, clearly relegated them to a distinct and inferior station in the life of the nation.

Commemoration would continue to provide a window into the long and rocky process of reconciliation as the twentieth century progressed. The United Daughters of the Confederacy remained dedicated to the project of inculcating and promoting a memory of the war and Reconstruction favorable to the [white] South. In 1922, a member of the UDC expressed to that group's annual convention her fears that "wrong" interpretations of history were entering "textbooks . . . encyclopedias and books of reference." These supposedly fallacious interpretations included the ideas that "the advocates of secession were traitors to the United States government . . . that the war was a 'Civil War' for we were not a republic of sovereign states but a nation . . . that the South fought to hold her slaves . . . that Abraham Lincoln freed the slaves."[12]

The 1961–65 centennial of the Civil War opened another window for commemorative activity that reflected the concerns and divisions of the civil rights era much as the Centennial had for the 1870s; there was even a national commission created to oversee the commemorations. The success of the groups like the UDC in shaping memory of the war into a Lost Cause mold can be seen in deputy commission head Karl Betts's reassurance to southern whites that Emancipation wouldn't feature heavily in the planned programs and activities. Betts added that "a lot of fine Negro people loved life as it was in the South."[13] Encouraged by such reassurance, southern state officials, in the words of historian Robert Cook, engaged readily in what they saw as a celebration of the Confederacy in the "expectation that efficient marketing would bring tourists flocking to the Southern battlefields."[14] Cook has also described how celebrations in Montgomery, Alabama, in 1961 caused a local man to reflect that the commemorations had given the city "a deeper appreciation of the things the Confederacy fought for." Using the commemoration of century-old events to comment on the ongoing struggle for Black freedom, the same man continued that "[the Civil War Centennial] had helped [the people of Montgomery] to realize that unrestrained federal power is destroying this nation."[15]

As South Carolina marked its tricentennial in 1970, the state was being forced to integrate its public schools, and once again, a confluence of the commemorative and the political was clear. In the town of Orangeburg, white and Black historical associations engaged in what Bruce Baker has described as "a behind-the-scenes contest over how to present the country's history and to what extent Orangeburg would integrate not only the present but also the past."[16] Excluded from a local (white) organizing committee, local Blacks set up their own group and used the state's anniversary as an "occasion to disseminate black history."[17]

Just as these commemorations were bound up with twentieth century concerns, so too was the Centennial Exhibition in Philadelphia with those of the 1870s. Intended as a patriotic endeavor to commemorate one hundred years of American independence—as well as a demonstration to the world of American unity, nationhood, and technological progress—the Centennial fell short in all but the last.

Overlapping with a divisive presidential election that served partly as a referendum on Reconstruction, the exhibition was a locus of political, racial, and sectional antagonism. The deep sectional and political divisions reflected in discourse around the exhibition make the case that those white southerners who did advocate engagement with the Centennial did so largely for pragmatic reasons, basing their positions on the putative economic and political advantages to be had. And in the same way that opportunistic southern enthusiasm for the Centennial fizzled into anticlimax, with only Mississippi and Arkansas having any official presence at the Philadelphia exposition, northern investment in the New South left the South economically shriveled and dependent for decades. For white southern visitors to Philadelphia, the American nationalism underpinning the Centennial only served to exacerbate their own sense of alienation from the Union and their own distinctive southern identity. Further, the exhibition provided a space for northern observers to exoticize and "other" both the South and southern visitors to the fair.

The importance of commemorative activity in a discussion of the 1870s white South lies not so much in the magnificent exhibits and revolutionary technology on display or the grand scale of the Centennial Exhibition or the barbecues and firecrackers of local Fourths of July but in what these commemorations meant to people and how they reflected the concerns of the day. The great exhibition was more than a site of memory and a declaration of technological advancement: it highlighted the divisions, the bitterness, and the complexities of a nation that was in many ways still at war with itself. The recalcitrance and bitterness of many southern whites in their reaction to and engagement with the commemorative activities of the Reconstruction era provide a foreshadowing of the conditional reconciliation of the coming century: Jim Crow, disfranchisement, massive resistance, and the "Solid South." Similarly, for Black Americans, these celebrations anticipated the struggles of Frederick Douglass, W.E.B. Du Bois, and others to highlight an emancipationist memory of the Civil War and to use the Fourth of July to assert their place as American citizens.

The Centennial was remarkable in its power to serve almost any rhetorical purpose and in the way it was simultaneously derided as a failure, a cynical Yankee ploy, held up as a potential (or missed) opportunity for state and local advancement, or extolled as the most marvelous, breathtaking human endeavor of all time. It also served as a looking glass in which Americans, North and South, Black and white, saw reflected back a nation that was tenuously reunited but far from reconciled.

Notes

INTRODUCTION

1. Linda P. Gross and Theresa R. Snyder, *Philadelphia's 1876 Centennial Exhibition* (Charleston, SC: Arcadia, 2005), 8.

2. Lally Weymouth, *America in 1876: The Way We Were* (New York: Vintage Books, 1976), 12.

3. See Gregory P. Downs, *After Appomattox: Military Occupations and the Ends of War* (Cambridge: Harvard University Press, 2015); Richard Zuczek, *State of Rebellion: Reconstruction in South Carolina* (Columbia: University of South Carolina Press, 2009); Anne Sarah Rubin, *A Shattered Nation: The Rise and Fall of the Confederacy, 1861–1868* (Chapel Hill: University of North Carolina Press, 2009); David W. Blight, *Race and Reunion: The Civil War in American Memory* (Cambridge: Harvard University Press, 2001); Caroline Janney, *Remembering the Civil War: Reunion and the Limits of Reconciliation* (Chapel Hill: University of North Carolina Press, 2013); W. Fitzhugh Brundage, *The Southern Past: A Clash of Race and Memory* (Cambridge: Harvard University Press, 2008); William Blair, *Cities of the Dead: Contesting the Memory of the Civil War in the South, 1865–1914* (Chapel Hill: University of North Carolina Press, 2004); Karen Cox, *Dixie's Daughters: The United Daughters of the Confederacy and the Preservation of Confederate Culture* (Gainesville: University Press of Florida, 2002); M. Keith Harris, *Across the Bloody Chasm: The Culture of Commemoration among Civil War Veterans* (Baton Rouge: Louisiana State University Press, 2014).

4. See Timothy J. Williams, "The Intellectual Roots of the Lost Cause: Camaraderie and Confederate Memory in Civil War Prisons," *Journal of Southern History* 86, no. 2 (2020): 253–82.

5. See Bruno Gilberti, *Designing the Centennial: A History of the 1876 International Exhibition in Philadelphia* (Lexington: University Press of Kentucky, 2002).

6. Philip Foner, "Black Participation in the Centennial of 1876," *Phylon* 39, no. 4 (1978): 283–96; Mitch Kachun, "Before the Eyes of All Nations: African-American Identity and Historical Memory at the Centennial Exposition of 1876," *Pennsylvania History* 65, no. 3 (1998): 300–323.

7. John Hepp, "Centennial Celebrations," in *A Companion to the Reconstruction Presidents*, ed. Edward O. Frantz (Malden, MA: John Wiley & Sons, 2014), 533.

8. Susanna W. Gold, *The Unfinished Exhibition: Visualizing Myth, Memory, and the Shadow of the Civil War in Centennial America* (London: Routledge, 2017), 43.

9. Lyn Spillman, *Nation and Commemoration: Creating National Identities in the United States and Australia* (Cambridge: Cambridge University Press, 1997), 71.

10. Kathleen Ann Clark, *Defining Moments: African American Commemoration and Political Culture in the South, 1863–1915* (Chapel Hill: University of North Carolina Press, 2005), 124.

11. Janney, *Remembering the Civil War*, 243.

12. W. Burlie Brown, "Louisiana and the Nation's One-Hundredth Birthday," *Journal of the Louisiana Historical Association* 18, no. 3 (1976): 271.

13. W. Fitzhugh Brundage, "No Deed but Memory," in *Where These Memories Grow: History, Memory, and Southern Identity*, ed. W. Fitzhugh Brundage (Chapel Hill: University of North Carolina Press, 2000), 5.

14. Ibid., 6.

15. Pierre Nora, "Between Memory and History," *Memory and Counter-Memory*, special issue no. 26 (1989): 7–24.

16. Bruce E. Baker, *What Reconstruction Meant: Historical Memory in the American South* (Charlottesville: University of Virginia Press, 2007), 6.

17. Matthew Dennis, *Red, White, and Blue Letter Days: An American Calendar* (Ithaca, NY: Cornell University Press, 2002), 6.

18. Cecilia Elizabeth O'Leary, *To Die For: The Paradox of American Patriotism* (Princeton: Princeton University Press, 1999), 11.

19. James McPherson, "Antebellum Southern Exceptionalism: A New Look at an Old Question." *Civil War History* 50 (2004): 433.

20. Robert E. Bonner *Mastering America: Southern Slaveholders and the Crisis of American Nationhood* (New York: Cambridge University Press, 2009), 41.

21. O'Leary, *To Die For*, 25.

22. Paul Nagel, *One Nation Indivisible: The Union in American Thought, 1776–1861* (New York: Oxford University Press, 1964), 15.

23. Ibid.; Thomas Jefferson to Joseph Priestley, 29 January 1804, at Founders Online, National Archives, https://founders.archives.gov/documents/Jefferson/01-42-02-0322.

24. Paul Quigley, *Shifting Grounds: Nationalism and the American South, 1848–1865* (Oxford: Oxford University Press, 2012), 215.

25. Nagel, *One Nation Indivisible*, 41.

26. Quoted in *Macon Weekly Telegraph,* 8 April 1851.

27. Avery O. Craven, *The Growth of Southern Nationalism: 1848–1861* (Baton Rouge: Louisiana State University Press, 1953), 8.

28. William Freehling, *The Road to Disunion, 1776–1854* (Oxford: Oxford University Press, 1990), 19.

29. William C. Harris, *The Day of the Carpetbagger: Republican Reconstruction in Mississippi* (Baton Rouge: Louisiana State University Press, 1979), 117.

30. Jonathon Holt Ingraham, *The South-West, by a Yankee in Two Volumes* (New York: Harper Brothers, 1835), 2:127, http://www.gutenberg.org/ebooks/35156.

31. Clement Eaton, "Calhoun and State Rights," *The Civilization of the Old South: Writings of Clement Eaton* (Lexington: University Press of Kentucky, 1968), 151.

32. Charles Grier Sellers, "The Travails of Slavery," in *The Southerner as American,* ed. Charles Sellers (Chapel Hill: University of North Carolina Press, 1960), 40.

33. William J. Cooper, *The American South: A History* (Boston: Rowman & Littlefield, 2002), 1:106.

34. Sellers, "Travails of Slavery," 43.

35. "The Cause of the South," *DeBow's Review,* July 1850: 120–28.

36. Ibid.

37. David Potter, *The Impending Crisis, 1848–1861* (New York: Harper & Row, 1976), 33.

38. Paul Escott, *After Secession: Jefferson Davis and the Failure of Confederate Nationalism* (Baton Rouge: Louisiana State University Press, 1978), 113.

39. Benjamin L. Carp, "Nations of American Rebels: Understanding Nationalism in Revolutionary North America and the Civil War South," *Civil War History* 23, no. 1 (2002): 11.

40. Drew Gilpin Faust, *The Creation of Confederate Nationalism: Ideology and Identity in the Civil War South* (Baton Rouge: Louisiana State University Press, 1988), 4.

41. Quigley, *Shifting Grounds,* 170.

42. See Gary Gallagher, *The Confederate War* (Cambridge: Harvard University Press, 1997), 75–88.

43. Escott, *After Secession,* 244. See also Gallagher, *Confederate War,* 74–77.

44. Escott, *After Secession,* 255.

45. Ibid.

46. Bonner, *Mastering America,* 319.

47. "Slavery as Connected with Our Present and Probable Future Exigencies," *Augusta Daily Constitutionalist,* 8 March 1865.

48. William C. Davis, *Jefferson Davis: The Man and His Hour* (Baton Rouge: Louisiana State University Press, 1992), 600.

49. Robert Durden, *The Gray and the Black: The Confederate Debate on Emancipation* (Baton Rouge: Louisiana State University Press, 1972), 188–89. Orchestrated by Maryland politician Francis Blair, this was a peace conference that took place aboard the

steamboat *River Queen* at Hampton Roads, Virginia. Lincoln himself attended, accompanied by Secretary of State William Seward, but Davis dispatched Vice President Stephens along with Assistant Secretary of State John Campbell. Davis's only unconditional demand was retention of southern independence, while Lincoln's only nonnegotiable condition was reunion; thus, the summit achieved nothing.

50. Don H. Doyle "Slavery, Secession, Reconstruction," in *The South as an American Problem*, ed. Larry J. Griffin and Don H. Doyle (Athens: University of Georgia Press, 1995), 118.

51. See Eric Foner, *Reconstruction: America's Unfinished Revolution, 1863–1877* (New York: HarperCollins, 1988), for some bleak statistics.

52. *Chester (SC) Reporter,* 4 September 1873, cited in Zuczek, *State of Rebellion,* 129.

1. ANTEBELLUM AND WARTIME FOURTHS OF JULY

1. "A Right Move in the Right Direction," *Shreveport (LA) South-Western,* 19 June 1861.

2. Ibid.

3. William Blair, *Cities of the Dead: Contesting the Memory of the Civil War in the South, 1865–1914* (Chapel Hill: University of North Carolina Press, 2004), 12.

4. Len Travers, *Celebrating the Fourth: Independence Day and the Rites of Nationalism in the Early Republic* (Amherst: University of Massachusetts Press, 1997), 152.

5. Andrew W. Robertson, "Look on This Picture . . . and on This! Nationalism, Localism, and Partisan Images of Otherness in the United States, 1787–1820," *American Historical Review* (October 2001): 1266.

6. David Waldstreicher, *In the Midst of Perpetual Fetes: The Making of American Nationalism, 1776–1820* (Chapel Hill: University of North Carolina Press, 1997), 129.

7. Philip F. Detweiler, "The Changing Reputation of the Declaration of Independence: The First Fifty Years," *William and Mary Quarterly* 19, no. 4 (October 1962): 573.

8. Jeffrey L. Pasley, "The Cheese and the Words," in *Beyond the Founders: New Approaches to the Political History of the Early American Republic,* ed. Jeffrey L. Pasley, Andrew W. Robertson, and David Waldstreicher (Chapel Hill: University of North Carolina Press 2004), 41.

9. Albrecht Koschnik, "Young Federalists, Masculinity and Partisanship during the War of 1812," in *Beyond the Founders: New Approaches to the Political History of the Early American Republic,* ed. Jeffrey L. Pasley, Andrew W. Robertson, and David Waldstreicher (Chapel Hill: University of North Carolina Press 2004), 166.

10. "Republican Celebration," *Vermont Republican and American Journal* (Windsor), 29 June 1812.

11. "Communications," *Vermont Watchman and State Journal* (Montpelier), 14 July 1814.

12. Travers, *Celebrating the Fourth,* 139.

13. Ibid., 141.

14. "The Fourth of July: Independence Forever!" *Mississippi Free Trader* (Natchez), 3 July 1838.

15. Isaiah Thomas, *Diary* (July 1817), 354, https://babel.hathitrust.org/cgi/pt?id=hvd .32044058136532&view=1up&seq=388.

16. Travers, *Celebrating the Fourth,* 10.

17. See Andrew Burstein, *America's Jubilee, July 4, 1826: A Generation Remembers the Revolution after Fifty Years of Independence* (New York: Vintage, 2002), 271–85.

18. Frederick Douglass, "What to the Slave Is the Fourth of July?" Teaching American History website, Ashbrook Center, https://teachingamericanhistory.org/library /document/what-to-the-slave-is-the-fourth-of-july-2/.

19. Mitch Kachun, *Festivals of Freedom: Memory and Meaning in African American Emancipation Celebrations, 1808–1915* (Amherst: University of Massachusetts Press, 2003), 54.

20. Ibid., 55.

21. "Original Communications," *Freedom's Journal* (New York), 13 July 1827. *Freedom's Journal* was the first African American–owned and operated newspaper published in the United States.

22. "The Fourth of July," *Frederick Douglass' Paper* (Rochester, NY), 7 July 1848.

23. "Gleanings of News," *Frederick Douglass' Paper* (Rochester, NY), 4 August 1854.

24. Kachun, *Festivals of Freedom,* 34.

25. Ibid., 35.

26. Kachun, "Before the Eyes of All Nations," 302.

27. Kachun, *Festivals of Freedom,* 62.

28. Ibid., 72.

29. Fletcher Green, "Listen to the Eagle Scream: One Hundred Years of the Fourth of July in North Carolina, 1776–1876," in *Democracy in the Old South and Other Essays by Fletcher Melvin Green,* ed. Isaac Copeland (Kingsport, TN: Vanderbilt University Press, 1969), 127.

30. Ibid.

31. Mary Lou Nemanic, *One Day for Democracy: Independence Day and the Americanization of Iron Range Immigrants* (Athens: Ohio University Press, 2007), 31.

32. Jack Larkin, *The Reshaping of Everyday Life: 1790–1840* (New York: Harper & Row, 1988), 275.

33. Kurt W. Ritter and James R. Andrews, *The American Ideology: Reflections of the Revolution in American Rhetoric* (Falls Church, VA: Speech Communication Association, 1978), 16–17.

34. Travers, *Celebrating the Fourth,* 6.

35. Kachun, *Festivals of Freedom,* 23.

36. Unknown to Louisa C. Harrison, 6 July 1847, Faunsdale Plantation Papers, 1805–1975, Birmingham Public Library Department of Archives and Manuscripts, Birmingham, AL.

37. "The Fourth of July," *Mississippi Free Trader* (Natchez), 22 July 1839.

38. Dennis, *Red, White, and Blue Letter Days*, 23.

39. Michael Kammen, *Mystic Chords of Memory: The Transformation of Tradition in American Culture* (New York: Vintage Books, 1991), 68. See *Anti-Slavery Picnic at Weymouth Landing*, by Susan Torrey Merritt, Civil War in Art website, https://www.civilwarinart.org/items/show/78.

40. Pauline Maier, *American Scripture: Making the Declaration of Independence* (New York: Knopf, 1997), 199.

41. Maier, *American Scripture*, 200.

42. Blair, *Cities of the Dead*, 12.

43. *Raleigh Register*, 7 July 1849, quoted in Green, "Listen to the Eagle Scream," 134.

44. "Fourth of July," *Knoxville Whig*, 26 May 1855.

45. Ibid.

46. *Wilmington Daily Journal*, 3 July 1856, quoted in Green, "Listen to the Eagle Scream," 135.

47. "A Fourth of July Manual," *Charleston Courier*, 15 July 1854.

48. Ibid.

49. "Anti-Slavery Celebration of the Fourth of July," *New York Herald*, 29 June 1856.

50. "The Fourth of July," *Texas State Gazette* (Austin), 4 July 1857.

51. Adam Criblez, *Parading Patriotism: Independence Day Celebrations in the Urban Midwest, 1826–1876* (DeKalb: Northern Illinois University Press, 2013), 72.

52. "The Fourth of July," *New Orleans Daily Picayune*, 29 June 1857.

53. "Fourth of July," *Richmond Whig*, 5 July 1858.

54. "Gov. Pettus on Bunker Hill Monuments and Fourth of Julys," *Montgomery (AL) Weekly Advertiser*, 14 November 1860.

55. *Indiana State Sentinel*, 4 July 1859, quoted in Criblez, *Parading Patriotism*.

56. Mrs. Mary Jones to Hon. Charles C. Jones Jr., 3 January 1861, in *Children of Pride: A True Story of Georgia and the Civil War*, ed. Robert Manson Myers (New Haven: Yale University Press, 1972), 38.

57. Williams, "Intellectual Roots of the Lost Cause," 264–65.

58. Rubin, *Shattered Nation*, 90.

59. Ibid. 93.

60. Ibid., 20.

61. George C. Rable, *The Confederate Republic: A Revolution against Politics* (Chapel Hill: University of North Carolina Press, 1994), 46.

62. "Anniversaries of Independence," *Charleston Mercury*, 27 June 1861.

63. Paul Quigley, "Independence Day Dilemmas in the American South, 1848–1865," *Journal of Southern History* 75, no. 2 (2009): 258.

64. "Fourth of July" reprinted in *Alexandria Gazette*, 29 December 1860.

65. "Abolition of the Fourth of July," *Massachusetts Spy* (Worcester), 12 December 1860.

66. "Fourth of July at the Pee Dee," *Charleston Courier,* 13 July 1861.

67. Ibid.

68. Ibid.

69. "Fourth of July," *Eastern Clarion* (Paulding, MS), 12 July 1861.

70. "The Fourth of July at Shreveport," *New Orleans Daily True Delta,* 29 June 1861.

71. "The Fourth of July," *Augusta Daily Constitutionalist,* 29 June 1861.

72. "American; Yankees; Declaration," *Richmond Whig,* 17 June 1862.

73. "The Fourth of July at Nashville," *Charleston Courier,* 19 July 1862.

74. "The Fourth," *Edgefield (SC) Advertiser,* 3 July 1861.

75. Ibid.

76. Ibid.

77. "The Fall of Vicksburg," *Gold Hill (NV) Daily News,* 5 May 1864.

78. "Freedom and the Fourth of July," *Southern Illustrated News* (Richmond, VA), 20 June 1863.

79. "The Fourth of July," *Augusta Daily Constitutionalist,* 3 July 1864.

80. Grace Brown Elmore, *A Heritage of Woe: The Civil War Diary of Grace Brown Elmore* (Athens: University of Georgia Press, 1997), 118, 123.

2. CONTESTING THE SOUTHERN FOURTH OF JULY

1. Mat Boyd to Alexander Boyd, 7 July 1860, in Alexander Boyd Papers, Birmingham Public Library Department of Archives and Manuscripts, Birmingham, AL.

2. Passage of the Thirteenth Amendment to the Constitution in 1865 ended slavery forever, and the Fourteenth and Fifteenth Amendments (1868 and 1870, respectively) guaranteed full citizenship and voting rights for all (male) African Americans.

3. Blight, *Race and Reunion,* 31.

4. David Goldfield, *Still Fighting the Civil War: The American South and Southern History* (Baton Rouge: Louisiana State University Press, 2013), 6.

5. Downs, *After Appomattox,* 39.

6. Maier, *American Scripture,* 207.

7. Rubin, *Shattered Nation,* 243.

8. Quigley, "Independence Day Dilemmas," 263.

9. *Weekly Southern Intelligencer* (Austin, TX), 7 July 1865.

10. "Letter from Mobile," *New Orleans Tribune,* 8 July 1865.

11. Ibid.

12. Ibid.

13. "The Fourth of July at Washington," *Daily Constitutionalist* (Augusta, GA), 12 July 1865.

14. "Reports of Conditions and Operations," Records of the Assistant Commissioner for the State of South Carolina, Bureau of Refugees, Freedmen and Abandoned Lands,

1865–1870, National Archives Microfilm Publication M869, roll 34, http://www.freed-mensbureau.com/southcarolina/scoperations4.htm.

15. "The Fourth of July: The Meeting at the Mechanics' Institute," *New Orleans Tribune,* 6 July 1867.

16. Ibid.

17. "South Carolina: Celebration of the Fourth—Speeches—Masquerade Procession—The Legislature—Sunstroke," *New York Times,* 10 July 1868.

18. Ibid.

19. Ibid.

20. "The Fourth in the South: Comments of the Southern Press on the Day and Its Observance," *New York Times,* 11 July 1870.

21. "Fourth of July in the South," *Macon Telegraph,* 23 July 1869.

22. Ibid.

23. "No Fourth of July," *Flake's Bulletin* (Galveston, TX), 30 June 1866.

24. "Fourth of July," *Honey-Grove (TX) Enterprise,* 9 July 1870.

25. "The Fourth of July: Its Practical Destruction" reprinted in *Memphis Daily Avalanche,* 3 July 1866.

26. "The Fourth of July," *Richmond Whig,* 5 July 1870.

27. "The Great Day," *Dallas Weekly Herald,* 11 July 1874.

28. Eric Foner, *Reconstruction: America's Unfinished Revolution, 1863–1877* (New York: HarperCollins, 1988), 412.

29. Ibid., 417.

30. Michael Perman, *The Road to Redemption: Southern Politics, 1869–1879* (Chapel Hill: University of North Carolina Press, 1984), 67.

31. *A Pamphlet Containing the Full History of the Celebration of the Ninety-Ninth Anniversary of American Independence in Atlanta, Ga., July 4th, 1875,* compiled from the *Atlanta Daily Herald,* https://archive.org/details/pamphletcontainioostep. Cited hereafter as "*Pamphlet.*"

32. Ibid.

33. Harris, *Across the Bloody Chasm,* 71.

34. Wm. H. Felton, "The Coming Fourth," in *Pamphlet.*

35. Ibid.

36. Ibid.

37. "From Judge James Jackson," in *Pamphlet.*

38. Ibid.

39. Thomas Norwood, in *Pamphlet.*

40. "The Blessed Fourth: What Thomas Hardman, Jr. Has to Say on the Subject," in *Pamphlet.*

41. "Our Brevet Fourth," in *Pamphlet.*

42. "From the Hon. Robert Toombs," in *Pamphlet.*

43. Ibid.

44. "Hon. A. H. Chappell: His Letter on the Fourth," in *Pamphlet.*

45. Ibid.

46. John Bodnar, *Remaking America: Public Memory, Commemoration, and Patriotism in the Twentieth Century* (Princeton: Princeton University Press, 1992), 15.

47. Rubin, *Shattered Nation*, 161.

48. Zuczek, *State of Rebellion*, 15.

49. "Gov. Smith's Remarks," in *Pamphlet.*

50. "The Fourth of July: The Great Celebration in Atlanta," *Augusta Chronicle*, 6 July 1875.

51. "The Fourth," *Macon Weekly Telegraph*, 11 July 1875.

52. "Burying the Hatchet," *Charleston News & Courier*, 7 July 1875.

53. Ibid.

54. Ibid.

55. "The Fourth in Augusta: Vidette's Letter to the News and Courier," *Augusta Chronicle*, 11 July 1875.

56. Ibid.

57. "The Excursion to Augusta—'Vidette' Pleads Guilty and Throws Himself on the Mercy of the Court- Sentence Suspended," *Augusta Chronicle*, 13 July 1875.

58. "The Fourth in Augusta: Vidette's Letter to the News and Courier," *Augusta Chronicle*, 11 July 1875.

59. "The Glorious Fourth," *Arkansas Gazette* (Little Rock), 18 June 1875.

60. Ibid.

61. "Fourth of July and Its Observance in Little Rock—The Substitute Celebration Day," *Arkansas Gazette* (Little Rock), 6 July 1875.

62. "The Day We Do Not Celebrate," *New Orleans Daily Picayune*, 4 July 1875.

63. Ibid.

64. "New Orleans Bulletin," LSU Libraries, http://www.lib.lsu.edu/collections/digital/dlnp/newspaper-histories/new-orleans-bulletin.

65. "Then and Now," *New Orleans Bulletin*, 6 July 1875.

66. Ibid.

67. "Letter from Manassas," *Alexandria Gazette*, 7 July 1875.

68. "The Fourth of July," *Montgomery (AL) Weekly Advertiser*, 3 July 1875.

69. Ibid.

70. Ibid.

71. "Fourth of July," *Knoxville Whig*, 20 June 1866.

72. Ellis Merton Coulter, *William G. Brownlow: Fighting Parson of the Southern Highlands* (Chapel Hill: University of North Carolina Press, 1937), 312. The Dunning School of Reconstruction historiography was prominent through much of the first half of the twentieth century. Sympathetic to white southerners, it framed the whole enterprise as

a tragic mistake in which vengeful Radical Republicans exploited "ignorant" freedmen for political gain.

73. "Celebration of the Fourth," *Brownlow's Knoxville Whig*, 26 June 1867.

74. "Fourth of July at Harrison," *Knoxville Whig*, 11 July 1866.

75. Ibid.

76. Charles Vincent, *Black Legislators in Louisiana during Reconstruction* (Baton Rouge: Louisiana State University Press, 1976), 118.

77. "Fourth of July Oration of Hon. T. B. Stamps at Hahnville," *Weekly Louisianian* (New Orleans), 10 July 1875.

78. Ibid.

79. Ibid.

80. "Fourth of July at Shreveport," *New Orleans Republican*, 7 July 1875.

81. "The Fourth at Shreveport," *Weekly Louisianian* (New Orleans), 24 July 1875.

82. Clark, *Defining Moments*, 67.

83. Ibid., 68.

84. "The Fourth at Cheraw," *Charleston News-Courier*, 8 July 1875.

85. "The Fourth," *New Orleans Daily Picayune*, 6 July 1875.

86. "A Fourth of July Row," *Macon Telegraph*, 13 July 1875.

87. "The Fourth of July at Vicksburg," *New Orleans Republican*, 8 July 1875.

88. "Another Chapter of Blood at Vicksburg," *Christian Recorder*, 22 July 1875.

89. "Fourth of July at Vicksburg."

90. Ibid.

91. "Another Chapter of Blood at Vicksburg."

92. Ibid.

93. "Fourth of July at Vicksburg."

94. Ibid.

95. Harris, *Day of the Carpetbagger*, 49. In the 1875 election, Mississippi Democrats staged a campaign of organized violence and intimidation in order to achieve "redemption," a model that would be used as a template by Democrats in other southern states. See 650–90.

96. "The Fourth," *Memphis Daily Appeal*, 6 July 1875.

97. Ibid.

98. Ibid.

99. Ibid.

100. "Southern Independence: Fourth of July at Memphis," *National Republican* (Washington, DC), 10 July 1875.

101. Ibid.

102. Ibid.

103. Downs, *After Appomattox*, 2.

104. Bodnar, *Remaking America*, 15.

105. Michael A. Ross, "The Commemoration of Robert E. Lee's Death and the Obstruction of Reconstruction in New Orleans," *Civil War History* 51, no. 2 (2005): 145.

106. Ibid., 150.

107. Bodnar, Remaking America, 13.

108. Susanna Michele Lee, "Reconciliation in Reconstruction Virginia," in *Crucible of Civil War: Virginia from Secession to Commemoration*, edited by Edward L. Ayers, Gary W. Gallagher, and Andrew J. Torget (Charlottesville: University of Virginia Press, 2006), 190.

109. Paul Gaston, *The New South Creed: A Study in Southern Mythmaking* (New York: Knopf, 1970), 96.

3. HUMBUG OR OPPORTUNITY

1. "Getting Ready in Time," *Macon Weekly Telegraph,* 30 July 1869.

2. A. H. Keller, "The Centennial," *North Alabamian* (Tuscumbia), 28 January 1874, clipping, United States Centennial Commission Papers, Philadelphia City Archives, Philadelphia. Cited hereafter as USCCP.

3. Robert Rydell, *All the World's a Fair: Visions of Empire at American International Expositions, 1876–1916* (Chicago: University of Chicago Press, 1987), 329.

4. Paul Greenhalgh, *Ephemeral Vistas: The Expositions Universelles, Great Exhibitions, and World's Fairs, 1851–1939* (Manchester: Manchester University Press, 1988), 1.

5. James D. McCabe, *The Illustrated History of the Centennial Exhibition* (Philadelphia: National Publishing Co., 1876), 197.

6. Ibid., 198.

7. Ibid., 733.

8. "The Centennial International Exhibition. An Address by the Centennial Commission," *Cincinnati Daily Gazette,* 4 December 1872.

9. Ibid.

10. William M. Byrd to Lewis Waln Smith, 28 April 1873, USCCP.

11. Ibid.

12. *The United States Centennial Commission: An Address* (Philadelphia: Baird & King, 1874), 22.

13. Ibid.

14. *Journal of the Proceedings of the United States Centennial Commission at Philadelphia, 1872* (Philadelphia: Markley & Sons, 1872), 153.

15. Ibid.

16. Ibid. Byrd did not live to see the opening of the exhibition he cared so deeply about; he was killed in a train accident in 1874.

17. *United States Centennial Almanac* (Philadelphia: Baird & King, 1874), 31.

18. State Correspondence, USCCP. See chapter 4 for a detailed discussion of William Parsons's stormy tenure on the Centennial Commission.

19. *Journal of the Proceedings of the United States Centennial Commission at Philadelphia, 1872* (Philadelphia: Markley & Sons, 1872), 150.

20. Reprinted in *Little Rock (AR) Morning Republican,* 11 September 1873.

21. Raphael Semmes, "Alabama at the Centennial: The Pirate of the 'Alabama' Denounces the Idea of His State Being Represented at the 'Radical Love-Feast'—A Typical Letter," *Mobile Register,* undated clipping, USCCP scrapbook.

22. Ibid.

23. "A Man Who Was Never Reconstructed," *San Francisco Bulletin,* 17 June 1875.

24. "The Centennial," *Augusta Chronicle and Sentinel,* 11 November 1873.

25. "Letter from Montgomery," *Mobile Daily Register,* 19 March 1875.

26. Ibid.

27. Ibid.

28. "A Quid Pro Quo," *Augusta Chronicle and Sentinel,* 16 May 1874.

29. "The Centennial Celebration," from the *Religious Herald,* reprinted in the *Richmond Whig,* 15 May 1874.

30. The Centennial Oath," *Arkansas Gazette* (Little Rock), 28 May 1875.

31. "The Centennial Oath," *New Orleans Daily Picayune,* 26 May 1875.

32. "The South and the Centennial Oath," *New Orleans Daily Picayune,* 27 May 1875.

33. Ibid.

34. A. H. Keller, "The Centennial," *North Alabamian* (Tuscumbia), 28 January 1874, clipping in USCCP scrapbook. Keller was the father of the renowned deaf and blind socialist writer and activist Helen Keller (1880–1968).

35. Ibid.

36. Ibid.

37. "The Centennial Exposition," quoted in *Macon Weekly Telegraph,* 20 April 1875.

38. "The Centennial," *Southern Planter & Farmer* (Richmond), May 1876.

39. Ibid.

40. "Southern Votes Wanted," *Atlanta Constitution,* reprinted in *Georgia Weekly Telegraph and Journal & Messenger* (Macon), 28 April 1874.

41. "The Centennial Humbug," *Hinds County Gazette* (Raymond, MS), 24 May 1876.

42. François Furstenburg, "What History Teaches Us about the Welfare State," *Washington Post,* 1 July 2011.

43. McCabe, *Illustrated History of the Centennial Exhibition,* 235.

44. "The Centennial," *Scribner's Monthly* (January 1876).

45. "The Centennial Commission," *Richmond Whig,* 31 May 1872.

46. Ibid.

47. Rydell, *All the World's a Fair,* 18.

48. Ibid.

49. Gross and Snyder, *Philadelphia's 1876 Centennial Exhibition*, 7.

50. Spillman, *Nation and Commemoration*, 80.

51. "The Centennial Exposition: Sale of Concessions," *Georgia Weekly Telegraph and Journal & Messenger* (Macon), 29 February 1876.

52. "The Centennial: A Practical View by a Practical Man," *Georgia Weekly Telegraph and Georgia Journal & Messenger* (Macon), 7 November 1876.

53. Gross and Snyder, *Philadelphia's Centennial Exhibition*, 25.

54. "Alabama Legislature, Centennial Exposition," *Montgomery Advertiser*, 17 March 1875.

55. "Letter from New York," *Alexandria Gazette & Virginia Advertiser*, 17 January 1876.

56. "About the *Alexandria Gazette*," Chronicling America, Library of Congress online, http://chroniclingamerica.loc.gov/lccn/sn85025007/.

57. "The Centennial Appropriation," *Georgia Weekly Telegraph and Journal & Messenger*, 25 January 1876.

58. Ibid.

59. "Georgia and the Centennial," *Macon Telegraph and Journal & Messenger*, 18 November 1873.

60. Ibid.

61. "The Centennial," *Augusta Chronicle and Sentinel*, 11 November 1873.

62. State Correspondence, USCCP.

63. Frederick Holliday to Alfred Goshorn, 17 June 1876, USCCP. Holliday demonstrated, in a postscript, that not all white southerners were clinging to the past at this point, describing Jefferson Davis as an "item of history."

64. *Journal of the Senate of the State of Alabama 1876*, 17.

65. "The Centennial," *Richmond Enquirer*, 17 February 1875.

66. Ibid.

67. Ibid. See also *Galveston Daily News*, 14 April 1875: "No Southern state has anything to gain by standing sullenly aloof from the Centennial. Texas is entitled to her share in the political legacy of 1876."

68. "July 4, 1876: The Centennial Movement Makes a Good Start in Tennessee," *Nashville Union and American*, 13 May 1875.

69. Ibid.

70. "Centennial Morbidity," *Mobile Register*, 19 January 1876.

71. "The S.A. Herald and the Centennial," *San Antonio Express*, 9 August 1875.

72. Ibid.

73. George E. Dodge to A. T. Goshorn, 20 August 1875, State Correspondence, US-CCP. The state did, in fact, appropriate five thousand dollars for a building in Fairmount Park, one of only two southern states to do so. Nonetheless, on 8 April 1876, the *Arkan-*

sas Gazette, commenting shortly before the fair opened, remarked that despite Dodge's "best exertions," a "dead sea of public apathy" prevailed that would rob Arkansas of the chance to "show to the whole world the capacities of our young state."

74. Joint Resolution of the Louisiana General Assembly, No. 99, 21 March 1874, USCCP.

75. Ibid.

76. H. Bonzano to Alfred Goshorn, 7 August 1875, USCCP.

77. J. L. Power to Alfred Goshorn, 13 October 1875, USCCP.

78. J. L. Power to Alfred Goshorn, 18 December 1875, USCCP.

79. James B. Lloyd, *Lives of Mississippi Authors, 1817–1967* (Jackson: University Press of Mississippi, 1981), 376.

80. Harris, *Day of the Carpetbagger,* 390.

81. Ibid., 388.

82. O'Leary, *To Die For,* 25.

83. Melinda Lawson, *Patriot Fires: Forging a New Nationalism in the Civil War North* (Lawrence: University Press of Kansas, 2002), 3.

84. "The South Snubs the Centennial," *Milwaukee Sentinel,* 17 October 1876.

85. "1776 and 1876," *Memphis Daily Appeal,* 7 June 1873.

86. Ibid.

87. "The Centennial," *South-Western-Telegram* (Shreveport, LA), 1 September 1875, clipping, USCCP scrapbook.

88. "The Centennial Exhibition: Should the South Be Represented?" *Columbus (GA) Daily Times,* 7 November 1875.

89. *Hot Springs Daily Telegraph,* 5 February 1875, clipping, USCCP scrapbook.

90. J. T. Bernard, "The Centennial Exhibition," *Tallahassee Sentinel,* 15 January 1876, clipping, USCCP scrapbook.

91. "Centennial," *Galveston News,* 2 September 1875.

92. Lewis B. Lesley, "A Southern Transcontinental Railroad into California: Texas Pacific vs. Southern Pacific, 1865–1885," *Pacific Historical Review* 5, no. 1 (March 1936): 53.

93. T. Lloyd Benson and Trina Rossman, "Re-Assessing Tom Scott: The Railroad Prince," paper prepared for the Mid-American Conference on History, Furman University, 16 September 1995, http://eweb.furman.edu/~benson/col-tom.html.

94. "The Proposed Constitution, the Railroad Ring, the Radical Party: Why?" *Austin (TX) Weekly Democratic Statesman,* 27 January 1876.

95. "How Tom Scott Went through the Constitutional Convention," *Austin (TX) Weekly Democratic Statesman,* 9 December 1875.

96. *Austin (TX) Weekly Democratic Statesman,* 24 February 1876.

97. Ibid.

98. *Austin (TX) Weekly Democratic Statesman,* 3 February 1876.

99. Ibid.

100. "Texas and the Centennial," *Dallas Daily Herald,* 12 September 1875.

101. Mary Frances Cordato, "Toward a New Century: Women and the Philadelphia Centennial Exhibition, 1876," *Pennsylvania Magazine of History and Biography* 17, no. 1 (1983): 116.

102. "An Appeal for the Centennial," in *The Second Annual Report of the Women's Centennial Executive Committee, March 1875,* 26, Historic Society of Pennsylvania, Philadelphia. Cited hereafter as HSP.

103. Bonner, *Mastering America,* 198.

104. Ibid., 204.

105. Ibid., 198.

106. Caroline Janney, *Burying the Dead but Not the Past* (Chapel Hill: University of North Carolina Press, 2008), 88.

107. Janney, *Remembering the Civil War,* 7.

108. Elizabeth Duane Gillespie to Ellen Call Long, 3 December 1874, Call Family Papers, Florida Memory, Division of Library and Information Services, Florida Department of State https://www.floridamemory.com/items/show/180897.

109. Ellen Call Long, "An Appeal to the Women of Florida," in The Second Annual Report of the Women's Centennial Executive Committee (Philadelphia: Thomas S. Dando Steam Power Printer, 1875), 18, HSP.

110. Ibid., 19.

111. Ibid.

112. Ibid., 20.

113. Ibid.

114. Ibid.

115. Ida Wood to Ellen Call Long, 8 April 1872, Call Family Papers, www.floridamemory.com/items/show/180888?id=2.

116. E. A. Perry to Ellen Call Long, 15 December 1875, Call Family Papers, https://www.floridamemory.com/items/show/180923. I believe this to be Edward Aylesworth Perry, Confederate officer and future Democratic governor of Florida.

117. Mrs. E. White to Ellen Call Long, 19 November 1875, Call Family Papers, https://www.floridamemory.com/items/show/180922.

118. Harriet Girardeau to Ellen Call Long, 20 December 1874, Call Family Papers, https://www.floridamemory.com/items/show/180901.

119. Joseph B. Browne to Ellen Call Long, 1 December 1874, Call Family Papers, https://www.floridamemory.com/items/show/180896.

120. Ibid.

121. Joseph B. Browne to Ellen Call Long, 13 January 1876, Call Family Papers, https://www.floridamemory.com/items/show/180925.

122. Jane Stockton to Ellen Call Long, 12 April 1876, Call Family Papers, https://www.floridamemory.com/items/show/180938. Anne Randall to Long, Call Family Papers, https://www.floridamemory.com/items/show/180929.

123. Harrison Reed to Ellen Call Long 15 December 1875, Call Family Papers, https://www.floridamemory.com/items/show/180924.

124. Ellen Call Long, *A History of the Memorial Association Founded in Tallahassee after the Late Civil War*, MS, Call Family Papers, https://www.floridamemory.com/items/show/180838?id=6. Emphasis mine.

125. Ellen Call Long to Carrie Brevard, undated, Brevard Family Papers, Florida Memory, Division of Library and Information Services, Florida Department of State, https://www.floridamemory.com/items/show/181438?id=2.

126. Tracy J. Revels, *Grander in Her Daughters: Florida's Women during the Civil War* (Columbia: University of South Carolina Press, 2004), 145.

127. "Centennial," *Dallas Weekly Herald*, 29 May 1875.

128. "Editorial Notes," *Dallas Weekly Herald*, 29 May 1875.

129. *Final Report of the Women's Centennial Executive Committee: March 22, 1877*, 81, HSP.

130. Ibid.

131. "The Centennial: A Discouraging Outlook for the Women of Tennessee," *Chattanooga Daily Times*, 11 March 1876.

132. Ibid.

133. Kammen, *Mystic Chords of Memory*, 255, 188.

134. *Final Report of the Women's Centennial Executive Committee: March 22, 1877*, 80–81.

135. Ibid.

136. Janney, *Remembering the Civil War*, 374.

137. Ibid.

138. Ibid.

139. Timothy B. Smith, *Mississippi in the Civil War: The Home Front* (Jackson: University Press of Mississippi, 2010), 128.

140. "The First Centennial Tea Party," *Memphis Daily Appeal*, 24 August 1875. Interestingly, this report contained a reminder to the ladies of Memphis that they were invited to a meeting to organize Centennial fundraising at the home of Mrs. Jefferson Davis.

141. Ibid.

142. Emma Westcott to Ellen Call Long, 3 February 1876, Call Family Papers, https://www.floridamemory.com/items/show/180928?id=2.

143. *Final Report of the Women's Centennial Executive Committee: March 22, 1877*, 8.

144. John McKee Barr, *Loathing Lincoln: An American Tradition from the Civil War to the Present* (Baton Rouge: Louisiana State University Press, 2014), 37.

145. See especially Rubin, *Shattered Nation*, chapter 7, "Gender and Southern Identity."

146. Janney, *Remembering the Civil War*, 9.

147. The only two southern women on the committee apart from those discussed here were Mattie Heck of North Carolina, whose husband, Jonathan, was described as "one of the men who built the New South and was extraordinarily successful in promoting the industrial and agricultural development of the state" (*Dictionary of North Carolina Biography* [Chapel Hill: University of North Carolina Press, 1988], 3:93); and Maria Ludeling of Louisiana, wife of that state's much excoriated (in the Democratic press) Republican chief justice.

148. *Journal of the Proceedings of the United States Centennial Commission, Sixth Session* (Philadelphia: Markley & Sons, 1875), 133–34.

149. Clark, *Defining Moments*, 130.

150. Craig Bruce Smith, "Claiming the Centennial: The American Revolution's Blood and Spirit in Boston, 1870–1876," *Massachusetts Historical Review* 15 (2013): 13.

151. "The Centennial," *Christian Recorder*, 16 March 1872.

152. Foner, "Black Participation in the Centennial of 1876," 286.

153. "Why Can't We Do It?" *Christian Recorder*, 5 March 1874.

154. Ibid.

155. Ibid.

156. "That Statue to Allen," *Christian Recorder*, 13 August 1874.

157. "Our History," African Methodist Episcopal Church official website, https://www.ame-church.com/our-church/our-history/.

158. Kachun, "Before the Eyes of All Nations," 311.

159. Mitch Kachun, "The Shaping of a Public Biography: Richard Allen and the AME Church," in *Black Lives: Essays in African American Biography*, ed. James L. Conyers (London: Routledge, 2015), 55.

160. *Christian Recorder*, 2 December 1874.

161. "Color at the Centennial," *Springfield Republican*, 5 May 1873.

162. Ibid.

163. Foner, "Black Participation in the Centennial of 1876," 287.

164. "A Tempest in a Teapot," *Camden Democrat*, 26 April 1873.

165. Ibid.

166. "For the Centennial," *San Francisco Weekly Alta*, 5 June 1875.

167. "The Centennial Management," *Los Angeles Herald*, 17 May 1874.

168. 43 Cong. Rec. H 250 (1874) (Rep. Josiah Walls), 250.

169. Ibid.,251.

170. Ibid., 252.

171. Ibid.

172. "Moral Insensibility," undated clipping, *Louisianian*, USCCP scrapbook.

173. Ibid.

4. THE CENTENNIAL AND THE POLITICS OF REPRESENTATION

1. *Brenham (TX) Banner,* 17 September 1875.

2. Paul Avrich, *The Haymarket Tragedy* (Princeton: Princeton University Press, 1984), 460.

3. Ibid.

4. Anne J. Bailey, "William Henry Parsons," in *The Handbook of Texas Online,* https://www.tshaonline.org/handbook/entries/parsons-william-henry. Some contemporary sources indicate that Parsons went to Brazil rather than Honduras.

5. Ernest William Winkler, *Platforms of Political Parties in Texas* (1916; reprint, London: Forgotten Books, 2013), 106.

6. Carl H. Moneyhon, "Edmund Jackson Davis," in *The Handbook of Texas Online,* http://www.tshaonline.org/handbook/online/articles/fda37.

7. Carl H. Moneyhon, *Republicanism in Reconstruction Texas* (College Station: Texas A&M University Press, 2001), xiii, xiv.

8. Bailey, "William Henry Parsons."

9. "Mr. William H. Parsons," *Dallas Daily Herald,* 1 September 1875.

10. "Gen. W. H. Parsons," *Waco Register,* 7 August 1876.

11. Carl Moneyhon, *Texas after the Civil War: The Struggle of Reconstruction* (College Station: Texas A&M University Press, 2007), 127.

12. Avrich, *Haymarket Tragedy,* 9.

13. Ibid., 46.

14. Ibid.

15. "Grand Army of the Republic in Texas," *Galveston Tri-Weekly News,* 8 March 1872.

16. Ibid.

17. Nancy Beck Young, "Democratic Party," in *The Handbook of Texas Online,* https://www.tshaonline.org/handbook/online/articles/wad01.

18. John W. Payne Jr., "Richard Coke," in *The Handbook of Texas Online,* https://www.tshaonline.org/handbook/online/articles/fco15.

19. James Marten, *Texas Divided: Loyalty and Dissent in the Lone Star State, 1856–1874* (Lexington: University Press of Kentucky, 1990), 145.

20. Curtis Bishop, "Coke-Davis Controversy," in *The Handbook of Texas Online,* http://www.tshaonline.org/handbook/online/articles/mqc01.

21. Carl H. Moneyhon, *Edmund Davis of Texas: Civil War General, Reconstruction Leader, Republican Governor* (Fort Worth: TCU Press, 2010), 223.

22. Marten, *Texas Divided,* 145.

23. Alwyn Barr, *Reconstruction to Reform: Texas Politics, 1876–1906* (Austin: University of Texas Press, 1971), 9.

24. "Our Centennial Commissioner," *Galveston Daily News,* 5 August 1875.

25. "Houston Local Items," *Galveston Daily News,* 24 July 1875.

26. John Y. Simon, ed., *The Papers of Ulysses S. Grant*, 32 vols. (Carbondale: Southern Illinois University Press, 1967), 26:44. Cited hereafter as *USG Papers*.

27. "Mr. William H. Parsons," *Dallas Daily Herald*, 1 September 1875.

28. Ibid.

29. "Houston Local Items," *Galveston Daily News*, 24 July 1875.

30. *Dallas Weekly Herald*, 17 July 1875.

31. *Brenham Banner*, 8 October 1875.

32. John Welsh to Ashbel Smith, 4 August 1875, Ashbel Smith Papers, Dolph Briscoe Center for American History, University of Texas at Austin. Cited hereafter as DBCAH.

33. Ibid. Smith's reply is as yet unknown, but he did write to former Tennessee governor John Brown, then a vice president of the Texas & Pacific Railroad, requesting a free ticket to Philadelphia for the exhibition. Ashbel Smith to John C. Brown, 14 August 1876, Smith Papers, DBCAH.

34. John Chew, "The International Exhibition," *Galveston Daily News*, 14 October 1875.

35. Richard Coke to Alfred Goshorn, 31 August 1875, Coke Gubernatorial Papers, Archives Division, Texas State Library, Austin.

36. "The 'Bloody Shirt' in the South," *Marshall (TX) Tri-Weekly Herald*, 20 April 1876.

37. Ibid.

38. "Gen. Parsons and the Centennial," *Austin Evening News*, 11 August 1875.

39. "Centennial," *Galveston Daily News*, 2 September 1875.

40. Hobart Huson, "Alfred Marmaduke Hobby," in *The Handbook of Texas Online*, https://tshaonline.org/handbook/online/articles/fho02.

41. *USG Papers*, 26:44.

42. Ibid.

43. "Texas and the Centennial," *Galveston Daily News*, 6 April 1876.

44. "Alfred M. Hobby," *New York Graphic*, 12 April 1876.

45. "Texas and the Centennial."

46. "Texas Centennial: State Commissioner A. M. Hobby Interviewed," *Galveston Daily News*, 20 April 1876.

47. Ibid.

48. "The South at Philadelphia," reprinted in *Nashville Union and American*, 21 May 1875.

49. W. H. Parsons, "The Councils of Robert E. Lee and Jefferson Davis," *Memphis Appeal*, 23 May 1875.

50. "Letter from Gen. Parsons," *Waco Register*, 21 August 1875.

51. "Our Centennial Commissioners," *San Antonio Daily Express*, 5 October 1875.

52. "From Our Centennial Commissioner," *Waco Daily Examiner*, 23 April 1876.

53. *Austin Weekly Democratic Statesman*, 23 March 1876.

54. John C. Chew, "The International Exhibition," *Galveston Daily News*, 14 October 1875.

55. John C. Chew, "Texas and the Centennial," *Galveston Daily News*, 23 September 1875.

56. "Editorial Notes," *Austin Weekly Democratic Statesman*, 6 April 1876.

57. *USG Papers*, 26:45.

58. "Pettiness," *National Republican* (Washington, DC), 2 May 1876.

59. Coke to Hobby, 14 March 1876, reprinted in "Texas Centennial Commissioners," *Galveston Daily News*, 17 March 1876.

60. "Pettiness," *National Republican* (Washington, DC), 2 May 1876.

61. Patrick G. Williams, *Beyond Redemption: Texas Democrats after Reconstruction* (College Station: Texas A&M University Press, 2007), location 193 of 3262, Kindle.

62. *Denison Daily News*, 9 April 1876. This piece of gossip notwithstanding, Parsons was at least popular enough with his fellow commissioners to have been elected to the National Centennial Commission's Executive Committee during its second session in 1873 and then, three years later, to a three-man committee overseeing the exhibition's closing ceremonies.

63. Ibid.

64. "Gen. William Gurney," *New York Times*, 3 February 1879.

65. David Dangerfield, "Dangerfield on Ginsberg, 'Moses of South Carolina: A Jewish Scalawag during Radical Reconstruction,'" Humanities and Social Science Online, https://networks.h-net.org/node/11282/reviews/11352/dangerfield-ginsberg-moses-south-carolina-jewish-scalawag-during.

66. "South Carolina," *Hartford Courant*, 8 July 1875.

67. "South Carolina and the Centennial," *Boston Daily Advertiser*, 12 July 1875.

68. "South Carolina at the Centennial," *Columbia (SC) Daily Phoenix*, 1 July 1875.

69. Ibid.

70. "Well Answered-Bravo! Woodward," *Macon Weekly Telegraph*, 6 July 1875.

71. "The State and the Centennial," *Charleston News &Courier*, 10 November 1875, clipping, USCCP scrapbook.

72. Ibid.

73. "The Centennial: Shall South Carolina Be Represented?" *Abbeville Press and Banner*, 7 July 1875.

74. "The Fourth of July," *Fairfield Herald* (Winnsboro, SC), 7 July 1875.

75. "No Place in the Picture," *Fairfield Herald* (Winnsboro, SC), 7 July 1875.

76. Ibid.

77. *USG Papers*, 26:45.

78. Ibid.

79. Harris, *Day of the Carpetbagger*, 468.

80. Ibid., 619.

81. "A Personal Card," *Jackson (MS) Weekly Clarion*, 13 April 1871.

82. *Hinds County Gazette* (Raymond, MS), 31 May 1876.

83. *New Orleans Times-Picayune,* 12 February 1875.

84. *Louisiana Democrat* (Alexandria), 10 May 1876.

85. *New Orleans Times,* 30 November 1876.

86. "The Centennial: The Speeches in Congress," *Austin Weekly Democratic States-man,* 24 February 1876.

87. "The Philadelphia Centennial Exposition," *Austin Weekly Democratic Statesman,* 3 February 1876.

88. "The Centennial Exposition," *San Antonio Daily Herald,* 10 May 1876.

89. State Correspondence, USCCP. Parsons's message read: "We assume that the celebration of the 100th Anniversary of American Independence is neither a sectional nor a party question, but one that should enlist the sympathy, excite the patriotism and ensure the cooperation of all sections and all parties of our common country."

90. "The Country's Worst Enemies," *Austin Weekly Democratic Statesman,* 13 May 1875.

91. Adam Fairclough, "'Scalawags,' Southern Honor, and the Lost Cause: Explaining the Fatal Encounter of James H. Cosgrove and Edward L. Pierson," *Journal of Southern History* 77, no. 4 (2011): 805.

5. WHITE SOUTHERNERS AND AFRICAN AMERICANS AT THE 1876 CENTENNIAL

1. "The Differences," *Holly Springs (MS) South,* 30 March 1876.

2. Kammen, *Mystic Chords of Memory,* 65.

3. "Lecture by Capt. Chas. P. Jones," *Pulaski (TN) Citizen,* 9 November 1876.

4. "Rev. Stoddert," in *Columbia (TN) Herald and Mail,* 18 August 1876.

5. "Ho! For the Centennial," *Columbia (TN) Herald and Mail,* 18 August 1876.

6. "Around Town," *Columbia (TN) Herald and Mail,* 18 August 1876.

7. "From Philadelphia," *Arkansas Gazette* (Little Rock), 8 April 1876.

8. "Centennial Notes," *Richmond Enquirer,* 13 May 1876.

9. "Local Brevities," *Dallas Daily Herald,* 18 June 1876.

10. "The Centennial Idiot," *Chicago Tribune,* 12 June 1876. Snodgrass's story was picked up by several other newspapers around the country, most of them derisory in tone.

11. Eliza Adams Robinson to Alice Marshall, 17 September 1876, Williams Family Papers, Virginia Historical Society, Richmond.

12. "Centennial," *Atlanta Weekly Constitution,* 11 July 1876.

13. "Centennial Notes: A Richmond Man's Observations at the Great Exhibition," *Richmond Enquirer,* 4 June 1876.

14. John S. Henderson to "Mother," 15 September 1876, John S. Henderson Papers, Southern Historical Collection, Wilson Library, University of North Carolina at Chapel Hill. Cited hereafter as SHC.

15. Harry Moss, "Harry Moss at the Centennial," *New Orleans Daily Picayune,* 25 June 1876.

16. "Centennial Failure," *Mobile Register,* 21 May 1876.

17. "Summering at Home," *Mobile Register,* 14 May 1876.

18. *Hinds County Gazette* (Raymond, MS), 14 June 1876.

19. Ibid., 24 May 1876.

20. "Centennial Notes," *Jackson (MS) Weekly Clarion,* 3 May 1876.

21. John S. Henderson to Elizabeth Henderson, 2 July 1876, John S. Henderson Papers, SHC.

22. *Jackson (MS) Weekly Clarion,* 16 August 1876. *Pennon* is an archaic form of *pennant.*

23. Unknown to "Dear Aunt," 2 December 1876, Larkin Newby Papers, SHC.

24. Ibid.

25. "The Insult to the South," *Bristol (TN and VA) News,* 23 May 1876.

26. Ibid.

27. Ibid.

28. Ibid.

29. "Centennial Notes: A Richmond Man's Observations at the Great Exhibition," *Richmond Enquirer,* 4 June 1876.

30. "Jottings by the Way," *New Orleans Daily Picayune,* 13 August 1876.

31. Ibid. "Cousin Nourma" prefaced these comments with a discussion of "the Radical political junta" and its alleged plans to use bayonets to ensure the Republicans carried southern states in the fall election, demonstrating again the intersection of politics and Centennial.

32. "Centennial Chat," *Galveston News,* 4 June 1876.

33. Gold, *Unfinished Exhibition,* 121–23.

34. Susanna Gold, "Fighting It Over Again: The Battle of Gettysburg at the 1876 Centennial Exhibition," *Civil War History* 54, no. 3 (2008): 281.

35. Gold, "Fighting It Over Again," 282–84.

36. "Centennial Chat: Observations on the Exhibition by a Galvestonian," *Galveston News,* 6 June 1876.

37. "Centennial Failure," *Mobile Register,* 21 May 1876.

38. "Centennial Correspondence Number 9," *Bristol (TN and VA) News,* 30 January 1877.

39. "Centennial Notes: A Richmond Man's Observations at the Great Exhibition," *Richmond Enquirer,* 4 June 1876.

40. Undated clipping enclosed with Hillyer letter, George Hillyer to Alfred Goshorn, 4 August 1876, USCCP.

41. George Hillyer to Alfred Goshorn, 4 August 1876, USCCP.

42. John Sartain to Alfred Goshorn, 8 August 1876, USCCP.

43. Gold, "Fighting It Over Again," 285.

44. Kachun, "Before the Eyes of All Nations," 314.

45. Stephen Salisbury, "Homecoming for a Piece of History," *Philadelphia Inquirer*, 11 June 2010.

46. Kachun, "Before the Eyes of All Nations," 316.

47. Andrew Chambers to Alfred Goshorn, 8 June 1876, USCCP.

48. Foner, "Black Participation in the Centennial of 1876," 283.

49. "The Allen Monument a Success!" *Christian Recorder*, 7 September 1876.

50. Ibid.

51. Ibid.

52. "Destruction of the Allen Monument," *Christian Recorder*, 5 October 1876.

53. Salisbury, "Homecoming for a Piece of History."

54. Ibid.

55. "No Redeeming Feature of the Exhibition for the Negro," *Alexandria (VA) People's Advocate*, 8 June 1876.

56. Ibid.

57. "Centennial–Negro Mechanism–Death of Cleopatra–Negro Education," *Alexandria (VA) People's Advocate*, 22 July 1876.

58. Ibid.

59. "No Nigger Need Apply," *Atlanta Weekly Constitution*, 23 May 1876.

60. Ibid.

61. "Centennial," *Atlanta Weekly Constitution*, 11 July 1876.

62. Theodore Bryant Kingsbury, *The International Exhibition Guide for the Southern States: The Only Guide-book Specially Suited to the Southern Visitor* (Raleigh: Fulgham, 1876), 5.

63. Kingsbury, *International Exhibition Guide for the Southern States*, 40.

64. Rydell, *All the World's a Fair*, 28.

65. McCabe, *Illustrated History of the Centennial Exhibition*, 695. Susanna Gold has cited a contemporary Italian account that claims that the Grand Southern Restaurant was the site of voter fraud, with white Democrats manipulating or defrauding Black men into swearing allegiance to the Democratic Party—another intersection of politics and the Centennial. See Gold, *Unfinished Exhibition*, 144.

66. Christopher Hayashida-Knight, "Philadelphia Plays Dixie: Accommodating the South at the 1876 Centennial," Conference paper, Mid-Atlantic Popular and American Culture Conference, Philadelphia, 3 November 2011.

67. Ibid.

68. "Colored Men and the Centennial," *Chicago Inter-Ocean*, 25 May 1876.

69. Ibid.

70. *Chicago Inter-Ocean*, 27 May 1876. Philip Foner has pointed out that there is no evidence of any Black employment in the construction of the Centennial grounds at

a time when the Black jobless rate in Philadelphia approached 70 percent. See Foner, "Black Participation in the Centennial of 1876," 288. More recently, undergraduate student Hope Hancock has used contemporary images from *Frank Leslie's Centennial Register* that do illustrate Black men working on construction of the exhibition as a corrective to Foner's argument. However, it seems clear that any Black employment, before or after the exhibition opened, was minimal. See Hope Hancock, "The 1876 Centennial Exposed: How Souvenir Publications Reveal Contrasting Attitudes of Race and Gender in the Post-Bellum United States," *Mellon Scholars' Works*, 2 March 2014, https://digitalcommons.hope.edu/cgi/viewcontent.cgi?article=1000&context=mellon.

71. "Ohio Day," *Cincinnati Daily Times*, 26 October 1876.

72. "Our Empire State," *Galveston Daily News*, 12 September 1876.

73. Ibid.

74. "Gov. Kemper's Letter on the Centennial," *Alexandria Gazette*, 10 October 1876.

75. Ibid.

76. Ibid. While Virginia had no official presence at Fairmount Park, there was a "Virginia House" on the exhibition grounds, erected at the expense of a private citizen, Edwin G. Booth. Booth was a native Virginian married to a Pennsylvania woman and residing in Philadelphia.

77. *New Hampshire Sentinel* (Keene), 19 October 1876.

78. "Virginia and the Centennial," *New York Tribune*, 12 October 1876.

79. "Centennial Reflections," *New Orleans Times*, 21 October 1876.

80. "Solid South: Shot-Gun Policy in South Carolina: Rabid Rebels on the Stump," *Cincinnati Daily Gazette*, 14 October 1876.

81. "Southern Day at the Centennial," *Frank Leslie's Illustrated Newspaper*, 4 November 1876.

82. "The Centennial Southern Day: The Solid South at Philadelphia," *New York Times*, 20 October 1876.

83. "The Exhibition: Virginia, Maryland and Delaware at the Great Show," *New York Herald*, 20 October 1876.

84. "The Centennial Southern Day: The Solid South at Philadelphia," *New York Times*, 20 October 1876.

85. See "The Tournament," Wilmington (DE) *Daily Gazette*, 20 October 1876; "Telegraphic Briefs," *Memphis Daily Appeal*, 20 October 1876.

86. "Exhibition: Virginia, Maryland and Delaware at the Great Show."

87. K. Stephen Prince, "The Burnt District: Making Sense of Ruins in the Postwar South," in *The World the Civil War Made: The Steven and Janice Brose Lectures in the Civil War Era*, ed. Gregory P. Downs and Kate Masur (Chapel Hill: University of North Carolina Press, 2015), 113.

88. Ibid.

89. "Centennial Successes," *New York Graphic*, 20 October 1876.

90. Ibid.

91. Ibid.

92. William Dean Howells, "A Sennight of the Centennial," *Atlantic Monthly,* July 1876.

93. Ibid. The white Mississippian Howells mentioned was J. W. Langley, whom the *Vicksburg Herald,* 30 May 1876, described as the Mississippi House's "courteous superintendent . . . constantly besieged by sight seekers, among whom the fair sex predominate." His Black colleague was Tazwell Jones, who, though answering "some ten thousand questions a day," remained as "serene as a huckleberry bush."

94. "The Centennial: A Practical View by a Practical Man," *Georgia Weekly Telegraph and Georgia Journal & Messenger* (Macon), 7 November 1876.

95. "Centennial Reflections," *New Orleans Times,* 21 October 1876.

96. Ibid.

97. Paul F. Boller Jr., *Presidential Campaigns* (New York: Oxford University Press, 1985), 133–37.

98. "Centennial: A Practical View by a Practical Man."

99. *Fayetteville Observer,* 18 May 1876.

100. "Local," *Fayetteville Observer,* 6 October 1876.

101. "Our Centennial Letter," *Cleveland (TN) Weekly Herald,* 13 October 1876.

102. "Letter from Philadelphia," *Sumter Weekly Republican* (Americus, GA), 6 October 1876.

103. Ibid.

104. "Centennial Correspondence Number 6," *Bristol (TN and VA) News,* 5 December 1876.

105. "Sow and Reap," *Mobile Register,* 23 January 1876.

106. Ibid. Senator James Blaine had spoken in Congress against extending amnesty to Jefferson Davis and was widely accused in the South of "waving the bloody shirt."

107. Unknown to "Dear Aunt," 2 December 1876.

108. *Journal of the Proceedings of the United States Centennial Commission at Philadelphia, 1872* (Philadelphia: Markley & Sons, 1872), app. 2, 52.

109. Keith Polakoff, *The Politics of Inertia: The Election of 1876 and the End of Reconstruction* (Baton Rouge: Louisiana State University Press, 1974), 145–46.

110. "The Country's Danger," *Christian Recorder,* 26 October 1876.

111. Ibid.

112. "Isolation," *Alexandria (VA) People's Advocate,* 1 July 1876.

113. William Leaphart to Lizzie Geiger, 13 November 1876, Lizzie K. Geiger Papers, 1858–97, South Caroliniana Library, University of South Carolina, Columbia.

114. "A Colored Brother on the Centennial," *Galveston News,* 20 January 1876.

115. "Lo, the Poor African!" *Richmond Enquirer,* 19 May 1876.

116. Ibid.

117. Kachun, "Before the Eyes of All Nations," 320.

118. William Leaphart to Lizzie Geiger, 13 November 1876.

119. Foner, "Black Participation in the Centennial of 1876," 294. Foner based his assumption that the white press had ignored the "Negro Declaration" on a search of newspapers for 5–6 July 1876 held by the Library of Congress. The declaration was dated 28 February 1876. Whether or not they reported on the actual declaration itself, southern white newspapers certainly gave coverage to the views of Garland White and his associates.

120. A 1997 article in *Civil War Times* recounts White's interesting career as a Black Union soldier but does not mention his Democratic activism in the 1870s.

121. Foner, "Black Participation in the Centennial of 1876," 293.

122. National Independent Political Union, *Negro Declaration of Independence: Republican Faithlessness and Corruptions Exposed and Scathingly Denounced by Colored Men* (Washington, DC, 1876), https://www.loc.gov/item/rbpe.20604600a/.

123. Garland H. White, "Negro Intimidation—Troubles of Colored Preacher Who Turned Democrat—He Is Denounced, Dismissed and His Flock Dispersed—Toleration of the Southern African—What Do Our Friends at the North Say to This?" August 1876, clipping, Frederick Holliday Scrapbook, David M. Rubenstein Rare Book and Manuscript Library, Duke University, Durham, NC.

124. Ibid.

125. "Colored Men for Tilden," undated clipping [1876], Holliday Scrapbook.

126. Ibid.

127. "Solid South: Shot-Gun Policy in South Carolina: Rabid Rebels on the Stump," *Cincinnati Daily Gazette*, 14 October 1876.

128. "Centennial Exhibition: The Grand Curtain Has Fallen," *Los Angeles Daily Star*, 5 December 1876.

129. "Arkansas' Future," *Arkansas Gazette* (Little Rock), 8 November 1876.

130. See, for example, "Arkansas at the Centennial," *Arkansas Gazette* (Little Rock), 6 July 1876; *Jackson (MS) Weekly Clarion*, 16 August 1876.

131. *Annual Reports of the Departments and Benevolent Institutions of the State of Mississippi for the Year Ending December 31, 1876* (Jackson, MS: Power & Barksdale, 1877), 21.

132. "The Centennial: A Practical View by a Practical Man," *Georgia Weekly Telegraph and Georgia Journal and Messenger* (Macon), 7 November 1876.

133. *Annual Reports . . . 1877*, 21.

6. JULY FOURTH 1876 IN THE SOUTH

1. "The Day We Do Not Celebrate," *New Orleans Daily Picayune*, 4 July 1875.

2. "Fourth of July," *New Orleans Daily Picayune*, 3 July 1876.

3. "Fourth of July: A Brilliant Procession," *New Orleans Daily Picayune*, 6 July 1876.

4. "Mere Mention," *Yorkville (SC) Enquirer*, 13 July 1876.

5. "The City," *Memphis Public Ledger*, 5 July 1876.

6. "The Centennial Fourth at Rocky Mount," *Tarborough (NC) Southerner*, 7 July 1876.

7. "The Fourth," *Bainbridge (GA) Weekly Democrat*, 22 June 1876.

8. "Perry County, Fourth of July Festivities," *Arkansas Gazette*, 14 July 1876.

9. "The National Holiday," *Nashville Daily American*, 6 July 1876.

10. Ibid.

11. Ibid.

12. "How the Fourth Was Celebrated," *Marshall (TX) Tri-Weekly Herald*, 8 July 1876.

13. Ibid.

14. Ibid.

15. See, for example, "To-morrow! How the Fourth Is to Be Celebrated," *Green Bay (WI) Press-Gazette*, 3 July 1878; or "The Fourth in Brandon," *Otter Creek News* (Brandon, VT), 27 June 1879.

16. Ibid.

17. "The Celebration: A Complete Success," *Brenham (TX) Weekly Banner*, 7 July 1876.

18. "The Fourth," *Macon Weekly Telegraph*, 11 July 1875.

19. "The Gala-orious Fourth," *Carroll County Times* (Carrollton, GA), 14 July 1876.

20. Ibid.

21. "Fourth of July Celebration," *Anderson (SC) Intelligencer*, 10 June 1876.

22. "Independence Day," *Montgomery Advertiser*, 22 June 1876.

23. *Our National Centennial Jubilee: Orations, Addresses and Poems Delivered on the Fourth of July 1876 in the Several States of the Union*, ed. Frederick Saunders (New York: E. B. Treat, 1877), 742. Watts is misidentified as John Watts in this source.

24. "The Fourth: How It Was Observed in Montgomery," *Montgomery Advertiser*, 6 July 1876.

25. "The City," *Memphis Public Ledger*, 5 July 1876.

26. "The Republican Barbecue," *Orangeburg (SC) Times*, 15 July 1876.

27. *Our National Centennial Jubilee*, 238.

28. Clark, *Defining Moments*, 79

29. Ibid.

30. John Thomas, "Word from Texas," *Christian Recorder* (Philadelphia), 20 July 1876.

31. "The Observance of the Centennial at Portsmouth and Oration by Prof. Langston," *People's Advocate* (Alexandria, VA), 22 July 1876.

32. Ibid. The *People's Advocate* did not report that Langston had also called for integrated public schools in Virginia; see "The National Utterances and Achievements of Our First Century by John M. Langston, 1876," Foundation Truths website, https://captain

jamesdavis.wordpress.com/2013/04/18/the-national-utterances-and-achievements-of
-our-first-century-by-john-m-langston-1876/. Langston was the great-uncle of poet
Langston Hughes.

33. "Special and Local," *Newberry (SC) Weekly Herald,* 5 July 1876.

34. "The Glorious Fourth," *Newberry (SC) Weekly Herald,* 12 July 1876.

35. Foner, *Reconstruction,* 570.

36. Ibid.

37. "The Hamburg Row," *Orangeburg (SC) Times,* 15 July 1876.

38. Reprinted in *Yorkville (SC) Enquirer,* 17 August 1876.

39. "Gen. Butler, the Hamburg Riot and the News & Courier," *Newberry (SC) Weekly
Herald,* 26 July 1876.

40. Ibid.

41. *Savannah Tribune,* 2 September 1876.

42. "Chamberlain to Grant," *Yorkville (SC) Enquirer,* 17 August 1876.

43. *USG Papers,* 27:199.

44. "The President's Libellous and Incendiary Message," *Huntsville (AL) Weekly
Democrat,* 9 August 1876.

45. Gasper Loren Toole II, *Ninety Years in Aiken County: Memoirs of Aiken County and
Its People* (1955), Genealogy Trails, http://genealogytrails.com/scar/aiken/aiken_hx2.htm.

46. "Image 1 of African American Pamphlet Collection Copy," in *A Centennial Fourth
of July Democratic Celebration: The Massacre of Six Colored Citizens of the United States at
Hamburgh, S.C., on July 4, Debate on the Hamburgh Massacre, in the U.S. House of Representatives, July 15th and 18th* [Washington, DC?], 1876, https://www.loc.gov/item/12007858/.

47. "A Beautiful Episode: A Fourth of July Scene in Georgia," *Columbus Daily Enquirer,* 11 August 1876.

48. Ibid.

49. "One Southern Word of Sense," *Waterloo (IA) Courier,* 9 August 1876. The *Courier*
reprinted, approvingly, the *Commercial's* article.

50. Ibid.

51. "The Intertwining Nonsense," *Chattanooga (TN) Daily Times,* 13 July 1876.

52. Ibid.

53. Ibid.

54. "Georgia Glimpses: Oglethorpe County Letter," *Augusta Chronicle,* 8 July 1876.

55. "The Feeling in Tallapoosa," *Montgomery Advertiser,* 12 July 1876.

CONCLUSION

1. Goldfield, *Still Fighting the Civil War,* 1.

2. Rubin, *Shattered Nation,* 147.

3. Ibid., 158.

4. "The True Bond of Union," *Nashville Republican Banner*, 24 April 1875.

5. "Georgia's Chance at the Centennial," *Atlanta Daily Herald*, "Tuesday 17," 1875, clipping, USCC Archives.

6. "Georgia's Cosey Quarters," *Macon Telegraph*, 11 March 1893.

7. See Rydell, *All the World's a Fair*, 52–53.

8. Ibid., 73.

9. Bruce Harvey, *World's Fairs in a Southern Accent* (Knoxville: University of Tennessee Press, 2014), 266.

10. Rydell, *All the World's a Fair*, 76.

11. See Howard Rabinowitz, "From Exclusion to Segregation: Southern Race Relations, 1865–1890," *Journal of American History* 63 (1976): 325–50.

12. "Delegate Flays," "Lincoln Cult," *Birmingham Age-Herald*, 19 November 1922.

13. Robert Cook, *Civil War Memories: Contesting the Past in the United States since 1865* (Baltimore: Johns Hopkins University Press, 2017), 165.

14. Cook, *Civil War Memories*, 166.

15. Ibid.

16. Bruce E. Baker, "Wade Hampton's Last Parade: Memory of Reconstruction in the 1970 South Carolina Tricentennial," *Remembering Reconstruction: Struggles over the Meaning of America's Most Turbulent Era* (Baton Rouge: Louisiana State University Press, 2017), 5798 of 6715, Kindle.

17. Ibid., 5843 of 6715.

Bibliography

PRIMARY SOURCES
Archival Primary Sources

Birmingham Public Library, Birmingham, Alabama
  Alexander Boyd Papers
  Faunsdale Plantation Papers
David M. Rubenstein Rare Book and Manuscript Library, Duke University,
  Durham, North Carolina
  Frederick W. Holliday Papers
Dolph Briscoe Center for American History, University of Texas at Austin
  Ashbel Smith Papers
  James P. Newcomb Papers
Historic Society of Pennsylvania, Philadelphia
  Final Report of the Women's Centennial Executive Committee: March 22,
    1877 The Second Annual Report of the Women's Centennial Executive
    Committee, March 1875
Philadelphia City Archives, Philadelphia
  United States Centennial Commission Papers
South Caroliniana Library, University of South Carolina, Columbia
  Lizzie K. Geiger Papers, 1858–97
Southern Historical Collection, Wilson Library, University of North Carolina
  at Chapel Hill
  John S. Henderson Papers
  Larkin Newby Papers

Texas State Library, Archives Division, Austin
     Coke Gubernatorial Papers
Virginia Historical Society, Richmond
     Williams Family Papers

Newspapers

The author consulted newspapers for the following towns and cities for the years indicated. Details can be found in the notes.

Abbeville, SC, 1875
Alexandria, LA, 1876
Alexandria, VA, 1860–76
Americus, GA, 1876
Anderson, SC, 1876
Atlanta, 1874–76
Augusta, GA, 1861–75
Austin, TX, 1857–76
Bainbridge, GA, 1876
Birmingham, AL, 1922
Boston, 1875
Brandon, VT, 1879
Brenham, TX, 1875–76
Bristol, TN and VA, 1876–79
Camden, NJ, 1873
Carrollton, GA, 1876
Charleston, SC, 1854–75
Chattanooga, TN, 1876
Chicago, 1876
Cincinnati, 1876
Cleveland, TN, 1876
Columbia, SC, 1875
Columbia, TN, 1876
Columbus, GA, 1875–76
Dallas, 1874–76
Denison, TX, 1876

Edgefield, SC, 1861

Fayetteville, TN, 1876

Galveston, TX, 1866–76

Gold Hill, NV, 1864

Green Bay, WS, 1878

Hartford, CT, 1875

Holly Springs, MS, 1876

Honey-Grove, TX, 1870

Hot Springs, AR, 1875

Huntsville, AL, 1876

Jackson, MS, 1871–76

Keene, NH, 1876

Knoxville, TN, 1855–67

Little Rock, AR, 1873–76

Los Angeles, 1874–76

Macon, GA, 1851–93

Marshall, TX, 1876

Memphis, 1866–76

Milwaukee, 1876

Mobile, AL, 1875–76

Montgomery, AL, 1860–76

Montpelier, VT, 1814

Nashville, 1875–76

Natchez, MS, 1838

New Orleans, 1857–76

New York, 1827–76

Newberry, SC, 1876

Orangeburg, SC, 1876

Paulding, MS, 1861

Philadelphia, PA, 1872–2010

Pulaski, TN, 1876

Raymond, MS, 1876

Richmond, VA, 1858–76

Rochester, NY, 1848–54

San Antonio, TX, 1875–76

San Francisco, 1875

Savannah, GA, 1876

Shreveport, LA, 1875

Springfield, MA, 1873

Tallahassee, FL, 1876

Tarboro, NC, 1876

Tuscumbia, AL, 1874

Vicksburg, MS, 1876

Waco, TX, 1875–76

Washington, DC, 1875–2011

Waterloo, IA, 1876

Wilmington, DE, 1876

Windsor, VT, 1812

Winnsboro, SC, 1875

Worcester, MA, 1860

York, SC, 1876

Online Primary Sources

African American Pamphlet Collection. Library of Congress. https://www.loc.
    gov/resource/rbaapc.31710/?sp=1.

Call and Brevard Family Papers. *Florida Memory.* Division of Library and Infor-
    mation Services. Florida Department of State. https://www.floridamemory
    .com/discover/historical_records/callbrevardpapers/.

The Handbook of Texas History. Texas State Historical Association. https://tsha-
    online.org/handbook.

Records of the Assistant Commissioner for the State of South Carolina Bureau of
    Refugees, Freedmen, and Abandoned Lands, 1865–70. "Reports of Condi-
    tions and Operations." National Archives Microfilm Publication M869, roll
    34. http://www.freedmensbureau.com/southcarolina/scoperations4.htm.

Toole, Gasper Loren II, *Ninety Years in Aiken County: Memoirs of Aiken County and
    Its People* (1955). Transcription. Genealogy Trails website. http://genealogy
    trails.com/scar/aiken/aiken_hx.htm.

Other Primary Sources

*Annual Reports of the Departments and Benevolent Institutions of the State of Mis-
    sissippi for the Year Ending 1877.* Jackson, MS: Power & Barksdale, 1878.

Centennial Oration of Gov. R. B. Hubbard, of Texas, Delivered at the National Exposition, Philadelphia, September 11, 1876. St. Louis: Texas Land & Immigration Co., 1876.

Elmore, Grace Brown. *A Heritage of Woe: The Civil War Diary of Grace Brown Elmore.* Athens: University of Georgia Press, 1997.

Ingraham, Jonathon Holt. *The South-West by a Yankee in Two Volumes.* Vol. 2. New York: Harper Brothers, 1835. http://www.gutenberg.org/ebooks/35156.

Kingsbury, Theodore Bryant, *The International Exhibition Guide for the Southern States: The Only Guide-Book Specially Suited to the Southern Visitor.* Raleigh, NC: Fulgham, 1876.

Journal of the Proceedings of the National Centennial Commission. Philadelphia, 1873.

Journal of the Proceedings of the United States Centennial Commission at Philadelphia, 1872. Philadelphia: Markley & Sons, 1872.

Journal of the Senate of the State of Alabama 1876.

McCabe, James Dabney. *The Illustrated History of the Centennial Exhibition.* Philadelphia: National Publishing Co., 1876.

Message from the Governor of Texas to the Fifteenth Legislature, First Session. Houston: A. C. Gray, 1876.

Myers, Robert Manson, ed. *Children of Pride: A True Story of Georgia and the Civil War.* New Haven: Yale University Press, 1972.

Our National Centennial Jubilee: Orations, Addresses and Poems Delivered on the Fourth of July 1876 in the Several States of the Union. Edited by Frederick Saunders. New York: E. B. Treat, 1877.

A Pamphlet Containing the Full History of the Celebration of the Ninety-Ninth Anniversary of American Independence in Atlanta, Ga., July 4th, 1875. Compiled from the *Atlanta Daily Herald.* https://archive.org/details/pamphletcontainioostep.

Simon, John Y., ed. *The Papers of Ulysses S. Grant.* 32 vols. Carbondale: Southern Illinois University Press, 1967.

United States Centennial Almanac. Philadelphia: King & Baird, 1874.

SECONDARY SOURCES
Books

Avrich, Paul. *The Haymarket Tragedy.* Princeton: Princeton University Press, 1984.

Baker, Bruce E. *What Reconstruction Meant: Historical Memory in the American South.* Charlottesville: University of Virginia Press, 2007.

Barr, Alwyn. *Reconstruction to Reform: Texas Politics, 1876–1906.* Austin: University of Texas Press, 1971.

Barr, John McKee. *Loathing Lincoln: An American Tradition from the Civil War to the Present.* Baton Rouge: Louisiana State University Press, 2014.

Blair, William. *Cities of the Dead: Contesting the Memory of the Civil War in the South, 1865–1914.* Chapel Hill: University of North Carolina Press, 2004.

Blight, David W. *Race and Reunion: The Civil War in American Memory.* Cambridge: Harvard University Press, 2001.

Bodnar, John. *Remaking America: Public Memory, Commemoration, and Patriotism in the Twentieth Century.* Princeton: Princeton University Press, 1992.

Boller, Paul F., Jr. *Presidential Campaigns.* New York: Oxford University Press, 1985.

Bonner, Robert E. *Mastering America: Southern Slaveholders and the Crisis of American Nationhood.* New York: Cambridge University Press, 2009.

Brundage, W. Fitzhugh. *The Southern Past: A Clash of Race and Memory.* Cambridge: Harvard University Press, 2008.

Burstein, Andrew. *America's Jubilee, July 4, 1826: A Generation Remembers the Revolution after Fifty Years of Independence.* New York: Vintage, 2002.

Clark, Kathleen Ann. *Defining Moments: African American Commemoration and Political Culture in the South, 1863–1915.* Chapel Hill: University of North Carolina Press, 2005.

Cook, Robert. *Civil War America: Making a Nation, 1848–1877.* London: Longman, 2003.

———. *Civil War Memories: Contesting the Past in the United States since 1865.* Baltimore: Johns Hopkins University Press, 2017.

Cooper, William J. *The American South: A History.* Vol. 1. Boston: Rowman & Littlefield, 2002.

Copeland, Isaac, ed. *Democracy in the Old South and Other Essays by Fletcher Melvin Green.* Kingsport, TN: Vanderbilt University Press, 1969.

Coulter, Ellis Merton. *William G. Brownlow: Fighting Parson of the Southern Highlands.* Chapel Hill: University of North Carolina Press, 1937.

Cox, Karen. *Dixie's Daughters: The United Daughters of the Confederacy and the Preservation of Confederate Culture.* Gainesville: University Press of Florida, 2002.

Craven, Avery O. *The Growth of Southern Nationalism: 1848–1861.* Baton Rouge: Louisiana State University Press, 1953.

Criblez, Adam. *Parading Patriotism: Independence Day Celebrations in the Urban Midwest, 1826–1876.* DeKalb: Northern Illinois University Press, 2013.

Davis, William C., *Jefferson Davis: The Man and His Hour*. Baton Rouge: Louisiana State University Press, 1992.

Dennis, Matthew. *Red, White, and Blue Letter Days: An American Calendar*. Ithaca, NY: Cornell University Press, 2002.

Downs, Gregory P. *After Appomattox: Military Occupations and the End of War*. Cambridge: Harvard University Press, 2015.

Durden, Robert F. *The Gray and the Black: The Confederate Debate on Emancipation*. Baton Rouge: Louisiana State University Press, 1972.

Escott, Paul D. *After Secession: Jefferson Davis and the Failure of Confederate Nationalism*. Baton Rouge: Louisiana State University Press, 1978.

Faust, Drew Gilpin. *The Creation of Confederate Nationalism: Ideology and Identity in the Civil War South*. Baton Rouge: Louisiana State University Press, 1988.

Foner, Eric. *Reconstruction: America's Unfinished Revolution, 1863–1877*. New York: HarperCollins, 1988.

Freehling, William. *The Road to Disunion, 1776–1854*. Oxford: Oxford University Press, 1990.

Gallagher, Gary W. *The Confederate War*. Cambridge: Harvard University Press, 1997.

Gaston, Paul. *The New South Creed: A Study in Southern Mythmaking*. New York: Knopf, 1970.

Gilberti, Bruno. *Designing the Centennial: A History of the 1876 International Exhibition in Philadelphia*. Lexington: University Press of Kentucky, 2002.

Gold, Susanna W. *The Unfinished Exhibition: Visualizing Myth, Memory, and the Shadow of the Civil War in Centennial America*. London: Routledge, 2017.

Goldfield, David. *Still Fighting the Civil War: The American South and Southern History*. Baton Rouge: Louisiana State University Press, 2013.

Greenhalgh, Paul. *Ephemeral Vistas: The Expositions Universelles, Great Exhibitions, and World's Fairs, 1851–1939*. Manchester: Manchester University Press, 1988.

Gross, Linda P., and Theresa R. Snyder. *Philadelphia's 1876 Centennial Exhibition*. Charleston, SC: Arcadia, 2005.

Harris, M. Keith. *Across the Bloody Chasm: The Culture of Commemoration among Civil War Veterans*. Baton Rouge: Louisiana State University Press, 2014.

Harris, William C. *The Day of the Carpetbagger: Republican Reconstruction in Mississippi*. Baton Rouge: Louisiana State University Press, 1979.

Harvey, Bruce. *World's Fairs in a Southern Accent*. Knoxville: University of Tennessee Press, 2014.

Janney, Caroline. *Burying the Dead but Not the Past.* Chapel Hill: University of North Carolina Press, 2008.

———. *Remembering the Civil War: Reunion and the Limits of Reconciliation.* Chapel Hill: The University of North Carolina Press, 2013.

Kachun, Mitch. *Festivals of Freedom: Memory and Meaning in African American Emancipation Celebrations, 1808–1915.* Amherst: University of Massachusetts Press, 2003.

Kammen, Michael. *Mystic Chords of Memory: The Transformation of Tradition in American Culture.* New York: Vintage Books, 1991.

Larkin, Jack. *The Reshaping of Everyday Life: 1790–1840.* New York: Harper & Row, 1988.

Lawson, Melinda. *Patriot Fires: Forging a New American Nationalism in the Civil War North.* Lawrence: University Press of Kansas, 2002.

Lloyd, James B. *Lives of Mississippi Authors, 1817–1967.* Jackson: University Press of Mississippi, 1981.

Maier, Pauline. *American Scripture: Making the Declaration of Independence.* New York: Knopf, 1997.

Marten, James. *Texas Divided: Loyalty and Dissent in the Lone Star State, 1856–1874.* Lexington: University Press of Kentucky, 1990.

Moneyhon, Carl H. *Edmund Davis of Texas: Civil War General, Reconstruction Leader, Republican Governor.* Fort Worth: TCU Press, 2010.

———. *Republicanism in Reconstruction Texas.* College Station: Texas A&M University Press, 2001.

Nagel, Paul. *One Nation Indivisible: The Union in American Thought, 1776–1861.* New York: Oxford University Press, 1964.

Nemanic, Mary Lou. *One Day for Democracy: Independence Day and the Americanization of Iron Range Immigrants.* Athens: Ohio University Press, 2007.

O'Leary, Cecilia. *To Die For: The Paradox of American Patriotism.* Princeton: Princeton University Press, 1999.

Perman, Michael. *Pursuit of Unity: A Political History of the American South.* Chapel Hill: University of North Carolina Press, 2009.

———. *The Road to Redemption: Southern Politics, 1869–1879.* Chapel Hill: University of North Carolina Press, 1984.

Polakoff, Keith. *The Politics of Inertia: The Election of 1876 and the End of Reconstruction.* Baton Rouge: Louisiana State University Press, 1974.

Potter, David. *The Impending Crisis, 1848–1861.* New York: Harper & Row, 1976.

Quigley, Paul. *Shifting Grounds: Nationalism and the American South, 1848–1865*. Oxford: Oxford University Press, 2012.

Rable, George C. *The Confederate Republic: A Revolution against Politics*. Chapel Hill: University of North Carolina Press, 1994.

Revels, Tracy J. *Grander in Her Daughters: Florida's Women during the Civil War*. Columbia: University of South Carolina Press, 2004.

Ritter, Kurt W., and James R. Andrews. *The American Ideology: Reflections of the Revolution in American Rhetoric*. Falls Church, VA: Speech Communication Association, 1978.

Rubin, Anne Sarah. *Shattered Nation: The Rise and Fall of the Confederacy, 1861–1868*. Chapel Hill: University of North Carolina Press, 2005.

Rydell, Robert. *All the World's a Fair: Visions of Empire at American International Expositions, 1876–1916*. Chicago: University of Chicago Press, 1987.

Smith, Timothy B. *Mississippi in the Civil War: The Home Front*. Jackson: University Press of Mississippi, 2010.

Spillman, Lyn. *Nation and Commemoration: Creating National Identities in the United States and Australia*. Cambridge: Cambridge University Press, 1997.

Stampp, Kenneth M. *The Imperiled Union*. Oxford: Oxford University Press, 1980.

Travers, Len. *Celebrating the Fourth: Independence Day and the Rites of Nationalism in the Early Republic*. Amherst: University of Massachusetts Press, 1997.

Vincent, Charles. *Black Legislators in Louisiana during Reconstruction*. Baton Rouge: Louisiana State University Press, 1976.

Waldstreicher, David. *In the Midst of Perpetual Fetes: The Making of American Nationalism, 1776–1820*. Chapel Hill: University of North Carolina Press, 1997.

Weymouth, Lally. *America in 1876: The Way We Were*. New York: Random House, 1976.

Williams, Patrick. *Beyond Redemption: Texas Democrats after Reconstruction*. College Station: Texas A&M University Press, 2007.

Winkler, Ernest. *Platforms of Political Parties in Texas*. London: Forgotten Books, 2013.

Zuczek, Richard. *State of Rebellion: Reconstruction in South Carolina*. Columbia: University of South Carolina Press, 2009.

Journal Articles and Book Chapters

Bailey, Anne J. "A Texas Cavalry Raid." In *Black Flag over Dixie: Racial Atrocities and Reprisals in the Civil War*, edited by Gregory Unwin, 19–33. Carbondale: Southern Illinois University Press, 2004.

Baker, Bruce E. "Wade Hampton's Last Parade: Memory of Reconstruction in the 1970 South Carolina Tricentennial." In *Remembering Reconstruction: Struggles over the Meaning of America's Most Turbulent Era,* edited by Carole Emberton and Bruce E. Baker, 5606–6034. Baton Rouge: Louisiana State University Press, 2017.

Brown, W. Burlie. "Louisiana and the Nation's One-Hundredth Birthday." *Journal of the Louisiana Historical Association* 18, no. 3 (1976): 261–75.

Brundage, W. Fitzhugh. "No Deed but Memory." In *Where These Memories Grow: History, Memory, and Southern Identity,* edited by W. Fitzhugh Brundage, 1–28. Chapel Hill: University of North Carolina Press, 2000.

Carp, Benjamin L. "Nations of American Rebels: Understanding Nationalism in Revolutionary North America and the Civil War South." *Civil War History* 23, no. 1 (2002): 5–33.

Cook, Robert. "The Quarrel Forgotten? Toward a Clearer Understanding of Sectional Reconciliation." *Journal of the Civil War Era* 6, no. 3 (2016): 413–36.

Cordato, Mary Frances. "Toward a New Century: Women and the Philadelphia Centennial Exhibition, 1876." *Pennsylvania Magazine of History and Biography* 107, no. 1 (1983): 113–35.

Detweiler, Philip F. "The Changing Reputation of the Declaration of Independence: The First Fifty Years." *William and Mary Quarterly* 19, no. 4 (1962): 557–74.

Doyle, Don H. "Slavery, Secession, Reconstruction." In *The South as an American Problem,* edited by Larry J. Griffin and Don H. Doyle, 102–25. Athens: University of Georgia Press, 1995.

Eaton, Clement. "Calhoun and State Rights." *The Civilization of the Old South: Writings of Clement Eaton,* 135–55. Lexington: University Press of Kentucky, 1968.

Fairclough, Adam. "'Scalawags,' Southern Honor, and the Lost Cause: Explaining the Fatal Encounter of James H. Cosgrove and Edward L. Pierson." *Journal of Southern History* 77, no. 4 (2011): 799–826.

Foner, Philip. "Black Participation in the Centennial of 1876." *Phylon* 39, no. 4 (1978): 283–96.

Foster, Gaines M. "Guilt over Slavery: A Historiographical Analysis." *Journal of Southern History* 56, no. 4 (1990): 665–94.

Genovese, Eugene, and Elizabeth Fox-Genovese. "The Divine Sanction of Social Order: Religious Foundations of the Southern Slaveholders' World View." *Journal of the American Academy of Religion* 55, no. 2 (1987): 211–33.

Gold, Susanna. "Fighting It Over Again: The Battle of Gettysburg at the 1876 Centennial Exhibition." *Civil War History* 54, no. 3 (2008): 277–310.

Green, Fletcher. "Listen to the Eagle Scream: One Hundred Years of the Fourth of July in North Carolina, 1776–1876." In *Democracy in the Old South and Other Essays by Fletcher Melvin Green,* edited by Isaac Copeland, 111–56. Kingsport, TN: Vanderbilt University Press, 1969.

Gurr, Steve. "Americus and the Centennial Year in the Sumter Republican." *Georgia Historical Quarterly* 60, no. 3 (1976): 239–50.

Hancock, Hope. "The 1876 Centennial Exposed: How Souvenir Publications Reveal Contrasting Attitudes of Race and Gender in the Post-Bellum United States." *Mellon Scholars' Works,* 2 March 2014. https://digitalcommons.hope .edu/cgi/viewcontent.cgi?article=1000&context=mellon.

Hayashida-Knight, Christopher. "Philadelphia Plays Dixie: Accommodating the South at the 1876 Centennial." Conference paper. Mid-Atlantic Popular and American Culture Conference, Philadelphia, 3 November 2011.

Hepp, John. "Centennial Celebrations." In *A Companion to the Reconstruction Presidents,* edited by Edward O. Frantz, 517–37. Malden, MA: John Wiley & Sons, 2014.

Howells, William Dean. "A Sennight of the Centennial." *Atlantic Monthly,* July 1876.

Kachun, Mitch. "Before the Eyes of All Nations: African-American Identity and Historical Memory at the Centennial Exposition of 1876." *Pennsylvania History* 65, no. 3 (1998): 300–323.

———. "The Shaping of a Public Biography: Richard Allen and the AME Church." In *Black Lives: Essays in African American Biography,* edited by James L. Conyers, 44–66. London: Routledge, 2015.

Koschnik, Albrecht. "Young Federalists, Masculinity and Partisanship during the War of 1812." In *Beyond the Founders: New Approaches to the Political History of the Early American Republic,* edited by Jeffrey L. Pasley, Andrew W. Robertson, and David Waldstreicher, 159–79. Chapel Hill: University of North Carolina Press 2004.

Lee, Susanna Michele. "Reconciliation in Reconstruction Virginia." In *Crucible of Civil War: Virginia from Secession to Commemoration,* edited by Edward L. Ayers, Gary W. Gallagher, and Andrew J. Torget. Charlottesville: University of Virginia Press, 2006.

Lesley, Lewis B. "A Southern Transcontinental Railroad into California: Texas Pacific vs. Southern Pacific, 1865–1885." *Pacific Historical Review* 5, no. 1 (1936): 52–60.

McPherson, James. "Antebellum Southern Exceptionalism: A New Look at an Old Question." *Civil War History* 50 (2004): 418–33.

Nora, Pierre. "Between Memory and History: Les Lieux de Mémoire." Special issue on "Memory and Counter-Memory." *Representations*, no. 26 (1989): 7–24.

Pasley, Jeffrey L. "The Cheese and the Words." In *Beyond the Founders: New Approaches to the Political History of the Early American Republic*, edited by Jeffrey L. Pasley, Andrew W. Robertson, and David Waldstreicher, 31–56. Chapel Hill: University of North Carolina Press 2004.

Potter, David M. "The Historian's Use of Nationalism and Vice Versa." *American Historical Review* 67, no. 4 (1962): 924–50.

Prince, K. Stephen. "The Burnt District: Making Sense of Ruins in the Postwar South." In *The World the Civil War Made: The Steven and Janice Brose Lectures in the Civil War Era*, edited by Gregory P. Downs and Kate Masur, 106–31. Chapel Hill: University of North Carolina Press, 2015.

Quigley, Paul. "Independence Day Dilemmas in the American South, 1848–1865." *Journal of Southern History* 75, no. 2 (2009): 235–66.

Rabinowitz, Howard. "From Exclusion to Segregation: Southern Race Relations, 1865–1890." *Journal of American History* 63 (1976): 325–50.

Robertson, Andrew W. "Look on This Picture . . . and on This! Nationalism, Localism, and Partisan Images of Otherness in the United States, 1787–1820." *American Historical Review* (October 2001): 1263–80.

Ross, Michael A. "The Commemoration of Robert E. Lee's Death and the Obstruction of Reconstruction in New Orleans." *Civil War History* 51, no. 2 (2005): 135–50.

Sellers, Charles Griers. "The Travails of Slavery." In *The Southerner as American*, edited by Charles Sellers, 40–77. Chapel Hill: University of North Carolina Press, 1960.

Smith, Craig Bruce. "Claiming the Centennial: The American Revolution's Blood and Spirit in Boston, 1870–1876." *Massachusetts Historical Review* 15 (2013): 7–53.

Thomas, Emory. "The Revolution Brings Revolutionary Change." In *Major Problems in the History of the American South*, vol. 1: *The Old South*, edited by Paul D. Escott, David R. Goldfield, and Sally G. McMillen, 383–86. Boston: Houghton Mifflin, 1999.

Waldstreicher, David. "Rites of Rebellion, Rites of Assent: Celebrations, Print Culture, and the Origins of American Nationalism." *Journal of American History* 82, no. 1 (1995): 37–61.

Williams, Timothy J. "The Intellectual Roots of the Lost Cause: Camaraderie and Confederate Memory in Civil War Prisons." *Journal of Southern History* 86, no. 2 (2020): 253–82.

Index

Abolitionists/abolitionism, 17–18

Adams, Dock, 165, 166

Adams, J. S., 61, 62

Adams, John, 16

African Methodist Episcopal Church
(AME), 90–91, 163

African Americans. *See* Black Americans

Alabama: and Centennial participation,
60, 63, 64, 66, 71; and "redemption,"
162

Alexandria Gazette (VA), 46, 69

Allen, Bishop Richard (bust of), 90, 93,
131–133

American Revolution: memory of, 25,
28, 36–37, 38, 40, 41, 45, 46, 47, 49,
89, 95, 114, 160, 168, 176

Ames, Adelbert, 53, 116

Andrews, Harvey, 50

Antoine, Caesar, 49–50

Appomattox, 13, 55, 61

Arkansas: and AME church, 91; and
Centennial participation, 62, 153, 178;
and "redemption," 36, 73–74

Atlanta Constitution, 123, 135

Atlanta Herald, 38–43, 56, 174

Attucks, Crispus, 51, 89

Augusta Chronicle & Sentinel, 43, 63, 70,
166, 171

Augusta Constitutionalist, 27

Austin Evening News, 105

Austin Democratic Statesman, 78, 79, 117,
118

Avrich, Paul, 100

Baker, Bruce, 5, 177

Baker, I. L, 69

Barr, Alwyn, 101

Bell, Alexander Graham, 1

Bell, James Hall, 106

Benjamin, Judah, 11

Bernard, J. T., 77

Betts, Karl, 177

Bigelow, John, 58

Black Americans: and antebellum
Fourths of July, 17–19; and the Centennial, 89–96, 131–135, 137, 138,
176, 178; and Democratic affiliation,
149–151; and employment at the Centennial, 137–138, 203n70; and later
world's fairs, 175–176; and national
identity, 89, 90, 131, 134, 156, 164; and
post-war Fourths of July, 32–35, 162–

Black Americans (*continued*)
165, 169; white southerners' views on, 32, 41, 46, 50; and Republican affiliation, 34, 49, 50, 148, 152, 167. *See also* women: Black women

Blaine, James G., 79, 144, 146

Blair, Francis, 183n49

Blair, William, 3, 22

Blake, William Phipps, 68

Blight, David, 2, 31

Bodnar, John, 41, 56

Bonner, Robert, 6, 11, 81

Bonzano, Hubert, 73

Booth, Edwin G., 204n76

Bourbon Democrats, 56, 63, 75, 111–112, 125, 152, 153, 173–174

Brenham Banner (TX), 97, 104

Bristol News (VA), 127

Brown, Cynthia, 85

Brown, John Bishop, 91

Brown, W. Burlie, 4

Browne, Joseph, 83

Brownlow, William, 47

Buchanan, James, 149

Butler, Matthew, 165, 166, 168

Byrd, William, 60, 62, 75, 191n16

Calhoun, John, 8, 22

Camden Democrat (NJ), 93

Campbell, John, 58

Carp, Benjamin, 10

Centennial Exhibition, 1–2, 13, 22, 57, 78; and African Americans, 89–96, 131–135, 138; and American identity, 2, 4, 61–62, 118; and the Civil War, 127–131; and economic concerns, 65–72, 77, 109, 117, 174; funding of, 59–61, 64, 79; jokes about, 121–122; planning of, 58–61; and political identity, 72–75, 144–145; and railroads, 79–80; as rhetorical arena, 63–65, 89–90, 97, 109–110, 118–119, 124, 125, 130–131, 134, 153, 202n31, 203n65; and sectional reconciliation, 61–63, 71, 108, 110, 117, 138, 139; sectionalism at, 130–131, 135–143; white southern impressions of, 123–127; and southern identity, 118, 126–127, 178; "State Days" at, 138–139; "Southern Day" at, 139–140; white southern impressions of, 123–127; white southern reaction to, 57–58, 63–65, 70–71, 151–152; wide coverage of, 121–122

Chamberlain, Daniel, 115, 167

Chambers, Andrew, 91–92, 132–133

Chappell, Absalom, 40–41, 42

Charleston Mercury (SC), 25

Charleston News & Courier (SC), 43

Chattanooga Commercial, 169, 170

Chattanooga Daily Times, 170

Chew, John Calhoun, 97, 100, 104, 109, 110, 112, 115

Chicago Inter-Ocean, 137, 138

Chicago Tribune, 122

Chicago World's Fair (1893), 174–175

Christian Recorder, 51, 90–91, 92, 93, 132, 146, 148, 163

Cincinnati Daily Gazette, 151

Cincinnati Daily Times, 138

Cincinnati Enquirer, 36

Civil War, the, 1, 6, 7, 11, 31, 98, 101, 113, 147, 173; centennial of, 176–177; end of, 29, 55; memory of, 127–130, 176–177; representation at the Centennial, 127–131

Clark, Kathleen Ann, 4, 50, 163

Cleveland Herald (TN), 144

Coke, Richard, 97, 98, 101, 102, 104, 105, 106, 107, 108, 111–112

Coldwell, Thomas, 72

Columbia Herald & Mail (TN), 121

Columbus Enquirer (GA), 35

commemoration, 5, 35, 42, 46, 91, 155; and historical memory, 21, 56, 81, 162, 168; and overlap with politics, 13, 14, 16, 18, 26, 28, 36, 38, 40, 41, 45, 55–56, 73–75, 81, 89, 106, 112, 156, 157, 160, 161–162, 171, 177–178; and reconciliation, 58, 84, 98, 176

Compromise of 1877, 152

Confederate States of America: and linkage to ideals of American Revolution, 24–25, 28, 41, 161; and Confederate nationalism, 10–12, 29, 118

Coombs, W. H. L., 151

Cooper, William, 9

Cordato, Mary Frances, 80

Coulter, Merton, 47

Cox, Karen, 3

Craven, Avery, 7–8

Criblez, Adam, 23

Crosby, Peter, 52

Cunningham, Pamela, 80

Dallas Herald, 37, 79, 84, 103, 122

Davenport, G. W., 50

Davis, Edmund J., 97–99, 100, 101, 104

Davis, Jefferson, 11–12, 146, 149

Death of Cleopatra, 134

Debow's Review, 9

Declaration of Independence, 15, 17, 21, 31, 32, 35, 39, 51

Degler, Carl, 10

Democratic Party, 10, 37, 38, 47, 52, 55, 75, 83, 106, 146, 148, 152, 156, 157, 167, 203n65; and African American supporters, 149–151; and Alabama, 162; and Arkansas, 74; "Bourbon" wing of, 56, 63, 75, 111–112, 152, 153, 173–174; and Mississippi, 74, 190n95; and

"New Departure," 37–38, 56, 75, 112, 173–174; and opposition to Republican policies, 99; and Texas, 37, 97, 105, 106, 99; and the 1876 election, 144, 149, 171

Democratic-Republican Party, 14–16

Dennis, Matthew, 5

Dodge, George, 73, 193n73

Douglass, Frederick, 17–19, 132, 178

Downs, Gregory, 2, 32, 55

Doyle, Don, 12

Du Bois, W. E. B., 178

Dunning School of Reconstruction historiography, 47, 168, 189n72

Early, Jubal, 119

Edgefield Advertiser (SC), 27

election of 1876, 138, 143–149, 151–152, 171

Emancipation Day (January 1), 18–19

Escott, Paul, 10

Fairfield Herald (SC), 115

Faust, Drew Gilpin, 11

Fayetteville Observer (TN), 144

Federalist Party, 15–16

Felton, William, 39

Fish, Hamilton, 65, 107, 111, 115–116

Florida: and Centennial participation, 77, 80, 82–84, 87, 88

Foner, Eric, 37, 165

Foner, Philip, 3, 93, 132, 149, 203n70, 206n119

Forrest, Nathan Bedford, 53

Fourth of July: antebellum celebrations of, 14–20; and Black Americans, 17–19, 162–165, 169, 171–172; and Black post-war celebrations, 34–35, 48–52; Black women and, 50, 165; and the Civil War, 24–30; and the Confederacy, 25–29; and identity, 55; linkage to

Fourth of July (*continued*)
  causes, 18, 19–21; partisan nature of
  celebrations, 14–17, 21, 26, 36, 45, 50,
  155–156, 171, 172; and reconciliation,
  159, 169–170; and "redemption," 37,
  156–160, 171; and sectionalism, 19, 21;
  and southern Republicans, 48–53; and
  white southerners, 35–47, 155–162,
  171–172; and white southern women,
  16, 160–161, 170–171
Freedman's Bureau, 33, 116
Freedom's Journal, 17
Freehling, William, 7–9
French, Obidiah C., 116–117

Galveston Daily News, 102, 106, 107,
  138, 148
Garrison, William Lloyd, 21, 23
Gaston, Paul, 56
Georgia: and Centennial participation,
  65, 70, 77, 153; and Chicago World's
  Fair, 174–175; and "redemption," 157
Gettysburg (painting), 129–130, 137
Gillespie, Elizabeth, 81, 92
Gilmer, J. W., 50
Girardeau, Harriet, 83
Gold, Susanna, 3, 128, 130, 203n65
Goldfield, David, 31, 173
Goshorn, Alfred, 59, 68, 74, 104, 132, 133
Grady, Henry W., 38, 174
Grant, Ulysses S., 37, 53, 66, 106–107,
  111, 115, 132, 144, 167
Gross, Linda, 68
Gurney, William, 113–116, 119

Hamburg, SC: 1876 massacre at, 165–
  168, 169
Hampton, Wade, III, 42, 147–148
Hancock, Hope, 204n70

Hancock, John, 105
Handy, Isaac, 24
Hardeman, Thomas, 40
Harris, M. Keith, 3, 39
Harris William C., 53, 116
Hartford Courant, 113
Harvey, Bruce, 175
Hawley, Joseph, 59, 61, 66, 138, 152
Hayashida-Knight, Christopher, 136
Hayes, Rutherford B., 138, 144, 145, 146,
  147, 152, 162
Henderson, John, 124, 125
Hendricks, Thomas, 150, 157, 160
Hepp, John, 3
Hill, James, 50
Hill, John, 50
Hillyer, George, 65, 130
Hinds County Gazette, 75, 116, 125
historical memory, 3, 4–5, 81, 161–162,
  168, 178; and the American Revolu-
  tion, 25, 28, 36–37, 38, 40, 41, 45, 46,
  47, 49, 89, 95, 114, 160, 168, 176; and
  the Civil War, 127–130, 176–177; and
  commemoration, 21, 56, 81, 161–162,
  168
Hobby, Alfred Marmaduke, 98, 106–111
Holliday, Frederick, 71, 150, 193n63
Honey-Grove Enterprise (TX), 36
Hoskins, James, 74
Houston, George, 71
Houston Telegraph, 35
Howells, William Dean, 141–142
Hubbard, Richard, 138
Hunter, William, 91–92
Huntsville Democrat (AL), 167

identity, 1, 2, 3, 7, 11, 19, 20, 24, 55, 118,
  127; and American national, 3, 6–7,
  32; and Black Americans, 2, 47, 89,

90, 134, 162, 164; and commemoration, 18, 32; Confederate, 10–12, 24, 26, 29; local and regional, 5, 10, 75, 76, 87, 109, 118, 120, 153; political identity at the Centennial, 72–75; southern identity at the Centennial, 126–127. See also nationalism
Independence Day. *See* Fourth of July
Indiana State Journal, 23
Ingraham, J. H., 8

Jackson Clarion (MS), 75, 116, 125
Jackson, James, 39
Janney, Caroline, 2, 4, 81, 86, 87
Jefferson, Thomas, 6, 7, 15, 16
Jennings, J. W., 98, 107–107, 109–111
Johnson, Andrew, 42, 48
Jones, Absalom, 18
Jones, Mary, 24
Jones, C. P., 121

Kachun, Mitch, 3, 18, 149
Kammen, Michael, 21, 85, 120
Keller, A. H., 66, 192n34
Keller, Helen, 192n34
Kellogg, William, 116
Kemper, James L., 138–139
Kingsbury, Theodore Bryant, 136
Knoxville Chronicle, 127
Knoxville Whig, 47
Ku Klux Klan, 53, 148

La Grange Planter (GA), 66
Langston, John Mercer, 164, 207n32
Lawson, Melinda, 75
Le Conte, Emma, 32
Leaphart, W. A., 149
Lee, Robert E., 55, 108, 119, 130
Lee, Susanna, 56

Lewis, Edmonia, 134
Lincoln, Abraham, 29, 32, 176, 184n49
Long, Ellen Call, 80–84, 86, 87, 88
Los Angeles Daily Star, 152
Los Angeles Herald, 94
"Lost Cause" mythology, 55–56, 177, 119
Louisiana: and Centennial participation, 73–74, 77; and controversy over Centennial Commission, 117; and Reconstruction politics, 37, 55, 74, 145
Louisville Courier-Journal, 35
Lynch, John Roy, 116–117, 137

McCabe, James Dabney, 67, 136
McPherson, James, 6
Mackey, T. J., 113–114
Macon Telegraph (GA), 51, 57, 70, 114
Madison, James, 6, 15
Maier, Pauline, 32
Manning, M. J., 74
Marryat, Frederick, 20
Marten, James, 101
Marshall Tri-Weekly Herald (TX), 105, 158
Memphis Daily Appeal, 53, 87, 156
Merriwether, McKie, 168
Mills, R. Q., 112
Minor, Kate, 86
Mississippi: and Centennial participation, 72, 74–75, 125, 141–142, 153–154, 188, 215n93; and controversy over the National Centennial Commission, 116; and "redemption," 74
Mobile Advertiser, 26
Mobile Register, 72, 124, 129, 145
Moneyhon, Carl, 99
Monroe, James, 16
Montgomery Advertiser, 46, 161, 171
Morrell, Daniel, 58
Moses, Franklin, 113, 115

Moss, Harry, 124
Mount Vernon Ladies' Association,
    80–81, 83, 85
Muckles, M. R., 58

Nagel, Paul, 7
Nashville Daily American, 157
Nashville Republican Banner, 174
National Centennial Commission, 97,
    104; controversies over in South
    Carolina, 113–116; controversies over
    in Mississippi, 116; controversies over
    in Texas, 102–112; political make-up
    of, 59–60, 66, 107, 109, 111
Nationalism: American, 2, 3, 5–6, 9, 14,
    25, 32, 55, 56, 69, 76, 118, 136, 159,
    162, 178; Confederate, 10–12, 24, 26,
    29, 118. *See also* identity
"Negro Declaration of Independence,"
    149–150, 206n119
Nemanic, Mary Lou, 20
"New Departure" Democrats, 37–38, 112,
    56, 75, 173–174
"New South" movement, 37–38, 56, 63,
    69, 84, 112, 143, 174, 178, 197n147
New Orleans Bee, 7
New Orleans Bulletin, 45–46
New Orleans *Daily True Delta,* 27
New Orleans Picayune, 23, 25, 45, 65, 124,
    128, 155
New Orleans Republican, 49, 51
New Orleans Times, 117
New Orleans Tribune, 32–34
New York Graphic, 107, 141
New York Herald, 108, 140
New York Times, 140
New York Tribune, 92, 129, 139
newspapers, 72–73, 75, 127
Nora, Pierre, 5
Norwood, Thomas M., 40

O'Leary, Cecilia, 5, 6

Palmer, Frederick, 163
Panic of 1873, 67–68
Parsons, Albert, 100
Parsons, Lucy, 100
Parsons, William Henry, 62, 97, 99–100,
    107, 108–110, 111, 112, 115, 117–118,
    119, 198n4, 200n62
Patton, Robert, 70
Pemberton, John, 28
People's Advocate, 133, 147, 207n32
Pezzicar, Francesco, 128
Perry, Edward A., 82, 195n116
Petersburg Post (VA), 128
Pettus, John, 23
Philadelphia Press, 93, 131
Pillow, Gideon, 53–54
Porter, James, 85
Potter, David, 9
Power, John Logan, 74–75
Powers, Ridgley, 116
Prince, Stephen K., 140

Quigley, Paul, 6, 11, 25, 28

Rabinowitz, Howard, 176
Raleigh Register, 22, 25
railroads, 78–80
reconciliation, 2, 3, 4, 13, 31, 32, 40, 43,
    44, 56, 80, 84, 111, 127, 137, 150, 156,
    159, 170, 176; and the Centennial, 62,
    108, 110, 138, 139; and commemora-
    tion, 176; conditionality of, 13, 55, 43,
    64, 71, 156, 159, 178; as distinct from
    reunion, 2–3, 32, 55; and white south-
    ern women, 82, 84, 87, 169
Reconstruction, 1, 2, 12, 13, 31, 35, 41, 42,
    48–49, 52, 54, 55, 57, 64, 65, 66, 77,
    81, 82, 95, 97, 99, 100, 102, 115, 118,

119, 135, 144, 145, 147, 152, 155, 159,
163, 165, 166, 168, 171, 178
"Redemption," 37, 74, 99, 101, 114, 156,
162, 163, 166, 174, 190n95
Reed, Harrison, 83
Religious Herald, 64
Republican Party, 35, 41, 75, 115, 149,
168, 170; and African Americans,
34, 49, 51, 52, 54, 135, 148, 162, 163;
radical faction of, 39, 42–43, 66, 93,
99, 106, 116, 118, 119, 135, 144, 148-
149, 151, 163, 167, 202n31; and Texas,
98–101
reunion, 12, 13, 39, 40, 44, 55, 58, 61, 63,
65, 67, 70, 71, 95, 108, 111, 117, 135,
137, 138, 168, 184n49; as distinct from
reconciliation, 3, 32, 55
Richardson, Ed., 116
Richmond Dispatch, 139
Richmond Enquirer, 7, 12, 71–72, 122, 123,
124, 128, 148
Richmond Whig, 36, 68
Ritter, Kurt, 20
Rivers, Prince, 165
Ross, Michael, 55
Rothermel, Peter, 129–130, 137
Rubin, Anne Sarah, 2, 41, 173
Rydell, Robert, 68, 175, 176

San Antonio Express, 72–73
San Antonio Herald, 72–73, 117
San Francisco Weekly Alta, 93
Sartain, John, 130–131
Savannah Tribune, 89, 152
Scott, Thomas, 78–80
Scribner's Monthly, 67
sectionalism, 5–10, 23, 24, 81, 120, 130–
131, 136, 139; and the Centennial, 119,
135–143; and political identity, 144
Sellers, Charles, 8–9

Semmes, Raphael, 63–64, 174
Seward, William, 7
Sherman, William T., 87
Smith, Ashbel, 104, 199n33
Smith, Craig Bruce, 89
Smith, James M., 42, 65
Smith, Lewis Waln, 60
Snodgrass, George Washington Americus
Vespucci, 122–123, 201n10
Snyder, Theresa, 68
South, the: definitions of, 7–10
South Carolina: and controversies over
the National Centennial Commission,
113–116
Southern Planter & Farmer, 66
Springfield Republican (MA), 92
Spillman, Lyn, 4, 68
Stampp, Kenneth, 10
Stamps, T. B., 48
Stearns, Marcellus Lovejoy, 88
Stephens, Alexander, 169
Stone, John, 153
Sullivan, T. O., 156

Tanner, Benjamin, 90
Tennessee: and Centennial participa-
tion, 72, 76, 85
Terrell, John, 64
Texas: and Centennial participation,
84–85, and controversies over
National Centennial Commission,
102–112, 117–119, 138; Reconstruction
politics in, 99–102; and "redemption,"
37, 101
Texas State Gazette, 23
Thomas, Isaiah, 16
Tilden, Samuel B., 144, 147, 150, 151, 152,
157, 158, 160, 161, 171
Tillman, Ben, 168
Toombs, Robert, 40, 149

Tyler, John, 22
Travers, Len, 14, 16, 20

union: as perceived threat to the south, 7
United Daughters of the Confederacy, 4, 81, 176, 177

Vicksburg Monitor, 52
Vicksburg Herald, 203n93
violence: electoral, 55, 147, 177, 190n95; and Fourth of July celebrations, 50–53
Virginia: and Centennial participation, 66, 70–71, 79, 138–139, 204n76

Waco Daily Examiner, 109
Waco Register, 99, 108
Waco Southwest, 98
Waco Spectator, 100
Walls, Josiah, 94–95
Watts, Thomas, 161–162
Warner, Alexander, 74
Washington, Booker T., 175
Washington National Republican, 111
Washington, George, 15, 24, 25, 41
Washington, Martha, 83
Webster, Daniel, 7
Wells, Ida B., 175
Welsh, John, 104
Wheeler, William A., 145, 167
White, Alfred, 131
White, Elizabeth, 82
White, Garland, 149–151, 206n120
white southerners: and antebellum July Fourth celebrations, 17, 21–24, 31; and Black Americans, 32, 33, 41, 54, 151; and the Centennial, 57–58, 60, 63–65, 70–71, 97, 151–152, 119, 120, 123–131, 135–143, 151–152, 153, 178, and the Chicago World's Fair, 174–175; and Democratic affiliation, 56, 143–148, 171; and "honor," 41–42, 118, 119, 140; and identity, 118, 143, 171and post-war Fourth celebrations, 35–47, 155–162, 169–172. *See also* women: white southern
white supremacy, 35
Wiley, Bell Irvin, 10
William, Timothy J., 3
Williams, Patrick, 112
women: Black women and the Centennial, 91, 92–93, 94; Black women and July Fourth celebrations, 50, 165; and commemoration, 4; white southern women and July Fourth celebrations, 16, 48, 87, 160–161, 170–171; white southern women and the Centennial, 80–88, 126–127, 197n147; as "custodians of tradition," 85–86
Women's Executive Committee, 80, 85, 86, 87–88; and Black women, 91, 92–93
Woodward, T. W., 113
Worcester (MA) *Spy,* 26
World's Columbian Exposition. *See* Chicago World's Fair
world's fairs, 58, 174–176
Wright, G. J., 40

Young, M. Jennie, 84–85

Zuczek, Richard, 2

CPSIA information can be obtained
at www.ICGtesting.com
Printed in the USA
LVHW092235041021
699540LV00001B/23